EIGHT DAYS A WEEK

An Illustrated Record of Rock 'n' Roll

By Kenneth Best

Photographs By Joseph Sia

Pomegranate Artbooks, San Francisco

For Lauren, Danielle, Jason and Ryan

Text © 1992 Kenneth Best
Photographs © 1992 Joseph Sia

Published by Pomegranate Artbooks, Inc.
Box 808022, Petaluma, CA 94975

Designed by Tim Lewis
Typography by Douglas Simpson
Printed in Hong Kong

ISBN 1-56640-026-0
Library of Congress Catalog Card Number: 92-82581

Front cover: Jimi Hendrix, 1968
Woolsey Hall, Yale University
New Haven, Connecticut

Preface and Acknowledgments

The idea for this book came from a feature story package written for *The Advocate* (Stamford, Connecticut) in March 1989 about an exhibition at the Museum of Art, Science & Industry in Bridgeport, Connecticut, called *Rock & Roll Art & Artifacts*. Because we did not have access at the time to any of the exhibition pieces, I was asked by one of the newspaper's graphic designers, Deena Murphy, if there was a way to include file photos of important rock musicians instead.

We decided that compiling a timeline of important events in the history of rock 'n' roll might be the answer. After doing some preliminary library research, I was surprised to discover that most of the resources needed to write the timeline were in my personal library of books on rock 'n' roll, which I had assembled over more than 20 years of reading and writing about rock music.

During the nearly three years I spent researching and writing this book, I had the opportunity to rediscover much of the music that I have written about for so many years. Most of the time I was working, I played many of the records, tapes and compact discs in my music collection.

The information in this book is a synthesis of a variety of data that have been available previously in many forms. What is different about the approach used here is the presentation of the history of rock 'n' roll in a daily chronicle for the entire calendar year, providing annotated biographies of important figures and noting landmark events.

I have taken the roles of reporter, historian and music fan in making decisions about whom to include in this volume. For the careful reader, there perhaps may seem to be too many references to events involving Elvis Presley and The Beatles. However, as the performers who have had the most impact on rock music, their recordings and activities merit special attention. Inductees into the Rock and Roll Hall of Fame also have been given special attention.

As always in rock 'n' roll, there were a great many inconsistencies. Where the conflicts were greatest, I used the sources that have proven to be the most authoritative along the way. In all instances, I cross-checked dates and details for the most consistent or generally accepted facts.

In order to keep the information listed somewhat manageable, I did not always include individual listings for all members of a band. The best-known member of the band is often used as the prime entry for a group, with other members of the group noted parenthetically within the biographical notation. Number One (No. 1) songs are listed on the dates on which they reached the top of the charts. The number in parentheses following each title and artist's name is the number of weeks the song stayed at the top of the charts.

The many solitary hours of preparing this book were made possible by the encouragement and support provided by friends and family. Thanks to Suzanne and Kira Skorpen, along with my colleagues from *The Advocate,* for their encouragement early on in the process. Thanks also to Bonnie Behar, Harvey Brooks, Gary Wesalo, David Zamba, Kathy Weydig, Bruce Markowitz and Sheila Burke for their ongoing support and to Dr. Bruce Harrah-Conforth and Bonnie Oviatt at the Rock and Roll Hall of Fame and Museum for their assistance in tracking down information. A special word of appreciation to the Dobosz-Rondeau family for their guidance, spirit and regular care and feeding during difficult times.

Kenneth Best
Bridgeport, Connecticut
August 1992

Rock History

TIMELINE

February 19, 1878
Thomas Edison obtains a patent for the phonograph.

1927
John Dopeyera develops the first working amplified guitar.

1933
John and Alan Lomax discover Huddie Ledbetter, better known as Leadbelly, at a Louisiana state prison farm.

1937
Charlie Christian changes jazz guitar-playing style with the electric guitar.

1940s

1940
Woody Guthrie is recorded for the first time, by Alan Lomax.

1941
Les Paul develops the prototype for his solid-body electric guitar.

June 21, 1948
Vinyl records are played in public for the first time, by Columbia Records in New York City.

July 11, 1951
Alan Freed begins his R&B radio show on WJW in Cleveland.

March 21, 1952
Alan Freed's The Moondog Coronation Ball in Cleveland ends in a near riot, signifying the beginning of the rock era.

January 14, 1954
Alan Freed's Rock 'n' Roll Jubilee marks the first time the term *rock 'n' roll* is used to describe an event.

July 5, 1954
Elvis Presley records his first record, *That's All Right, Mama,* at Sun Records.

July 10, 1954
WHBQ (Memphis) DJ Dewey Phillips plays *That's All Right, Mama* by Elvis Presley for the first time anywhere.

July 9, 1955
Rock Around the Clock by Bill Haley & The Comets becomes the first rock 'n' roll record to reach No. 1.

August 20, 1955
Maybellene by Chuck Berry enters the Top 40 charts.

February 4, 1956
James Brown records his first record for Federal, *Please, Please*.

June 15, 1956
John Lennon and Paul McCartney meet at a church picnic.

September 9, 1956
Elvis Presley performs on *Toast of the Town*, Ed Sullivan's show, for the first time.

August 5, 1957
American Bandstand debuts on ABC television.

August 4, 1958
Billboard magazine begins the Hot 100 chart.

February 3, 1959
Buddy Holly, Ritchie Valens and The Big Bopper die in a plane crash.

1960
Leo Fender files the patent for the Stratocaster guitar.

August 1, 1960
Aretha Franklin makes her first secular recordings, in New York City.

1961
Berry Gordy, Jr. begins the Motown Record label in Detroit.

March 21, 1961
The Beatles perform at The Cavern Club in Liverpool for the first time.

April 11, 1961
Bob Dylan performs for the first time, at Gere's Folk City in New York City.

November 29, 1963
I Want to Hold Your Hand by The Beatles is released in England.

February 9, 1964
The Beatles appear on *The Ed Sullivan Show* for the first time.

April 4, 1964
Beatlemania peaks when The Beatles hold the top five positions on Billboard's Hot 100.

April 26, 1964
The Rolling Stones release their first album, *The Rolling Stones*.

May 6, 1966
The Beach Boys release *Pet Sounds*.

August 29, 1966
The Beatles perform in concert for the last time, in San Francisco.

June 1, 1967
The Beatles' *Sgt. Pepper's Lonely Hearts Club Band* is released.

June 16, 1967
The Monterey Pop Festival begins.

November 9, 1967
Rolling Stone magazine begins publication.

January 17, 1969
Led Zeppelin releases its first album, *Led Zeppelin*, opening the age of heavy metal.

August 15, 1969
The Woodstock Music and Art Festival begins on Max Yasgur's farm in Bethel, New York.

December 31, 1970
The Beatles break up.

May 31, 1976
The Who is declared the loudest band in the world by the *Guinness Book of Records.*

August 16, 1977
Elvis Presley dies at Graceland.

December 8, 1980
John Lennon is shot and killed by Mark David Chapman in New York City.

August 1, 1981
MTV begins broadcasting.

December 1, 1982
Thriller by Michael Jackson is released.

March 5, 1985
We Are the World is broadcast on 5,000 radio stations around the world.

July 13, 1985
Live Aid concerts take place at Wembley Stadium in London and J.F.K. Stadium in Philadelphia.

January 20, 1986
The Rock and Roll Hall of Fame holds its first induction ceremony, in New York City.

1988
Compact discs outsell records for the first time.

. . . .

AN ILLUSTRATED RECORD OF ROCK 'N' ROLL

1

1942
Country Joe McDonald is born in El Monte, California. Leader of the highly political San Francisco-based '60s group Country Joe and the Fish (Chicken Hirsch, Bruce Barthol, Barry Melton, David Cohen), whose best-known song was the antiwar *Feel-Like-I'm-Fixin'-to-Die-Rag*.

1953
Hank Williams, country music star who penned such classics as *Hey, Good Lookin'* and *Your Cheatin' Heart*, influenced early rock 'n' roll development and is a member of the Rock and Roll Hall of Fame, dies in Oak Hill, West Virginia, at age 29 from excessive drinking and drug use.

1962
The Beatles audition at Decca Records in London for a recording contract. They fail the audition.

1964
Top of the Pops debuts on BBC-TV in England, where it becomes the longest-running rock showcase.

1970
Jimi Hendrix welcomes the new year with the second of his two shows at The Fillmore East in New York City with his group The Band of Gypsies, featuring Billy Cox on bass and Buddy Miles on drums.

1973
In Concert debuts on ABC television.

1985
Video Hits One (VH-1), the music video network aimed at the so-called "Baby Boom" generation (25 to 49), is launched by the Music Television Network (MTV).

NUMBER ONE SONGS:

1960
The Sounds of Silence by Simon & Garfunkel (1)

2

1949
Chick Churchill is born in Flintshire, England. Keyboard player for the English rock-blues band Ten Years After (Alvin Lee, Leo Lyons, Ric Lee), which had five Top 40 albums between 1969 and 1973 and a Top 40 single, *I'd Love to Change the World*, in 1971. The group is remembered for its performance at the Woodstock Music and Art Festival in 1969, particularly *Goin' Home*, which featured Alvin Lee's nimble guitar and vocals.

1969
The Beatles begin filming *Let It Be*, originally titled *Get Back*, at Twickenham Film Studios in England.

3

1926
George Martin, producer for The Beatles, is born in London. His interest in the raw talent of The Beatles helped get the band an audition for a recording contract with British Parlophone. His knowledge of classical music and recording techniques influenced The Beatles' landmark records, particularly *Sgt. Pepper's Lonely Hearts Club Band*.

1945
Stephen Stills is born in Dallas, Texas. A founding member of the influential band Buffalo Springfield (Neil Young, Richie Furay, Dewey Martin, Bruce Palmer, Jim Messina), he enhanced his reputation on the landmark *Super Session* album with Mike Bloomfield, Harvey Brooks and Al Kooper before joining with David Crosby and Graham Nash to form the supergroup Crosby, Stills & Nash. Neil Young later joined CSN. Stills wrote Buffalo Springfield's only Top 10 song, *For What It's Worth*. CSN had six Top 30 hits in its early days and four more with Neil Young, including *Woodstock* and *Teach Your Children*. Stills also had two Top 40 records as a solo, *Love the One You're With* and *Sit Yourself Down*.

1974
Bob Dylan returns to performing with a two-month American tour opening at The Chicago Amphitheater. He is backed up by The Band.

NUMBER ONE SONGS:

1969
Raindrops Keep Fallin' on My Head by B. J. Thomas (4)

1976
Saturday Night by The Bay City Rollers (1)

4

1954
Elvis Presley meets Sam Phillips, owner of Sun Records, when he goes to the Memphis Recording Service. Presley records *Casual Love Affair* and *I'll Never Stand in Your Way*.

1962
The Beatles are rated the most popular group in the newest poll by *Mersey Beat*, soon after their return from Hamburg, Germany.

NUMBER ONE SONGS:

1960
El Paso by Marty Robbins (2)
1964
There! I've Said It Again by Bobby Vinton (4)
1975
Lucy in the Sky with Diamonds by Elton John (2)
1983
Down Under by Men at Work (4)

5

1923
Sam Phillips is born in Florence, Alabama. Pioneering record company executive who opened Sun Records in Memphis, Tennessee, where he was the first to record such performers as Elvis Presley, Jerry Lee Lewis, Roy Orbison, Carl Perkins, Johnny Cash, Charlie Rich and others. He was one of the first white men to record seminal black R&B artists such as Howlin' Wolf. Inducted into the Rock and Roll Hall of Fame January 20, 1986.

NUMBER ONE SONGS:

1980
Please Don't Go by KC & The Sunshine Band (1)

6

1929
Wilbert Harrison is born in Charlotte, North Carolina. Had a No. 1 hit in 1959 with the classic version of Jerry Leiber and Mike Stoller's *Kansas City*. Also had a Top 40 record in 1970 with *Let's Work Together*, which was later covered by both Canned Heat and Bryan Ferry.

1945
Syd Barrett is born Roger Barrett in Cambridge, England. Guitarist and vocalist for the innovative rock group Pink Floyd (Richard Wright, Roger Waters, Nick Mason, later David Gilmour). The group produced seven Top 40 albums, including one of the all-time best-selling LPs, the No. 1 *The Dark Side of the Moon*, which sold more than 10 million copies. Also had No. 1 LPs with *Wish You Were Here* in 1975 and *The Wall* in 1979 and a No. 1 single in 1980 with *Another Brick in The Wall (Part II)*.

1957
Elvis Presley's last performance on *The Ed Sullivan Show*. He sings *Peace in the Valley, Hound Dog, Too Much, Paralyzed* and *When My Blue Moon Turns to Gold Again*.

1958
Chuck Berry records *Sweet Little Sixteen*, a No. 2 hit on the Top 40 charts.

NUMBER ONE SONGS:

1958
At the Hop by Danny & The Juniors (7)
1973
You're So Vain by Carly Simon (3)
1979
Too Much Heaven by The Bee Gees (2)

7

1942
Paul Revere is born in Boise, Idaho. Keyboard player and founder (with Mark Lindsay) of Paul Revere and the Raiders (Phil Volk, Michael Smith, Drake Levin), later known as The Raiders. The

quintet, known for lively stage shows in which the band was dressed in Revolutionary War costumes, had 15 Top 40 hits between 1961 and 1971, including *Kicks, Good Thing* and the No. 1 *Indian Reservation (The Lament of the Cherokee Reservation Indian)*.

1946
Jann Wenner is born in New York City. Cofounder of *Rolling Stone*, the magazine dedicated to rock music that became a voice for the rising youth culture of the 1960s.

1948
Kenny Loggins is born in Everett, Washington. Singer-songwriter who had six Top 40 albums and three hit singles with Jim Messina as Loggins & Messina and subsequently has had 11 Top 40 records as a solo artist. His No. 1 single was *Footloose* in 1984.

1955
Rock Around the Clock by Bill Haley & The Comets enters the U.K. singles charts.

JIMI HENDRIX, 1969
New Year's Eve

AN ILLUSTRATED RECORD OF ROCK 'N' ROLL

8

1935

Elvis Presley is born in Tupelo, Mississippi. Rock 'n' roll's first real star, he changed the direction of popular music and established rock 'n' roll as an accepted art form. He had 107 Top 40 single hit records, including 17 gold records. Among his most popular singles were *Heartbreak Hotel; I Want You, I Need You; Hound Dog; Don't Be Cruel* and *All Shook Up.* He died August 16, 1977, at his home in Memphis, Tennessee, at age 42. Inducted into the Rock and Roll Hall of Fame January 20, 1986.

1941

Little Anthony is born Anthony Gourdine in New York City. Lead vocalist for Little Anthony and The Imperials (Ernest Wright, Jr., Clarence Collins, Tracy Lord, Glouster Rogers), a doo-wop group that had seven Top 35 singles, including the Top 10 hits *Tears on My Pillow, Goin' out of My Head* and *Hurt So Bad.*

1945

Terry Sylvester is born in Liverpool, England. Guitarist and vocalist who replaced Graham Nash in The Hollies in 1968 and remained with the band until 1981. Hits during that time included five Top 30 songs, including *He Ain't Heavy, He's My Brother; Long Cool Woman (in a Black Dress)* and *The Air That I Breathe.*

1946

Robby Krieger is born in Los Angeles. Guitarist for The Doors and writer of the group's No. 1 hit *Light My Fire.* The Doors (Ray Manzarek, Jim Morrison, John Densmore) had 11 Top 40 albums and eight Top 40 singles, including the Top 10 records *Hello, I Love You* and *Touch Me.* The band disbanded soon after Morrison's death in 1971. Krieger performed with Densmore as the Butts Band and later toured as a solo based on an instrumental album released in 1982.

1947

David Bowie is born David Robert Jones in London. Chameleonlike singer-songwriter and musician who has changed his image and music with almost every album and tour. Always on the cutting edge of the avant-garde, he has had 14 Top 40 albums and eight Top 30 singles, including the No. 1 hits *Fame* and *Let's Dance.* He also has had a career as an actor in film and on the stage.

1960

Eddie Cochran's last recording session, at Goldstar Studios in Los Angeles, includes Sonny Curtis and Jerry Allison of The Crickets.

NUMBER ONE SONGS

1966

We Can Work It Out by The Beatles (3)

1977

You Don't Have to Be a Star (to Be on My Show) by Marilyn McCoo and Billy Davis (1)

9

1915

Les Paul is born Lester Polfus in Waukesha, Wisconsin. Guitar pioneer who invented the solid-body electric guitar and created multitrack recording and other modern recording techniques. He and his wife, Mary Ford, had a successful recording career in the 1950s with top hits such as *How High the Moon* and *Vaya Con Dios.*

1944

Jimmy Page is born in Middlesex, England. Influential guitarist and founder of Led Zeppelin (John Paul Jones, Robert Plant, John Bonham). He began his famed career with The Yardbirds, a seminal rock blues group that also had as lead guitarist at various times Eric Clapton and Jeff Beck. (See Paul Samwell-Smith, May 8; John Paul Jones, June 3.)

1944

Scott Walker is born Scott Engel in Hamilton, Ohio. Vocalist and multi-instrumentalist for The Walker Brothers (John Maus, Gary Leeds), who had two Top 20 hits in 1965–1966, *Make It Easy on Yourself* and *The Sun Ain't Gonna Shine Anymore.*

1971

The U.S. Jaycees name Elvis Presley one of the 10 Outstanding Young Men of the Year.

NUMBER ONE SONGS

1988

So Emotional by Whitney Houston (1)

10

1917

Jerry Wexler is born in New York City. Musician, record company executive and producer who helped create soul music from R&B at Atlantic Records. Among those he worked with were LaVern Baker, Joe Turner, Phil Spector, Aretha Franklin and Wilson Pickett, Dr. John, Jose Feliciano, Jackie DeShannon and others. Inducted into the Rock and Roll Hall of Fame January 21, 1987.

1935

Ronnie Hawkins is born in Fayetteville, Arkansas. Veteran rockabilly performer who had a Top 30 hit in 1959 with *Mary Lou.* He assembled a group of musicians who would later become The Band (Levon Helm, Robbie Robertson, Garth Hudson, Rick Danko, Richard Manuel) as part of his backup band, The Hawks, in the early '60s.

1943

Jim Croce is born in Philadelphia. Singer-songwriter and guitarist who had two No. 1 singles—*Bad, Bad Leroy Brown* and *Time in a Bottle*—and the No. 1 album *You Don't Mess Around with Jim* within two years as his career began to show promise. He died in a plane crash September 20, 1973, in Natchitoches, Louisiana.

1945

Rod Stewart is born in London. Raspy-voiced singer-songwriter who began his career with a variety of bands before gaining a reputation with The Jeff Beck Group and with Faces. His solo career began in 1970 while he was still with Faces and has included more than 15 Top 40 albums, including the No. 1 records *Every Picture Tells a Story* and *Blonds Have More Fun.* His more than 20 Top 40 singles include the No. 1 hits *Maggie May, Tonight's the Night* and *Da Ya Think I'm Sexy.*

1946

Aynsley Dunbar is born in England. Highly respected drummer who has played with John Mayall (1966), The Jeff Beck Group (1967), Journey (1974–1979) and Jefferson Starship (1979–1982).

1956

Elvis Presley's first recording session for RCA Records includes *I Got a Woman* and *Heartbreak Hotel.*

1976

Howlin' Wolf, influential Delta bluesman and member of the Rock and Roll Hall of Fame whose electric guitar and deep-throated vocals helped shape rock 'n' roll, dies in Hines, Illinois, at age 66.

NUMBER ONE SONGS

1976

Convoy by C. W. McCall (1)

11

1924

Slim Harpo is born James Moore in Lobdell, Louisiana. Influential bluesman whose song *I'm a King Bee* was an early showpiece for The Rolling Stones. He had two hits in the '60s, with *Rainin' in My Heart* in 1961 and *Baby, Scratch My Back,* a No. 1 on the R&B charts, in 1966. He died January 31, 1970, of a heart attack in Baton Rouge, Louisiana.

1963

The Beatles release *Please Please Me* as a single in England. It becomes a No. 3 hit in the United States in 1964.

1965

The Rolling Stones' recording session at RCA Studios in Hollywood includes *The Last Time,* which became a No. 1 hit in England, and the B-side tune *Play with Fire,* which was included on the group's album *Big Hits: High Tide and Green Grass.*

12

1941

Long John Baldry is born in East Maddon-Doveshire, England. Blues vocalist who was one of the most influential musicians on the British music scene in the 1960s. He helped organize Alexis Korner's Blues Incorporated, whose roster included at various times Ginger Baker and Jack Bruce of Cream, Brian Auger, guitarist Vic Briggs of The Animals, Charlie Watts and Mick Jagger of The Rolling Stones, and keyboardist Reg Dwight, who later changed his name to Elton John. Baldry's best-known song in America was the Top

JIMMY PAGE, 1969
Led Zeppelin

100 single *Don't Try to Lay No Boogie-Woogie on the King of Rock 'n' Roll*.

1965
Hullabaloo debuts on NBC television.

1974
The Joker by The Steve Miller Band (1)

13

1963
The Beatles perform *Please Please Me* while recording their debut on *Thank Your Lucky Stars* for ABC television.

1962
The Twist by Chubby Checker (2)

14

1938
Allen Toussaint is born in New Orleans, Louisiana. Talented singer, songwriter, arranger, producer and pianist whose songs have been recorded by a wide range of performers from The Rolling Songs (*Fortune Teller*) to Glen Campbell (*Southern Nights*), Bonnie Raitt (*What Do You Want the Boy to Do?*) and Herman's Hermits (*A Certain Girl*). An early song, *Java*, was a No. 4 hit for trumpeter Al Hirt.

1948
Tim Harris is born in London. Drummer for The Foundations (Alan Warner, Clem Curtis, Eric Dale, Tony Gomez, Pat Burke, Peter Macbeth, Mike Elliott, Colin Young), a mid-'60s group that had two Top 15 hits: *Baby, Now That I've Found You* and *Build Me Up Buttercup*.

1954
Alan Freed holds his first Rock 'n' Roll Jubilee Ball in New York City at the St. Nicholas Arena. Performers include Fats Domino, Clyde McPhatter and the Drifters, Joe Turner, Ruth Brown and the Harptones. It is the first time the term *rock 'n' roll* is used to describe a concert/dance event.

1964
Chuck Berry records nine songs, including *Nadine*, a No. 23 hit on the Top 40 charts.

1970
Monterey Pop, a documentary on the 1967 Monterey Pop Festival, opens in Los Angeles.

1978
The last performance by the punk-rock band The Sex Pistols takes place at Winterland in San Francisco. The band breaks up the next day.

1979
Donnie Hathaway, singer best known for his work with Roberta Flack, dies in New York City at age 34 after falling from his hotel room.

1978
Baby Come Back by Player (3)
1989
My Prerogative by Bobby Brown (1)

AN ILLUSTRATED RECORD OF ROCK 'N' ROLL

15

1941
Captain Beefhart is born Don Van Vliet in Glendale, California. Founder of The Magic Band, Beefhart is known for his wide-ranging blues vocals. Performed with Frank Zappa and the Mothers of Invention and toured through the 1980s.

1964
The Beatles perform in France for the first time, at the Cinema Cyrano in Versailles.

1967
Roy Orbison attends the premiere of his film *The Fastest Gun Alive* in New York City.

1970
An exhibition of John Lennon's lithographs opens at the London Arts Gallery.

NUMBER ONE SONGS:

1972
American Pie by Don McLean (4)
1977
You Make Me Feel Like Dancing by Leo Sayer (1)

16

1941
Sandy Denny is born in Wimbledon, England. Best known as singer for the electric folk group Fairport Convention (Judy Dyble, Simon Nichol, Ashley Hutchings, Martin Lamble, Ian Matthews, Richard Thompson, Dave Pegg) in the early 1970s. She died April 21, 1978, in London of head injuries after a fall in her home.

1957
The Cavern Club opens in Liverpool, England. The club becomes a mecca for local bands, including The Beatles.

1959
The Everly Brothers go to England for their first visit and appear on the television show *Cool for Cats*. They later receive an award from *New Musical Express* magazine as World's No. 1 Vocal Group.

1960
Eddie Cochran makes his English TV

debut on the live rock 'n' roll show *Boy Meets Girl*.

1976
Donny and Marie, starring Donny and Marie Osmond, debuts on ABC television.

1976
Frampton Comes Alive!, a concert album by Peter Frampton, is released. It will spend 10 weeks as the No. 1 LP.

NUMBER ONE SONGS:

1988
Got My Mind Set on You by George Harrison (1)

17

1930
Bobby "Blue" Bland is born in Rosemark, Tennessee. Influential vocalist and pioneer of modern soul who was a member of B. B. King's informal blues gathering The Beale Streeters (Johnny Ace, Willie Nix, Roscoe Gordon). He had four Top 35 singles in the early 1960s, including *Turn on Your Love Light*, *Call on Me*, *That's the Way Love Is* and *Ain't Nothing You Can Do*. Inducted into the Rock and Roll Hall of Fame in 1992.

1944
Chris Montez is born in Los Angeles. Singer and guitarist who had five Top 40 hits in the 1960s, including *Call Me* and *The More I See You*.

1945
William Hart is born in Washington, D.C. Founder of The Delfonics (Wilbert Hart, Randy Cain, Ritchie Daniels), 1960s Philadelphia vocal group that set the standards for sophisticated black pop. Recorded six Top 40 hits, including *La - La Means I Love You* and *Didn't I (Blow Your Mind This Time)*.

1948
Mick Taylor is born in Hertfordshire, England. Guitarist who replaced Brian Jones in The Rolling Stones in 1969. Also played with John Mayall's Bluesbreakers from 1967 to 1969.

1969
The soundtrack album of The Beatles' *Yellow Submarine* is released in England.

1969
Led Zeppelin releases its first album, *Led Zeppelin*, opening the age of heavy metal.

NUMBER ONE SONGS:

1976
I Write the Songs by Barry Manilow (1)
1987
Shake You Down by Gregory Abbott (1)

18

1941
David Ruffin is born in Whyknot, Mississippi. Primary singer with The Temptations (Otis Williams, Eddie Kendricks, Paul Williams, Melvin Franklin, Eldridge Bryant, later Dennis Edwards), one of Motown's pioneering vocal groups, from 1964 to 1968, when the group had more than 15 Top 40 hits, including the No. 1 song *My Girl*. He had two Top 10 singles as a solo, *My Whole World Ended (the Moment You Left)* and *Walk Away from Love*. He died June 1, 1991, in Philadelphia at age 50 of a drug overdose. Inducted into the Rock and Roll Hall of Fame January 18, 1989, as a member of the original Temptations.

1964
I Want to Hold Your Hand by The Beatles first appears on the Billboard charts at No. 45.

1988
Westwood One radio network begins broadcast of *The Lost Lennon Tapes*, a year-long series based on material from John Lennon's personal archives.

NUMBER ONE SONGS:

1975
Mandy by Barry Manilow (1)
1986
That's What Friends Are For by Dionne Warwick & Friends (4)

19

1939
Phil Everly is born in Brownie, Kentucky. With his brother, Don, originated as a country duo, The Everly Brothers, and moved to pop as rock 'n' roll began to flourish.

Their floating harmonies, supported by a driving backbeat, resulted in a remarkable Top 10 record every four months from 1957 to 1960, including *Bye Bye Love*, *Wake Up Little Susie*, *All I Have to Do Is Dream*, *Bird Dog* and *Cathy's Clown*. Inducted into the Rock and Roll Hall of Fame January 20, 1986.

1943
Janis Joplin is born in Port Arthur, Texas. Lead singer for the San Francisco blues band Big Brother and the Holding Company (Peter Albin, Sam Andrews, James Gurley, David Getz), she has been called the best white blues singer of the 1960s. Her gritty vocals pushed Big Brother to the top of the charts in 1968 with the *Cheap Thrills* LP and the Top 15 single *Piece of My Heart*. Her brief solo career before her death at age 27 from a drug overdose (October 4, 1970, in Hollywood) yielded four Top 40 albums, including *Pearl*, the No. 1 record that produced the No. 1 hit *Me and Bobby McGee*.

1949
Robert Palmer is born in Batley, England. British R&B singer-songwriter who began his career with Vinegar Joe before reaching solo success with the Top 20 single *Every Kinda People*. His 1986 album *Riptide* produced the No. 1 hit *Addicted to Love*.

1952
Dewey Bunnell is born in Yorkshire, England. One of three guitarist-vocalists who made up the trio America (Gerry Beckley, Dan Peek), which had 11 Top 35 singles, including *I Need You*, *Ventura Highway*, *Tin Man* and two No. 1 hits, *A Horse with No Name* and *Sister Golden Hair*, between 1972 and 1983.

1973
The Bobby Darin Show debuts on NBC television.

1977
Aretha Franklin sings an a cappella version of *God Bless America* at the Inaugural Eve Gala for President Jimmy Carter in Washington, D.C.

1981
Simon & Garfunkel reunite for the first time in four years before 400,000 people in Central Park in New York City.

JANIS JOPLIN c. 1968

20

1889
Leadbelly is born Huddie Ledbetter in Mooringsport, Louisiana. Pioneering folk-blues singer-songwriter whose music and style inspired Woody Guthrie, Pete Seeger and other 20th-century folk artists, who in turn influenced the activist folk and folk-rock performers of the 1960s. Author of classics such as *The Rock Island Line, The Midnight Special* and *Goodnight Irene.* He died December 6, 1949, in New York City. Inducted into the Rock and Roll Hall of Fame January 20, 1988.

1948
Melvin Pritchard is born in Oldham, England. Drummer for the 1960s art-rock band Barclay James Harvest (Stewart Wolstenholme, John Lees, Les Holroyd).

1958
After its staff destroys all of its rock records, St. Louis radio station KWK announces it no longer will play rock 'n' roll.

1964
Meet The Beatles LP, which includes *I Want to Hold Your Hand,* is released in the United States.

1965
Disc jockey Alan Freed, who is credited with coining the phrase *rock 'n' roll* and is a member of the Rock and Roll Hall of Fame, dies in Palm Springs, California.

1986
First induction ceremony of the Rock and Roll Hall of Fame, which was organized in 1984, is held in New York City. The first group of inductees includes Elvis Presley, Chuck Berry, Little Richard, Jerry Lee Lewis, James Brown, Buddy Holly, Ray Charles, Fats Domino, The Everly Brothers and Sam Cooke as artists; Alan Freed and Sam Phillips as nonperformance inductees;

Robert Johnson, Jimmie Rogers, John Hammond and Jimmy Yancey as early influences.

21

1941
Richie Havens is born in Brooklyn, New York. Folksinger and activist whose percussive guitar style opened the performances at the Woodstock Music and Art Festival in August 1969. His covers of songs by rock and folk artists such as The Beatles, Van Morrison and James Taylor are typified by his 1967 classic LP *Mixed Bag.* He had a Top 20 single in 1971 with his cover of George Harrison's *Here Comes the Sun.*

1942
Edwin Starr is born Charles Hatcher in Nashville, Tennessee. Powerful vocalist who had four Top 40 pop hits, including the No. 1 antiwar song *War* in 1970, and several R&B chart successes. On May 7, 1966, Starr had a hand in three songs on the Hot 100: *Headline News* (his single), *I'll Love You Forever* (vocal with The Holidays) and *Oh How Happy* (producer for Shades of Blue).

1947
Jimmy Ibbotson is born in Philadelphia. Drummer for the Nitty Gritty Dirt Band (Jeff Hanna, Jimmie Fadden, Jackson Browne, Ralph Barr, John McEuen, Les Thompson, Bruce Kunkel), later The Dirt Band, from 1969 to 1976, when the diverse country-rock group had its greatest pop success with the Top 10 single *Mr. Bojangles.*

1957
Chuck Berry records *School Days,* which reached No. 3 on the Top 40 charts.

1962
Jackie Wilson appears on *The Ed Sullivan Show.*

1963
The Beatles sign a contract with Vee-Jay Records to record in the United States.

1982
B. B. King donates his collection of 20,000 records to the Center for the Study of Southern Culture at the University of Mississippi.

1984
Jackie Wilson dies in a Mount Holly, New Jersey, hospital at age 50 while recovering from a disabling heart attack he suffered while performing in September 1975.

CARL PERKINS, 1969

AN ILLUSTRATED RECORD OF ROCK 'N' ROLL

22

1935

Sam Cooke is born in Chicago. Helped pioneer soul music by blending gospel music and secular themes through his widely imitated vocal style. He had Top 10 hits with *You Send Me, Chain Gang, Twistin' the Night Away* and *Shake.* Cooke died in Los Angeles December 11, 1964, after he was shot following an argument with a woman. Inducted into the Rock and Roll Hall of Fame January 20, 1986.

1940

Micki Harris is born in Passaic, New Jersey. Vocalist with The Shirelles (Shirley Owens Alston, Doris Coley Kenner, Beverly Lee), the pioneering female vocal group that was one of the first to write its own hit songs. Between 1960 and 1963, the group had a dozen Top 40 hits, including *Mama Said, Dedicated to the One I Love* and the No. 1 singles *Will You Love Me Tomorrow* and *Soldier Boy.* Harris died June 10, 1982, in Los Angeles.

1955

Carl Perkins begins his first recording session for Sun Records, resulting in two singles, *Movie Mugg* and *Turn Around.*

1969

George Harrison asks Billy Preston to play on the *Let It Be* sessions.

1971

John Lennon and Yoko Ono record *Power to the People,* which becomes a No. 11 Top 40 hit.

NUMBER ONE SONGS:

1977
I Wish by Stevie Wonder (1)

23

1944

Jerry Lawson is born in Fort Lauderdale, Florida. Baritone vocalist for the unique a cappella group The Persuasions (Jayotis Washington, Joseph Jesse Russell, Herbert Rhoad, Jimmy Hayes, Willie Daniels), who have performed in concert continuously since 1962 and as backup vocalists on recording

sessions with artists such as Stevie Wonder, Phoebe Snow, Don McLean and many others.

1950

Bill Cunningham is born in Memphis, Tennessee. Keyboardist and bass player for the blue-eyed soul band The Box Tops (Alex Chilton, Tom Boggs, Rick Allen, Gary Talley), which had seven Top 40 hits between 1967 and 1969, including the No. 1 single *The Letter* and the No. 2 *Cry Like a Baby.*

1978

Terry Kath, guitarist and cofounder with Walter Parazaider of the jazz-rock group Chicago Transit Authority, later known as Chicago, dies in Woodland Hills, California, from an accidental gunshot wound.

NUMBER ONE SONGS:

1965
Downtown by Petula Clark (2)
1971
Knock Three Times by Dawn (3)
1988
The Way You Make Me Feel by Michael Jackson (1)

24

1936

Doug Kershaw is born in Tiel Ridge, Louisiana. Veteran fiddler who made a reputation in country music before becoming a highly sought session player with rock musicians. He has performed with Johnny Cash, Bob Dylan and Grand Funk Railroad, among others.

1941

Neil Diamond is born in Brooklyn, New York. Prolific singer-songwriter and guitarist who has recorded 36 Top 40 singles and 21 hit albums. His two No. 1 singles were *Cracklin' Rosie* in 1970 and *Song Sung Blue* in 1972.

NUMBER ONE SONGS:

1976
Theme from Mahogany (Do You Know Where You're Going To) by Diana Ross (1)
1987
At This Moment by Billy Vera & The Beaters (2)

25

1976

Ringo Starr surprises the audience by coming onstage during Bob Dylan's "Rolling Thunder" tour at the Astrodome in Houston.

NUMBER ONE SONGS:

1975 *Please Mr. Postman* by The Carpenters (1)

26

1956

Buddy Holly & The Crickets record in Nashville for the first time at Bradley's Barn Studio as "Buddy Holly & The Three Tunes."

1957

Eddie Van Halen is born in Nijmegan, Holland. Guitarist for the influential heavy metal band Van Halen (Alex Van Halen, Michael Anthony, David Lee Roth, later Sammy Hagar), which has had more than 10 Top 40 hits showcasing Eddie's distinctive guitar work, including the No. 1 hit *Jump,* from the band's LPs, among them *1984, Women and Children First* and the No. 1 *5150.*

NUMBER ONE SONGS:

1963
Walk Right In by The Rooftop Singers (2)
1974
You're Sixteen by Ringo Starr (1)

27

1918

Elmore James is born Elmore Brooks in Richland, Mississippi. Innovative guitarist and bluesman whose slide-guitar style helped bridge the way from blues to rock. He died May 24, 1963, of a heart attack in Chicago. Inducted into the Rock and Roll Hall of Fame in 1992.

1945

Nick Mason is born in Birmingham, England. Drummer for Pink Floyd (Syd Barrett, Richard Wright, Roger Waters, later David Gilmour). (See Syd Barrett, January 6.)

1946

Nedra Talley is born in New York City. Member of the mid-'60s vocal trio The Ronettes (Ronnie Spector, Estelle Bennett), which had five Top 40 singles produced by Phil Spector, including the No. 2 hit *Be My Baby* in 1963.

1968

The Bee Gees perform their first U.S. concert, at the Anaheim Convention Center in California.

1986

Paul McCartney is presented with "The Award of Merit" during the American Music Awards.

NUMBER ONE SONGS:

1962
Peppermint Twist by Joey Dee & The Starlighters (3)
1973
Superstition by Stevie Wonder (1)

28

1946

Rick Allen is born in Little Rock, Arkansas. Organ and bass player for The Box Tops (Alex Chilton, Bill Cunningham, Tom Boggs, Gary Talley). (See Bill Cunningham, January 23.)

1948

Corky Laing is born in Montreal, Quebec. Drummer for the power rock trio Mountain (Felix Pappalardi, Leslie West) from 1970 to 1977, during its most popular incarnation, when the group had three Top 40 LPs and its only pop single, *Mississippi Queen.*

1956

Elvis Presley makes his national television debut on *Stage Show,* which is hosted by Tommy and Jimmy Dorsey. He plays *Heartbreak Hotel* and *Blue Suede Shoes.*

1985

We Are the World is recorded in Los Angeles by USA for Africa, led by Harry Belafonte to benefit Ethiopia. Musicians include Michael Jackson, Lionel Richie, Ray Charles, Bruce Springsteen, Hall & Oates, Tina Turner, Cyndi Lauper, Diana Ross, the Pointer Sisters, Sheila E and Bob Dylan.

AN ILLUSTRATED RECORD OF ROCK 'N' ROLL

29

1947

David Byron is born in Essex, England. Lead singer for the English heavy metal group Uriah Heep (Mick Box, Ken Hensley, Paul Newton, Alan Napier), which had five Top 40 LPs between 1972 and 1974 and a single hit, *Easy Livin'*, in 1972.

1964

The Beatles record *Can't Buy Me Love*, a No. 1 single, and the German versions of *I Want to Hold Your Hand* and *She Loves You* at Pate Marconi Studios in Paris.

NUMBER ONE SONGS:

1977

Car Wash by Rose Royce (1)

30

1941

Joe Terranova is born in Philadelphia. Baritone vocalist for Danny and The Juniors (Danny Rapp, Frank Mattei, Dave White), the Philadelphia vocal quartet that produced four Top 40 singles between 1957 and 1960, including the No. 1 *At the Hop* and the anthem *Rock and Roll Is Here to Stay*.

1942

Marty Balin is born in Cincinnati, Ohio. Vocalist for Jefferson Airplane (Paul Kantner, Jorma Kaukonen, Signe Anderson, Bob Harvey, Skip Spence, later Jack Casady, Grace Slick, Spencer Dryden, Papa John Creach, John Barbata, Aynsley Dunbar, among others), later renamed Jefferson Starship, one of the San Francisco-based rock groups that used diverse styles of music successfully and helped usher in the era of psychedelia in the mid 1960s. The band had more than 30 hit albums, with a variety of cast members, including the Airplane's landmark LP *Surrealistic Pillow* in 1967, which included two hit singles, *Somebody to Love* and *White Rabbit*, and the No. 1 *Red Octopus* in 1975 as Starship. Balin had a brief solo career, which included the Top 10 single *Hearts* from his album *Balin*.

1947

Steve Marriott is born in London. Lead singer, guitarist, keyboardist

and harmonica player for the hard-rock band Humble Pie (Peter Frampton, Greg Ridley, Jerry Shirley) and for Small Faces (1966 to 1969). Humble Pie had four Top 40 albums, including the live LP *Eat It* and the No. 6 *Smokin'*.

1969

The Beatles play together for the last time, in an impromptu session on the roof of Apple Records in London, after the *Let It Be* recording session breaks down into disagreements. Five songs are played (*Get Back* is done twice) in less than 30 minutes.

1976

Lightnin' Hopkins, influential blues artist who was one of the traditional blues musicians most frequently recorded by R&B-based rock performers, dies in Houston at age 64.

1980

Professor Longhair, innovative piano stylist who pioneered early rock 'n' roll piano techniques, dies in New Orleans at age 62.

NUMBER ONE SONGS:

1961

Will You Love Me Tomorrow by the Shirelles (2)

1982

I Can't Go for That (No Can Do) by Hall & Oates (1)

1988

Need You Tonight by INXS (1)

31

1946

Terry Kath is born in Chicago, Illinois. Guitarist and cofounder, with Walter Parazaider, of the jazz-rock group Chicago Transit Authority (Walt Perry, Peter Cetera, Robert Lamm, Danny Seraphine, James Pankow, Lee Loughnane), which later became known as Chicago. The group had more than 30 Top 40 hits and 15 Top 25 LPs, including five No. 1 albums, *Chicago V* through *Chicago IX*. Kath died January 23, 1978, of an accidental gunshot wound.

1951

Phil Collins is born in London. Drummer, vocalist and songwriter for Genesis (Tony Banks, Mike Rutherford), one of the most successful bands of the 1980s, with

the albums *Invisible Touch*, *Three Sides Live*, *Abacab* and *Genesis* and the singles *Misunderstanding*, *Man on the Corner* and the No. 1 *Invisible Touch*. His parallel solo career has included the No. 1 singles *Against All Odds (Take a Look at Me Now)*, *One More Night*, *Sussudio*, *Another Day in Paradise* and *Two Hearts* and the No. 1 LP *No Jacket Required*.

1951

Phil Manzanera is born in London. Guitarist for the innovative English art-rock group Roxy Music, led by Bryan Ferry. More popular in England than in the U.S., the group had three Top 40 albums and one Top 30 single, *Love Is the Drug*.

1970

Slim Harpo, influential bluesman whose song *I'm a King Bee* was an early showpiece for The Rolling Stones, dies of a heart attack in Baton Rouge, Louisiana.

1973

Bruce Springsteen performs for the first time in New York City, at The Gaslight.

NUMBER ONE SONGS:

1970

I Want You Back by The Jackson 5 (1)

1976

Love Rollercoaster by Ohio Players (1)

1981

The Tide Is High by Blondie (1)

1

1937

Don Everly (The Everly Brothers) is born in Brownie, Kentucky. Inducted into the Rock and Roll Hall of Fame January 29, 1986. (See Phil Everly, January 19.)

1937

Ray Sawyer is born in Chickasaw, Alabama. Lead singer and guitarist for Dr. Hook and The Medicine Show (Dennis Locorriere, William Francis, George Cummings, John Jay David), which had 10 Top 35 singles between 1972 and 1982 but is best known for its satirical No. 6 hit *The Cover of Rolling Stone*.

NUMBER ONE SONGS:

1964

I Want to Hold Your Hand by The Beatles (7)

1969

Crimson and Clover by Tommy James & The Shondells (2)

1975

Laughter in the Rain by Neil Sedaka (1)

2

1939

Roberta Flack is born in Asheville, North Carolina. Pianist and vocalist who had nine Top 30 singles ballads as a solo or as a duo with Donny Hathaway between 1972 and 1982, including three No. 1 solo hits: *The First Time Ever I Saw Your Face*, *Killing Me Softly with His Song* and *Feel Like Makin' Love*.

1942

Graham Nash is born in Blackpool, England. Guitarist, vocalist and founding member of The Hollies (Anthony Hicks, Allan Clarke, Donald Rathbone, Eric Haydock), second only to The Beatles as singles hitmakers in Britain. The group had 12 Top 40 singles between 1966 and 1983, including *Bus Stop*; *Carrie-Anne*; *Stop Stop Stop*; *On a Carousel*; *He Ain't Heavy, He's My Brother*; *Long Cool Woman (in a Black Dress)* and *The Air That I Breathe*. He left The Hollies in 1968 to form the supergroup Crosby, Stills & Nash with David Crosby and Stephen Stills. CSN had six Top 30 hits in its early days and four more with Neil Young, including *Woodstock* and *Teach Your Children*. Nash also performed as a duo with Crosby.

1943

Peter Macbeth is born in London. Bassist for The Foundations. (See Tim Harris, January 14.)

1956

Atlantic Records signs The Coasters (Carl Gardner, Leon Hughes, Billy Guy, Bobby Nunn), who had just changed their name from The Robins.

1973

Midnight Special debuts on NBC television.

1979

Sid Vicious of The Sex Pistols dies in

PHIL COLLINS, 1977
Genesis

Richardson decide to fly ahead to Moorhead, Minnesota, instead of riding the tour bus and are killed when the plane crashes in a field near Mason City, Iowa. The event was recalled as "The Day the Music Died" in Don McLean's No. 1 hit *American Pie* in 1972.

1968
Green Tambourine by The Lemon Pipers (1)
1973
Crocodile Rock by Elton John (3)

4

1941
John Steel is born in Newcastle-upon-Tyne, England. Drummer for The Animals (Alan Price, Eric Burdon, Chas Chandler, Hilton Valentine), the British Invasion group based in R&B. The group had 14 Top 40 singles and is best known for the No. 1 hit *The House of the Rising Sun*.

1948
Alice Cooper is born Vincent Furnier in Detroit. Theatrical shock-rock performer who had 10 Top 40 singles and eight Top 35 LPs in the 1970s, including the No. 1 album *Billion Dollar Babies* and the No. 2 LP *School's Out*.

1956
James Brown makes his first record, on the Federal label at radio station WIBB in Macon, Georgia, titled *Please, Please*.

1975
Louis Jordan, shuffle-boogie rhythm stylist who is a member of the Rock and Roll Hall of Fame, dies at age 67 in Chicago.

1983
Karen Carpenter, who with her brother, Richard, formed the 1970s pop duo The Carpenters, dies in Los Angeles at age 33 of a heart attack.

1978
Stayin' Alive by The Bee Gees (4)
1984
Karma Chameleon by Culture Club (3)
1989
When I'm with You by Sheriff (1)

New York City at age 22 from a heroin overdose.

1974
The Way We Were by Barbra Streisand (3)
1985
I Want to Know What Love Is by Foreigner (2)

3

1935
Johnny "Guitar" Watson is born in Houston, Texas. Influential blues guitarist whose style was important to the development of many 1960s musicians, most notably Jimi Hendrix.

1943
Dennis Edwards is born in Birmingham, Alabama. Vocalist who replaced David Ruffin in The Temptations (Otis Williams, Eddie Kendricks, Paul Williams, Melvin Franklin, Eldridge Bryant), the most popular male vocal group of the 1960s and early 1970s. The Temptations had 35 Top 40 songs, including *I Wish It Would Rain, Cloud Nine, Psychedelic Shack* and *Ball of Confusion (That's What the World Is Today)*, and four No. 1 hits—*My Girl, I Can't Get Next to You, Just My Imagination (Running Away with Me)* and *Papa Was a Rollin' Stone*. Inducted into the Rock and Roll Hall of Fame January 18, 1989.

1947
Dave Davies is born in London. Guitarist and vocalist for The Kinks (Ray Davies, Mick Avory, Pete Quaife), the British Invasion band that had 12 Top 40 singles hits and as many albums over nearly 20 years. The group's most popular songs were *You Really Got Me, Lola, All Day and All of the Night, Tired of Waiting for You* and *Come Dancing*.

1947
Melanie Safka is born in New York City. Known by her first name, Melanie had six Top 40 songs in the 1970s, including *Lay Down (Candles in the Rain)* and the No. 1 single *Brand New Key*.

1959
The Winter Dance Party Tour, which includes Dion & The Belmonts, Ritchie Valens, Buddy Holly, The Big Bopper (J. P. Richardson) and Waylon Jennings, plays The Surf Ballroom in Clear Lake, Iowa. Holly, Valens and

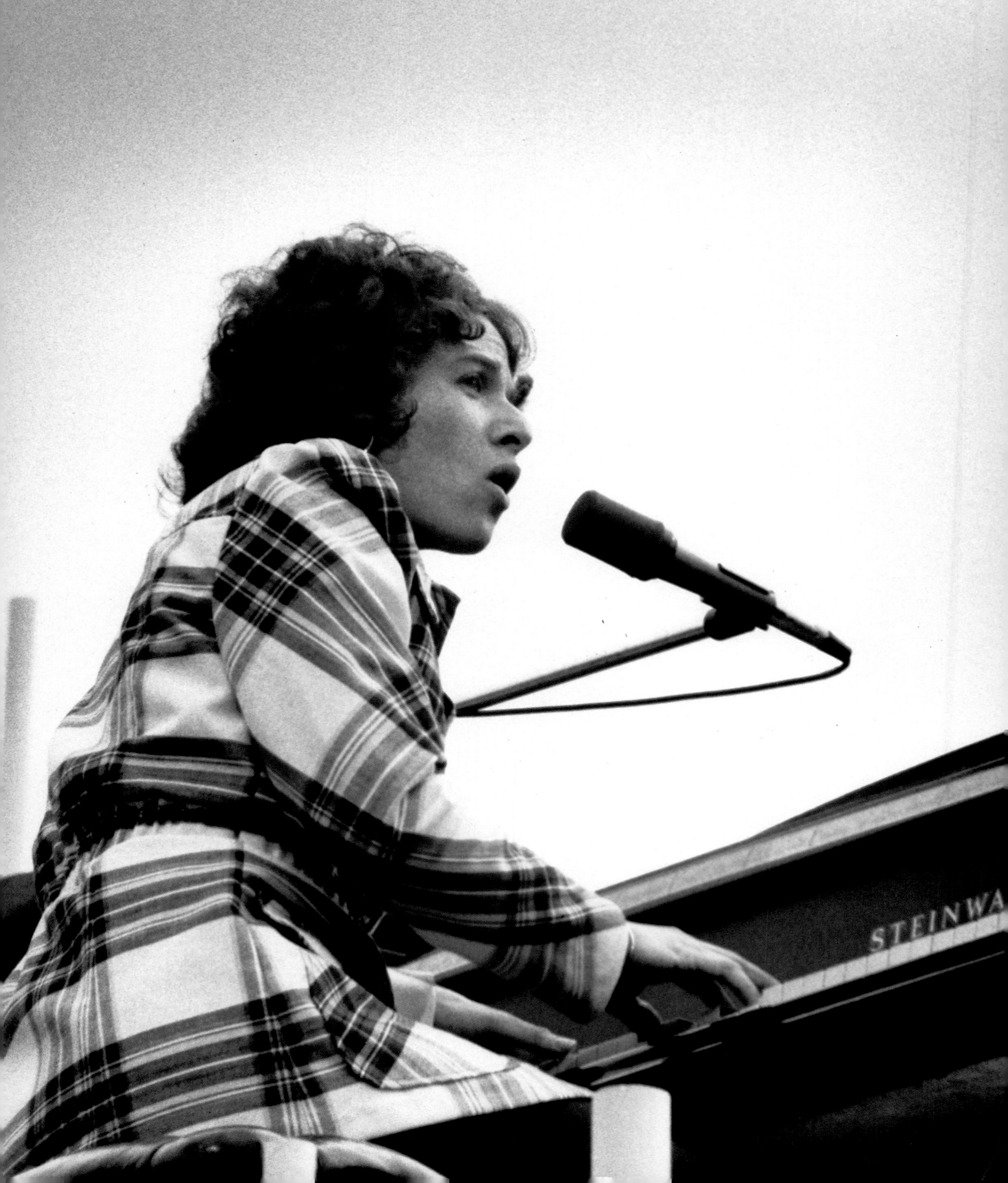

CAROLE KING, 1973

AN ILLUSTRATED RECORD OF ROCK 'N' ROLL

5

1944
Al Kooper is born in New York City. Influential keyboard player, arranger and producer. He was a founding member of Blood, Sweat & Tears (Steve Katz, Fred Lipsius, Jim Fielder, Bobby Colomby, Dick Halligan, Randy Brecker, Jerry Weiss), which influenced jazz-rock fusion, and was a sought-after session player after adding the organ to Bob Dylan's *Like a Rolling Stone* and the *Highway 61* sessions, along with session work for The Rolling Stones' *Let It Bleed* and with Jimi Hendrix on *Electric Ladyland*. One of his best-known recordings is *Super Session* with Mike Bloomfield, Stephen Stills and Harvey Brooks. He later produced albums for Lynyrd Skynard and The Tubes.

1945
Corey Wells is born in Buffalo, New York. Vocalist for Three Dog Night (Danny Hutton, Chuck Negron, Mike Allsup, Jimmy Greenspoon, Joe Schermie, Floyd Sneed), the pop band in the late 1960s and early 1970s that had 21 Top 40 singles and 12 Top 30 LPs by covering songs written by a variety of songwriters, including Harry Nilsson, Hoyt Axton, Elton John, Randy Newman, Laura Nyro and others. The group's No. 1 singles include *Mama Told Me (Not to Come)*, *Joy to the World* and *Black & White*.

1972
Mother and Child Reunion becomes Paul Simon's first single release since the breakup of Simon & Garfunkel.

NUMBER ONE SONGS:

1966
My Love by Petula Clark (2)
1977
Torn Between Two Lovers by Mary MacGregor (2)
1983
Africa by Toto (1)

6

1943
Fabian Forte is born in Philadelphia. One of several teen idols from Philadelphia in the 1950s, he was known by his first name and had eight Top 40 hits, including *Tiger*, *Hound Dog Man* and *Turn Me Loose*.

1957
Bill Haley & The Comets perform at the Dominion Theatre in London, the first time an American rock 'n' roll group plays in England.

1970
The Everly Brothers Show LP is recorded at the Grand Hotel in Anaheim, California.

NUMBER ONE SONGS:

1965
You've Lost That Lovin' Feelin' by The Righteous Brothers (2)
1982
Centerfold by The J. Geils Band (6)
1987
Open Your Heart by Madonna (1)
1988
Could've Been by Tiffany (2)

7

1960
Warner Brothers Records signs The Everly Brothers to a 10-year contract for $1 million.

1964
The Beatles fly to the United States for the first time and are met by thousands of screaming fans at Kennedy Airport.

1966
Crawdaddy magazine publishes its first edition in New York City.

1980
Pink Floyd opens its tour to promote the album *The Wall* with a three-dimensional stage show at the Sports Arena in Los Angeles.

NUMBER ONE SONGS:

1970
Venus by The Shocking Blue (1)
1976
50 Ways to Leave Your Lover by Paul Simon (3)

8

1941
Tom Rush is born in Portsmouth, New Hampshire. Primarily a folksinger, Rush helped introduce the songs of James Taylor, Jackson Browne and Joni Mitchell to mass audiences during his performances in the 1960s and 1970s.

1973
Max Yasgur, who owned the farm where the Woodstock Music and Art Festival was held in August 1969, dies.

NUMBER ONE SONGS:

1960
Teen Angel by Mark Dinning (2)
1975
Fire by Ohio Players (1)

9

1949
Carole King is born in New York City. Singer-songwriter who with her husband, Gerry Goffin, co-wrote more than 100 hits, including many of the 1960s' best-known pop songs for other artists, such as *Will You Love Me Tomorrow* (The Shirelles), *Wasn't Born to Follow* (The Byrds), *I'm into Something Good* (Herman's Hermits), *Chains* (Cookies) and *The Loco-Motion* (Little Eva). She helped launch the age of the singer-songwriter in the 1970s with her landmark best-selling album *Tapestry*. Her solo career has included 13 Top 40 singles, such as the No. 1 *It's Too Late/I Feel the Earth Move*, and eight Top 20 LPs, including the No. 1 sellers *Tapestry*, *Music* and *Wrap Around Joy*.

1964
The Beatles make their U.S. television debut on *The Ed Sullivan Show* to an estimated audience of 73 million.

1981
Bill Haley dies of a heart attack in Harlington, Texas, at age 55.

NUMBER ONE SONGS:

1957
Too Much by Elvis Presley (3)
1959
Stagger Lee by Lloyd Price (4)
1963
Hey Paula by Paul & Paula (3)

1974
Love's Theme by Love Unlimited Orchestra (1)

10

NUMBER ONE SONGS:

1958
Don't by Elvis Presley (5)
1968
Love Is Blue by Paul Mauriat (5)
1979
Da Ya Think I'm Sexy by Rod Stewart (4)
1990
Opposites Attract by Paula Abdul with The Wild Pair (3)

11

1935
Gene Vincent is born Eugene Vincent Craddock in Norfolk, Virginia. Early rock 'n' roll singer who had a Top 10 hit with Be-Bop-A-Lula. He died October 12, 1971, at age 36 from a bleeding ulcer.

1963
The Beatles record their first LP, *Please Please Me*, at Abbey Road studios in London. Original songs include *I Saw Her Standing There*, *Please Please Me*, *Love Me Do*, *P.S. I Love You* and covers of *Twist and Shout* and *Chains*.

1964
The Beatles play their first U.S. concert, at the Washington, D.C. Coliseum.

NUMBER ONE SONGS:

1989
Straight Up by Paula Abdul (3)

AN ILLUSTRATED RECORD OF ROCK 'N' ROLL

12

1935
Ray Manzarek is born in Chicago. Keyboardist for The Doors (Robby Krieger, Jim Morrison, John Densmore). The band had 11 Top 40 albums and eight Top 40 singles, including the Top 10 records *Hello, I Love You* and *Touch Me* and the No. 1 hit *Light My Fire*. The band disbanded soon after Morrison's death in 1971.

1964
The Beatles perform at Carnegie Hall in New York City.

NUMBER ONE SONGS:

1972
Let's Stay Together by Al Green (1)

13

1942
Peter Tork is born in Washington, D.C. Vocalist and bass player for The Monkees (Mickey Dolenz, Davy Jones, Mike Nesmith), the made-for-TV pop group styled after The Beatles. The group had 12 Top 40 singles, including three No. 1 hits—*Last Train to Clarksville*, *I'm a Believer* and *Daydream Believer*—and seven Top 35 LPs, including four consecutive No. 1 albums—*The Monkees*, *More of the Monkees*, *Headquarters* and *Pisces, Aquarius, Capricorn & Jones, Ltd.*

1966
The Rolling Stones appear on *The Ed Sullivan Show*.

1972
The 1950s nostalgia musical *Grease* opens off-Broadway in New York City.

NUMBER ONE SONGS:

1971
One Bad Apple by The Osmonds (5)

14

1943
Eric Anderson is born in Pittsburgh. Folksinger and songwriter whose songs, such as *Thirsty Boots*, have been recorded by Judy Collins, Johnny Cash, Joan Baez and Peter, Paul and Mary. His best-known solo LP is *Blue River*.

NUMBER ONE SONGS:

1970
Thank You by Sly & The Family Stone (2)
1987
Livin' on a Prayer by Bon Jovi (4)

15

1941
Brian Holland is born in Detroit. One-third of the team of Holland- (Lamont) Dozier- (brother Eddie) Holland, which wrote and produced most of Motown's biggest hits in the 1960s for performers such as The Supremes, Marvin Gaye, The Four Tops, The Temptations and The Isley Brothers. Their hit songs include *Heat Wave*, *Baby Love*, *I Can't Help Myself*, *Reach Out, I'll Be There* and *You Keep Me Hangin' On*. Inducted into the Rock and Roll Hall of Fame in 1990.

1944
Mick Avory is born in London. Drummer for The Kinks (Ray Davies, Dave Davies, Pete Quaife). (See Dave Davies, February 3.)

1951
Melissa Manchester is born in New York City. Singer-songwriter who began as a backup singer for Bette Midler. She had seven Top 40 singles, including the Top 10 hits *Midnight Blue*, *Don't Cry Out Loud* and *You Should Hear How She Talks About You*, from her four Top 35 LPs.

1957
The Greatest Show of 1957 tour begins with featured performers Chuck Berry, Fats Domino, Clyde McPhatter and LaVern Baker.

1961
Jackie Wilson is shot by fan Juanita Jones and spends two weeks in the hospital.

NUMBER ONE SONGS:

1969
Everyday People by Sly & The Family Stone (4)
1975
You're No Good by Linda Ronstadt (1)
1986
How Will I Know by Whitney Houston (1)

16

1935
Sonny Bono is born Salvatore Bono in Detroit. Singer-songwriter who gained fame with his wife, Cherilyn Sarkasian LaPier, known as Cher, in the 1960s as a duo with 10 Top 35 singles, including the No. 1 hit *I Got You Babe*. They had a network television series from 1971 to 1975 before their divorce ended their success and Cher went on to a solo career as a singer and actor. Sonny won election as mayor of Palm Springs, California, in 1988.

1958
The Dick Clark Show, a prime time version of *American Bandstand*, debuts on ABC television.

1964
The Beatles make their second appearance on *The Ed Sullivan Show*.

1968
The Beatles go to India to study with the Maharish Mahesh Yogi.

NUMBER ONE SONGS:

1980
Do That to Me One More Time by The Captain & Tennille (1)
1985
Careless Whisper by Wham! (3)

17

1933
Bobby Lewis is born in Indianapolis. Singer who recorded both the No. 1 hit *Tossin' and Turnin'* and the Top 10 single *One Track Mind* in 1961.

18

1941
Gene Pitney is born in Hartford, Connecticut. Singer-songwriter who had 16 Top 40 singles in the 1960s, including *Town Without Pity*, *(The Man Who Shot) Liberty Valance*, *It Hurts to Be in Love* and *I'm Gonna Be Strong*.

1971
James Taylor performs *Fire and Rain* during his first major television appearance, on *The Johnny Cash Show*.

1972
Pink Floyd performs the first of four shows premiering the LP *Dark Side of the Moon* at the Rainbow in London.

NUMBER ONE SONGS:

1962
Duke of Earl by Gene Chandler

1933
Yoko Ono is born in Tokyo. Conceptual artist who married John Lennon March 20, 1969. Lennon credited his wife with expanding his creative horizons into film, art and music. She recorded with Lennon as part of the Plastic Ono Band and on his last album, the No. 1 *Double Fantasy*.

1980
Bon Scott, vocalist for AC/DC, dies at age 34 after an all-night drinking binge.

NUMBER ONE SONGS:

1956
The Great Pretender by The Platters (2)
1967
Kind of a Drag by The Buckinghams (2)

JOHNNY WINTER, 1969

19

1878
Thomas Edison obtains U.S. patent number 200,521 for his latest invention, the phonograph.

1940
William "Smokey" Robinson is born in Detroit, Michigan. Leader and musical force behind The Miracles (Ronnie White, Bobby Rogers, Peter Moore, Claudette Rogers Robinson), one of the earliest Motown Records groups, with hits like *Shop Around*, *The Tears of a Clown* and *I Second That Emotion*. His solo career includes the Top 10 hits *Being with You* and *Cruisin'*. Inducted into the Rock and Roll Hall of Fame January 21, 1987.

1943
Lou Christie is born Lugee Geno Saco in Glen Willard, Pennsylvania. Falsetto-style singer who had a No. 1 hit in 1966 with *Lightnin' Strikes*, one of five Top 25 singles he had between 1963 and 1969.

1948
Tony Iommi is born in Birmingham, England. Guitarist and songwriter for Black Sabbath (Ozzy Osbourne, Geezer Butler, Bill Ward), the English heavy metal band that had 10 Top 40 LPs, including the Top 10 albums *Master of Reality* and *Sabbath Bloody Sabbath*.

1955
Pat Boone is introduced by Dot Records as "a great new voice."

NUMBER ONE SONGS:

1972
Without You by Nilsson (4)
1977
Blinded by the Light by Manfred Mann's Earth Band (1)
1983
Baby, Come to Me by Patti Austin with James Ingram (2)

February

20

1898
Jimmy Yancey is born in Chicago. Innovative pianist who developed the boogie-woogie style of playing, which emphasized bass lines and influenced the playing of early rockers such as Fats Domino. He died September 17, 1951, in Chicago at age 53. Inducted into the Rock and Roll Hall of Fame January 20, 1986.

1940
Barbara Ellis is born in Olympia, Washington. Member of the vocal trio The Fleetwoods (Gary Troxel, Gretchen Diane Christopher), which had nine Top 40 singles between 1959 and 1963, including two No.1 hits, *Come Softly to Me* and *Mr. Blue*.

1946
J. Geils is born Jerome Geils in New York City. Founder of and guitarist for The J. Geils Band (Peter Wolf, Magic Dick, Danny Klein, Stephen Jo Bladd), an R&B band known for its live performances. The group had 10 Top 40 singles, including the No. 1 hit *Centerfold*, and seven Top 10 LPs, including the No. 1 *Freeze-Frame*, in the late 1970s and early 1980s.

1951
Randy California is born in Los Angeles. Guitarist for the rock fusion group Spirit (Jay Ferguson, John Locke, Mark Andes, Ed Cassidy), which had a Top 25 single, *I Got a Line On You*, in 1969 but is best known for its continual touring over the years.

NUMBER ONE SONGS:

1965
This Diamond Ring by Gary Lewis & The Playboys (2)
1988
Seasons Change by Expose (1)

21

1976
Florence Ballard, founder of The Supremes, dies at age 32 in Detroit of a heart attack.

1982
Murray The K (Kaufman), pioneering disc jockey who was the original host of the *Soundtrack of the '60s* syndicated radio program and host of The Beatles' concerts at Carnegie Hall and Shea Stadium in New York City, dies of cancer at age 60 in Los Angeles.

NUMBER ONE SONGS:

1981
9 to 5 by Dolly Parton (3)

22

1963
Northern Songs, the Beatles' music-publishing company, is formed.

NUMBER ONE SONGS:

1960
The Theme from a Summer Place by Percy Faith (9)
1975
Pick up the Pieces by Average White Band (1)

23

1944
Johnny Winter is born in Leland, Mississippi. Blues guitarist who has played with Mike Bloomfield, Rick Derringer and his brother, Edgar Winter, over a long career. He had three Top 25 LPs between 1969 and 1973.

1946
Rusty Young is born in Long Beach, California. Pedal steel guitarist for Poco (Richie Furay, Jim Messina, George Grantham, Randy Meisner), the country-rock band formed out of the breakup of Buffalo Springfield. The band had two Top 20 singles, *Crazy Love* and *Heart of the Night*.

1952
Brad Whitford is born in Winchester, Massachusetts. Guitarist for Aerosmith (Joe Perry, Tom Hamilton, Steven Tyler, Joey Kramer), the heavy metal band based in the blues that has had seven Top 40 singles and nine Top 40 LPs. The band's top singles include *Dream On, Walk This Way* and *Janie's Got a Gun*.

1979
Dire Straits begins its first U.S. tour at the Paradise Club in Boston.

NUMBER ONE SONGS:

1980
Crazy Little Thing Called Love by Queen (4)

24

1944
Nicky Hopkins is born in London. Keyboard player known for his session work and for touring with major groups. He has played with Jeff Beck, Rod Stewart, The Beatles, The Rolling Stones, The Who, The Kinks and Quicksilver Messenger Service, among others.

1958
Good Golly, Miss Molly by Little Richard enters the Billboard Top 40 charts, where it reaches No. 10. It is on the charts for 10 weeks.

1965
The Beatles begin filming *Help!* in the Bahamas.

25

1987
B. B. King is presented a Lifetime Achievement Award at the 29th annual Grammy Awards.

NUMBER ONE SONGS:

1958
Get a Job by The Silhouettes (2)
1973
Killing Me Softly with His Song by Roberta Flack (5)

1943
George Harrison is born in Liverpool, England. Lead guitarist for The Beatles (John Lennon, Paul McCartney, Ringo Starr), the most influential band in rock 'n' roll history. The group expanded the possibilities of writing, recording and sound and was the first band to perform almost exclusively its own compositions. The all-time greatest recording group had 21 No. 1 hits and 15 No. 1 albums in the decade of the 1960s. As a solo performer, Harrison has had two No. 1 singles, *My Sweet Lord* and *Give Me Love (Give Me Peace on Earth)*, as part of 11 Top 40 records. He also has had two No. 1 LPs, *All Things Must Pass* and *Living in the Material World*, among his 10 solo LPs. Later formed The Traveling Wilburys with Bob Dylan, Tom Petty, Roy Orbison and Jeff Lynne. Inducted into the Rock and Roll Hall of Fame with The Beatles January 20, 1988.

1957
Buddy Holly and his group, The Crickets, record *That'll Be the Day* at Norman Petty's studio in Clovis, Texas. The record stayed on the charts for 16 weeks and reached No. 1.

1963
Please Please Me becomes the first Beatles record released in the U.S.

1983
Marvin Gaye wins his first Grammy Award, for *(Sexual) Healing* as Best Male Vocal Performance of the Year.

NUMBER ONE SONGS:

1984
Jump by Van Halen (5)

AN ILLUSTRATED RECORD OF ROCK 'N' ROLL

26

1928
Antoine "Fats" Domino is born in New Orleans, Louisiana. An established R&B performer by the time rock 'n' roll began, he became one of rock's top hitmakers with his first Top 10 record, *Ain't That a Shame*, and continued with songs like *Blueberry Hill*, *I'm Walkin'* and *Walkin' to New Orleans*. Inducted into the Rock and Roll Hall of Fame January 20, 1986.

1932
Johnny Cash is born in Kingsland, Arkansas. Singer, songwriter and guitarist known as the "Man in Black," his style and sound influenced country-rock performers. He had 12 Top 40 singles hits, including *I Walk the Line*, *Ring of Fire*, *Folsom Prison Blues* and the No. 2 *A Boy Named Sue*, from the No. 1 LP *Johnny Cash at San Quentin*. Inducted into the Rock and Roll Hall of Fame in 1992.

1954
U.S. Rep. Ruth Thompson of Michigan introduces a bill in Congress to prohibit the mailing of "obscene, lewd, lascivious or filthy discs or other articles capable of producing sound" in an effort to cut the popularity of R&B singles.

1955
Billboard reports that 45 rpm singles outsell 78 rpm LPs for the first time.

NUMBER ONE SONGS:

1966
These Boots Are Made for Walkin' by Nancy Sinatra (1)
1977
New Kid in Town by The Eagles (1)

27

NUMBER ONE SONGS:

1961
Pony Time by Chubby Checker (3)
1988
Father Figure by George Michael (2)

28

1942
Brian Jones is born Lewis Brian Hopkins-Jones in Cheltenham, England. Guitarist and founding member of The Rolling Stones (Mick Jagger, Charlie Watts, Bill Wyman, Keith Richards), the R&B-based rock group that proclaimed itself the "world's greatest rock 'n' roll band" and has lived up to that claim for over 25 years with more than 40 top LPs and more than 30 Top 40 singles. Among the No. 1 hits during Jones's time with the band were *(I Can't Get No) Satisfaction*, *Get off of My Cloud*, *Paint It Black* and *Ruby Tuesday*. He died at age 27 on July 3, 1969 (shortly after leaving the Stones), drowned in his swimming pool.

1942
Joe South is born in Atlanta, Georgia. Singer-songwriter who had brief success in 1969 to 1970 with two Top 15 singles, *Games People Play* and *Walk a Mile in My Shoes*.

1966
Authorities in Liverpool close down the Cavern Club, where The Beatles first built their reputation, because of high debts.

NUMBER ONE SONGS:

1970
Bridge Over Troubled Water by Simon & Garfunkel (6)
1976
Theme from S.W.A.T. by Rhythm Heritage (1)
1981
I Love a Rainy Night by Eddie Rabbitt (2)

29

1968
Aretha Franklin wins her first Grammy Award, for *Respect*, the Best Female R&B Vocal Performance, the first time the category is included in the awards.

1

1917
Ralph J. Gleason is born in San Francisco. Influential music critic and writer who was cofounder of the first jazz magazine, *Jazz Information*, and of the first rock magazine, *Rolling Stone*. He died June 3, 1975, in Berkeley, California, of a heart attack at age 58.

1944
Roger Daltrey is born in London. Lead singer for The Who (Pete Townshend, John Entwistle, Keith Moon, later Kenny Jones), which personified 1960s teenage rebellion in its music and its actions, becoming known for smashing its instruments after performing during the band's early days. The Who created the first rock opera, *Tommy*, one of its 12 Top 40 LPs, which also included *Who Are You* and the No. 2 *Quadrophenia*. The albums produced 16 Top 40 singles, with *I Can See for Miles* as a Top 10 hit. Daltrey's solo career resulted in two Top 30 LPs before he concentrated on acting. Inducted into the Rock and Roll Hall of Fame in 1990.

1958
Buddy Holly & The Crickets open their only tour of England at The Trocadero Elephant and Castle in London.

1969
Police arrest Jim Morrison after he is charged with exposing himself during a show at the Dinner Key Auditorium in Miami.

1975
Aretha Franklin wins her 10th Grammy Award, for *Ain't Nothing Like the Real Thing*, as the Best Female R&B Vocal Performance of 1974.

NUMBER ONE SONGS:

1975
Best of My Love by The Eagles (1)
1986
Kyrie by Mr. Mister (3)

2

1942
Charlie Christian, pioneering guitarist and member of the Rock and Roll Hall of Fame, dies in New York City of pneumonia at age 26.

1943
Lou Reed is born in Brooklyn, New York. Avant-garde singer-songwriter who founded The Velvet Undergroud (John Cale, Sterling Morrison, Maureen Tucker, Nico), which was known for its bleak, alienated outlook on the world. His solo career is best known for the Top 20 single *Walk on the Wild Side* and the concert album *Rock 'n' Roll Animal*.

1950
Karen Carpenter is born in New Haven, Connecticut. With her brother, Richard, formed the 1970s pop duo The Carpenters, which had 20 Top 35 singles, including the No. 1 songs *(They Long to Be) Close to You*, *Top of the World* and *Please Mr. Postman* and the No. 2 hits *We've Only Just Begun*, *Superstar*, *Hurting Each Other* and *Yesterday Once More*. She died February 4, 1983, in Los Angeles of a heart attack resulting from anorexia nervosa.

1958
Buddy Holly & The Crickets appear on live television in England for the first time, on *Sunday Night at the London Palladium*.

NUMBER ONE SONGS:

1974
Seasons in the Sun by Terry Jacks (3)

3

1927
Junior Parker is born Herman Parker in West Memphis, Arkansas. Blues vocalist and harmonica player who performed with Howlin' Wolf, B. B. King and Johnny Ace but is better known for writing *Mystery Train*, the 1955 classic recorded by Elvis Presley. He died November 19, 1971, following brain surgery.

1938
Willie Chambers is born in Mississippi. One of the four Chambers Brothers

JOHNNY CASH, 1969
*with June Carter Cash
and Carl Perkins*

(Lester, George, Joe), the pioneering and innovative funk/psychedelic band that had the Top 40 hits *I Can't Turn You Loose* and *Time Has Come Today* in the late 1960s.

1966
Stephen Stills invites Neil Young, Richie Furay, Bruce Palmer and Dewey Martin to Los Angeles to discuss forming a new band, which becomes Buffalo Springfield.

NUMBER ONE SONGS:

1990
Escapade by Janet Jackson (3)

1944
Bobby Womack is born in Cleveland, Ohio. Singer, songwriter and guitarist who had a successful solo career as a vocalist but is known as a top-flight session guitarist, playing with and writing for Sam Cooke and Wilson Pickett. As a performer, he had four Top 35 hits, including the Top 10 hit *Lookin' for a Love*.

1948
Chris Squire is born in London. Bass player and founding member of Yes (Jon Anderson, Peter Banks, Tony Kaye, Bill Bruford, later Rick Wakeman, Steve Howe), one of the most important progressive-rock bands of the 1970s, which combined vocal harmonies with superb musicianship. Yes had more than 10 Top 40 albums but is best known for its early works, *Fragile* and *Close to the Edge*. In 1983 the band had its only No. 1 hit, *Owner of a Lonely Heart*.

1966
John Lennon says that The Beatles "are now more popular than Christ" in an interview with Maureen Cleave of the *London Evening Standard*.

When the quote is reported out of context in the U.S., Beatle effigies and the band's records are burned.

NUMBER ONE SONGS:

1967
Ruby Tuesday by The Rolling Stones (1)

1978
(Love Is) Thicker Than Water by Andy Gibb (2)

1989
Lost in Your Eyes by Debbie Gibson (3)

AN ILLUSTRATED RECORD OF ROCK 'N' ROLL

5

1955
Elvis Presley's first television appearance takes place on *The Louisiana Hayride*.

1960
Eddie Cochran makes his only live radio broadcast in England on the BBC's *Saturday Club*, where he sings *C'mon Everybody*.

1960
Elvis Presley is discharged from the U.S. Army at Fort Dix, New Jersey.

1971
Aretha Franklin, Ray Charles, King Curtis and Tower of Power open a three-night stand at the Fillmore West in San Francisco.

1977
The British series *Rock Follies* debuts on U.S. television.

1985
5,000 radio stations around the world broadcast *We Are the World* by USA for Africa at 5:30 p.m. GMT.

NUMBER ONE SONGS:

1966
The Ballad of the Green Berets by Sgt. Barry Sadler (5)
1977
Love Theme from A Star Is Born (Evergreen) by Barbra Streisand (3)
1983
Billie Jean by Michael Jackson (7)

6

1944
David Gilmour is born in Cambridge, England. Guitarist and vocalist for Pink Floyd (Syd Barrett, Richard Wright, Roger Waters, Nick Mason). (See Syd Barrett, January 6.)

1944
Mary Wilson is born in Detroit. Founding member of The Supremes (Diana Ross, Florence Ballard), the most successful female group of the 1960s, which helped establish the Motown Sound. The Supremes had 30 Top 40 hits between 1963 and 1976, including the No. 1 hits *Where Did Our Love Go, Baby Love, Come See About Me,*

Stop! In the Name of Love, I Hear a Symphony and *You Can't Hurry Love*. Inducted into the Rock and Roll Hall of Fame January 20, 1988.

1947
Kiki Dee is born Pauline Matthews in Yorkshire, England. Vocalist who gave Elton John his first No. 1 single in England with the duet *Don't Go Breaking My Love*.

NUMBER ONE SONGS:

1965
My Girl by The Temptations (1)
1976
Love Machine (Part 1) by The Miracles (1)

7

1946
Peter Wolf is born Peter Blankfield in New York City. Vocalist for The J. Geils Band (J. Geils, Magic Dick, Danny Klein, Stephen Jo Bladd). (See J. Geils, February 20.)

1948
Peggy March is born in Philadelphia. As "Little Peggy March" she had a No. 1 hit with *I Will Follow Him* at age 15. She also had Top 35 single hits with *I Wish I Were a Princess* and *Hello Heartache, Goodbye Love*.

1958
U.S. disc jockeys gather in Kansas for the first Disc Jockey Convention.

1971
Aretha Franklin and Ray Charles sing an encore duet on the final night of their Fillmore West concerts.

1983
The Nashville Network (TNN), a country music and country life-style entertainment television network that features country-rock stars, is launched by Group W, the Westinghouse Broadcasting Company, Inc.

8

1945
Mickey Dolenz is born in Los Angeles. Drummer and vocalist for The Monkees (Mike Nesmith, Davy Jones, Peter Tork). (See Peter Tork, February 13.)

1946

Randy Meisner is born in Scottsbluff, Nebraska. Bass player and vocalist who was a member of Poco (Richie Furay, Jim Messina, Rusty Young, George Grantham) and later joined Rick Nelson's Stone Canyon Band before becoming a founding member of The Eagles (Don Henley, Bernie Leadon, Glenn Frey, later Don Felder). The quintessential California rock band of the 1970s, The Eagles had seven Top 25 albums, including four consecutive No. 1 LPs—*One of These Nights, Eagles: Their Greatest Hits 1971–1975, Hotel California* and *The Long Run*—and 16 Top 40 singles, including five No. 1 songs: *Best of My Love, One of These Nights, New Kid in Town, Hotel California* and *Heartache Tonight*.

1968
The Fillmore East opens in New York City with performances by Big Brother and the Holding Company, Tim Buckley and Albert King.

1973
Rod "Pigpen" McKernan, keyboardist and vocalist for The Grateful Dead, dies of liver disease in San Francisco at age 30.

NUMBER ONE SONGS:

1975
Have You Never Been Mellow by Olivia Newton-John (1)

9

1934
Lloyd Price is born in New Orleans. Pioneering singer-songwriter who had early R&B hits with *Ain't It a Shame* and *Lawdy Miss Clawdy* before having Top 40 pop success with *Personality, I'm Gonna Get Married* and the No. 1 *Stagger Lee*.

1945
Robin Trower is born in London. Innovative and influential guitarist who began with Procol Harum (Gary Brooker, Matthew Fisher, B. J. Wilson, Dave Knights) but later moved into power guitar, expanding his work as a disciple of Jimi Hendrix. He had eight Top 40 LPs as a solo, including three Top 10 albums: *Bridge of Sighs, For Earth Below* and *Robin Trower Live!*

1948

Jimmie Fadden is born in Long Beach, California. Guitarist, harmonica player and vocalist for the country-rock group The Dirt Band, originally the Nitty Gritty Dirt Band (Jeff Hanna, John McEuen, Jackson Browne, Jimmy Ibbotson, Ralph Barr, Les Thompson, Bruce Kunkel). The group had a Top 10 single hit with *Mr. Bojangles* but is known for its landmark album *Will the Circle Be Unbroken*, which brought together many of country music's biggest names.

NUMBER ONE SONGS:

1959
Venus by Frankie Avalon (5)
1962
Hey! Baby by Bruce Channel (3)
1985
Can't Fight This Feeling by REO Speedwagon (3)

10

1941
Dean Torrence is born in Los Angeles. Half of the vocal group Jan & Dean, with Jan Berry, which created the 1960s "surfing sound" with 14 Top 40 singles, including the No. 1 *Surf City* and the Top 10 singles *Dead Man's Curve* and *The Little Old Lady (from Pasadena)*. Following the automobile accident that nearly killed Berry, Torrence became a successful album cover designer.

1956
Blue Suede Shoes by Carl Perkins enters the Billboard Top 40 charts, where it will stay for 17 weeks, reaching No. 2.

1956
Elvis Presley's *Heartbreak Hotel* is released. It becomes the first of his 18 No. 1 records, staying on the charts for 22 weeks, with eight weeks at the top.

NUMBER ONE SONGS:

1979
I Will Survive by Gloria Gaynor (3)

DAVID GILMOUR, 1973
Pink Floyd

11

1947

Mark Stein is born in Bayonne, New Jersey. Keyboardist and vocalist for Vanilla Fudge (Vince Martell, Tim Bogert, Carmine Appice), pioneering heavy-rock band that popularized recording the long version of songs on albums. The band's best-known song is *You Keep Me Hangin' On*, a No. 6 single, from its debut album, *Vanilla Fudge*.

1967

The Beatles win three Grammy Awards, for the singles *Michelle* and *Eleanor Rigby* and the LP *Revolver*.

1989

Rock & Roll Art & Artifacts exhibition opens at the Museum of Art, Science & Industry in Bridgeport, Connecticut. It is the first time a museum devotes a major exhibit to rock 'n' roll, and it features art works created by musicians such as Joni Mitchell, Ron Wood and Richie Havens, along with album cover and poster art, photos, T-shirts, guitars and other rock memorabilia.

NUMBER ONE SONGS:

1967

Love Is Here and Now You're Gone by The Supremes (1)

AN ILLUSTRATED RECORD OF ROCK 'N' ROLL

12

1917
Leonard Chess is born in Poland. Pioneering record company executive who provided an early forum for black performers such as Chuck Berry, Howlin' Wolf, Elmore James and Willie Dixon on Chess Records, which he co-owned with his brother, Phil. He died October 16, 1969, at age 52. Inducted into the Rock and Roll Hall of Fame January 21, 1987.

1942
Paul Kantner is born in San Francisco. Guitarist and vocalist who was an original member of Jefferson Airplane (Marty Balin, Jorma Kaukonen, Signe Anderson, Bob Harvey, Skip Spence, later Jack Casady, Grace Slick, Spencer Dryden, Papa John Creach, Aynsley Dunbar, among others) when the group had its first success with the Top 10 singles *Somebody to Love* and *White Rabbit*. After the group became Jefferson Starship, it had hits with the Top 10 singles *Miracles* and *Count on Me;* as Starship it had No. 1 hits with *We Built This City* and *Sara*. The various incarnations of the band have had 19 Top 35 LPs, including the No. 1 *Red Octopus*. Kantner had modest solo success with Slick on early 1970s albums.

1948
James Taylor is born in Boston. Singer-songwriter who helped usher in the 1970s folk-rock movement. During his peak years in the '70s, he had 10 Top 40 singles and 10 Top 25 LPs. His biggest hits were *Fire and Rain, How Sweet It Is (to Be Loved by You), Handy Man* and the No. 1 *You've Got a Friend.*

1969
Paul McCartney marries Linda Eastman in London, at the Marylebone Register Office.

NUMBER ONE SONGS:

1988
Never Gonna Give You Up by Rick Astley (2)

13

1933
Mike Stoller is born in Belle Harbor, New York. Along with Jerry Leiber, wrote classic rock 'n' roll songs in the 1950s and '60s, such as *Kansas City, Hound Dog, Yakety-Yak, On Broadway* and *Young Blood,* which have been recorded by major rock performers from Elvis Presley and The Drifters to The Beatles and The Rolling Stones. Inducted into the Rock and Roll Hall of Fame January 21, 1987.

1939
Neil Sedaka is born in Brooklyn, New York. Singer-songwriter who had performing success in the 1960s with a dozen Top 30 singles, including the No. 1 *Breaking Up Is Hard to Do* before reviving his career in the mid 1970s with the No. 1 hits *Laughter in the Rain* and *Bad Blood* (with Elton John).

1965
Eric Clapton decides that The Yardbirds are moving too far from the blues, and he leaves the band.

NUMBER ONE SONGS:

1965
Eight Days a Week by The Beatles (2)
1976
December, 1963 (Oh, What a Night) by The Four Seasons (3)

14

1933
Quincy Jones is born in Chicago. Trumpeter, arranger, composer and producer who has influenced pop music for more than 25 years. He has worked with dozens of musicians, including Ray Charles, LaVern Baker, B. B. King, Little Richard, Paul Simon, Frank Sinatra, Jose Feliciano, Chaka Kahn, James Ingram and Donna Summer. He produced the No. 1 single *We Are the World,* which featured an all-star group of singers, and the best-selling LP of all time, Michael Jackson's *Thriller.*

1960
Sam Cooke begins his first tour of the West Indies in Montego Bay, Jamaica. The tour influences later Jamaican musicians, including Bob Marley and Jimmy Cliff.

1991
Jerome "Doc" Pomus, innovative songwriter who wrote many classic rock hits and is a member of the Rock and Roll Hall of Fame, dies in New York City at age 66 of lung cancer.

NUMBER ONE SONGS:

1987
Jacob's Ladder by Huey Lewis & The News (1)

15

1912
Sam (Lightnin') Hopkins is born in Centerville, Texas. One of the traditional blues musicians most frequently recorded by R&B-based rock performers, including Van Morrison and The Rolling Stones. He died January 30, 1976, at age 63.

1940
Phil Lesh is born Philip Chapman in Berkeley, California. Bassist and vocalist for The Grateful Dead (Jerry Garcia, Bob Weir, Pigpen McKernan, Bill Kreutzmann, later Mickey Hart, Keith Godchaux), one of the longest-running bands in history. An improvisational group from the beginning, the Dead displayed a diversity of musical influences even when they were a psychedelic band. Until *Touch of Grey* the band never had a Top 40 single, but it had 10 Top 30 LPs over the years due to the loyal tour following of its fans, known as Deadheads.

1941
Mike Love is born in Los Angeles. Vocalist for The Beach Boys (Brian Wilson, Carl Wilson, Dennis Wilson, Alan Jardine), the group that established California rock and expanded Jan & Dean's "Surfing Sound" in the 1960s. The Beach Boys had 34 Top 15 singles and 20 Top 35 LPs. Their No. 1 hits include *I Get Around; Help Me, Rhonda; Good Vibrations* and *Kokomo.* Inducted into the Rock and Roll Hall of Fame with The Beach Boys January 20, 1988.

1944
Sly Stone is born Sylvester Stewart in Dallas. Guitarist, keyboardist and vocalist for Sly and the Family Stone (Freddie Stone, Larry Graham, Cynthia Robinson, Greg Errico, Rosie Stone, Jerry Martini), the soul-rock-pop band that had 11 Top 40 singles,

including the No. 1 hits *Everyday People, Thank You (Falettinme Be Mice Elf Agin)* and *Family Affair* from five Top 15 LPs, including the No. 1 album *There's a Riot Goin' On.*

1946
Howard Scott is born in San Pedro, California. Guitarist and vocalist for the Latin-jazz-funk band War (Harold Brown, Papa Dee Allen, B. B. Dickerson, Charles Miller, Lee Oskar, Lonnie Jordan). The group's nine Top 25 albums in the 1970s included the No. 1 *The World Is a Ghetto,* which produced two of the group's 11 singles, *The World Is a Ghetto* and *The Cisco Kid.*

1947
Ry Cooder is born in Los Angeles. Versatile musician who is known for his guitar session work with Taj Mahal, Gordon Lightfoot, Randy Newman, Arlo Guthrie and Little Feat. He later went on to success as an album and film score producer.

1956
Colonel Tom Parker becomes Elvis Presley's manager.

1990
Police in Sarasota, Florida, arrest a record store clerk for selling *As Nasty As They Wanna Be* by 2 Live Crew to an 11-year-old girl. Later that day, a judge rules the LP obscene and bans the sale of the record in Broward County, Florida.

NUMBER ONE SONGS:

1969
Dizzy by Tommy Roe (4)
1986
Sara by Starship (1)

16

1942
Jerry Jeff Walker is born in Oneonta, New York. Singer-songwriter who began his career as a member of the psychedelic band Circus Maximus but is known for writing *Mr. Bojangles,* a song about the lengendary New Orleans street dancer Bill Robinson.

1954
Nancy Wilson is born in San Francisco. Singer and guitarist for Heart (Ann Wilson, Roger Fisher, Howard Leese, Steve Fossen, Michael Derosier), the

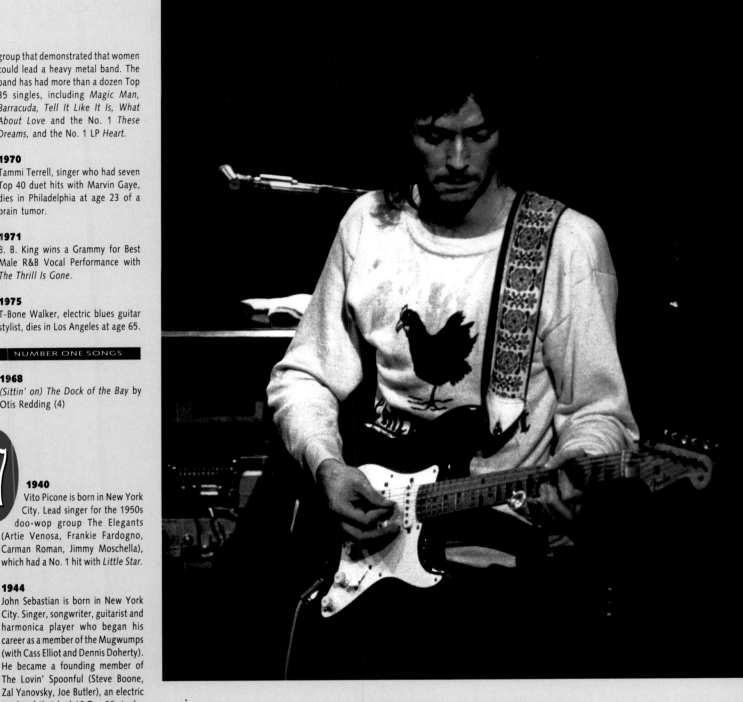

group that demonstrated that women could lead a heavy metal band. The band has had more than a dozen Top 35 singles, including *Magic Man, Barracuda, Tell It Like It Is, What About Love* and the No. 1 *These Dreams,* and the No. 1 LP *Heart.*

1970
Tammi Terrell, singer who had seven Top 40 duet hits with Marvin Gaye, dies in Philadelphia at age 23 of a brain tumor.

1971
B. B. King wins a Grammy for Best Male R&B Vocal Performance with *The Thrill Is Gone.*

1975
T-Bone Walker, electric blues guitar stylist, dies in Los Angeles at age 65.

NUMBER ONE SONGS:

1968
(Sittin' on) The Dock of the Bay by Otis Redding (4)

17

1940
Vito Picone is born in New York City. Lead singer for the 1950s doo-wop group The Elegants (Artie Venosa, Frankie Fardogno, Carman Roman, Jimmy Moschella), which had a No. 1 hit with *Little Star.*

1944
John Sebastian is born in New York City. Singer, songwriter, guitarist and harmonica player who began his career as a member of the Mugwumps (with Cass Elliot and Dennis Doherty). He became a founding member of The Lovin' Spoonful (Steve Boone, Zal Yanovsky, Joe Butler), an electric jug band that had 10 Top 30 singles between 1965 and 1967, including *Do You Believe in Magic, Daydream, Nashville Cats* and the No. 1 *Summer in the City.* His solo career has included the No. 1 single *Welcome Back,* the theme from the TV show *Welcome Back Kotter.*

1946
Harold Brown is born in Long Beach, California. Drummer for War (Howard Scott, Papa Dee Allen, B. B. Dickerson, Charles Miller, Lee Oskar, Lonnie Jordan). (See Howard Scott, March 15.)

1956
Carl Perkins gives his first television performance, on *Ozark Jubilee,* hosted by Red Foley.

1978
American Hot Wax, a film based on the early days of Alan Freed, opens.

1981
The Blues Project, including Al Kooper, Andy Kulberg, Danny Kalb, Steve Katz and Roy Blumenfeld, reunites for a concert at Bond's in New York City.

NUMBER ONE SONGS:

1958
Tequila by The Champs (5)

18

1941
Wilson Pickett is born in Prattville, Alabama. One of the great soul singers of the 1960s, he had 16 Top 35 singles, including *In the Midnight Hour* and *Mustang Sally* and the Top 10 hits *Land of 1000 Dances* and *Funky Broadway.* Inducted into the Rock and Roll Hall of Fame in 1991.

NUMBER ONE SONGS:

1967
Penny Lane by The Beatles (1)
1972
Heart of Gold by Neil Young (1)
1978
Night Fever by The Bee Gees (8)

AN ILLUSTRATED RECORD OF ROCK 'N' ROLL

19

1957
Elvis Presley buys the Graceland estate, located in the Memphis suburb of Whitehaven.

20

1951
Carl Palmer is born in Birmingham, England. Percussionist who with guitarist Greg Lake and keyboardist Keith Emerson formed the 1970s classically influenced progressive band Emerson, Lake & Palmer. ELP produced eight Top 40 albums, including *Pictures at an Exhibition*, based on Mussorgsky's classical work, and a Top 40 single, *From the Beginning*.

1965
Motown Records moves to widen its visibility in the U.K. with a tour featuring The Miracles, Stevie Wonder, Martha & The Vandellas, The Temptations and The Supremes.

1969
John Lennon marries Yoko Ono in the British Consulate building on the island of Gibraltar.

NUMBER ONE SONGS:

1961
Surrender by Elvis Presley (2)
1971
Me and Bobby McGee by Janis Joplin (2)
1982
I Love Rock 'n' Roll by Joan Jett & The Blackhearts (7)

21

1952
Alan Freed's first Moondog Coronation Ball at the Cleveland Arena ends in a riot as an unruly crowd tries to get into the sold-out 10,000-seat arena to hear Paul Williams, The Dominoes and Varetta Dillard. This event is generally regarded as the beginning of the rock 'n' roll era.

1961
The Beatles perform at the Cavern Club in Liverpool for the first time.

1991
Electric guitar pioneer and Rock and Roll Hall of Fame member Leo Fender dies at age 82.

NUMBER ONE SONGS:

1964
She Loves You by The Beatles (2)
1981
Keep on Loving You by REO Speedwagon (1)
1987
Lean on Me by Club Nouveau (2)

22

1945
Jeremy Clyde is born in England. With Chad Stuart formed the vocal duo Chad & Jeremy, which had seven Top 35 singles between 1964 and 1966, including *Yesterday's Gone* and *A Summer Song*.

NUMBER ONE SONGS:

1975
My Eyes Adored You by Frankie Valli (1)
1980
Another Brick in The Wall (Part II) by Pink Floyd (4)
1986
These Dreams by Heart (1)

23

1964
John Lennon's first book, *In His Own Write*, wins the prestigious Foyle's Literary Prize.

NUMBER ONE SONGS:

1963
Our Day Will Come by Ruby & The Romantics (1)
1974
Dark Lady by Cher (1)

24

1946
Lee Oskar is born in Copenhagen, Denmark. Harmonica player for War (Howard Scott, Papa Dee Allen, B. B. Dickerson, Charles Miller, Harold Brown, Lonnie Jordan). (See Howard Scott, March 15.)

1958
Elvis Presley enters the U.S. Army as a private at the Memphis office of the Selective Service. He serves two years and is discharged March 3, 1960, at Fort Dix, New Jersey.

NUMBER ONE SONGS:

1973
Love Train by The O'Jays (1)
1979
Tragedy by The Bee Gees (2)
1990
Black Velvet by Alannah Myles (2)

25

1942
Aretha Franklin is born in Memphis, Tennessee. With a background in gospel music, she fused pop, gospel and R&B to become the all-time female hitmaker with songs like *Respect, Think, Spanish Harlem, Chain of Fools* and *Natural Woman* as part of her string of more than 35 Top 40 records. Known as the Queen of Soul, she was inducted into the Rock and Roll Hall of Fame January 21, 1987.

1947
Elton John is born Reginald Kenneth Dwight in Pinner, England. Singer, songwriter and pianist who with lyricist Bernie Taupin created some of the biggest hits of the 1970s, 15 of which were Top 10 hits, including *Your Song, Rocket Man, Honkey Cat, Daniel* and *The Bitch Is Back*. He has had almost 40 Top 40 singles, with five No. 1 hits—*Crocodile Rock, Bennie and the Jets, Lucy in the Sky with Diamonds, Philadelphia Freedom* and *Island Girl*. His 23 top-selling albums include seven No. 1 LPs: *Honky Chateau, Don't Shoot Me I'm Only the Piano Player, Goodbye Yellow Brick Road, Caribou, Greatest Hits, Captain Fantastic and the Brown Dirt Cowboy* and *Rock of the Westies*.

1969
John Lennon and Yoko Ono begin their seven-day Bed-In for Peace in the Amsterdam Hilton.

NUMBER ONE SONGS:

1972
A Horse with No Name by America (3)
1989
The Living Years by Mike & The Mechanics (1)

JOHN LENNON
and YOKO ONO, 1971

STEVEN TYLER, 1976
Aerosmith

AN ILLUSTRATED RECORD OF ROCK 'N' ROLL

26

1936
Fred Parris is born in New Haven, Connecticut. Lead singer with The Five Satins (Rich Freeman, Al Denby, Ed Martin, Jessie Murphy), the 1950s doo-wop group that recorded *In the Still of the Nite* and *To the Aisle*.

1944
Diana Ross is born in Detroit. Lead singer and founding member of The Supremes (Mary Wilson, Florence Ballard). The group was renamed Diana Ross and the Supremes in 1967, and Ross left for a solo career in 1970. She has had 23 Top 40 singles, including five No. 1 hits: *Ain't No Mountain High Enough, Touch Me in the Morning, Love Hangover, Theme from Mahogany* and *Upside Down.* Inducted into the Rock and Roll Hall of Fame January 20, 1988. (See Mary Wilson, March 6.)

1948
Steven Tyler is born in New York City. Lead vocalist for Aerosmith (Joe Perry, Brad Whitford, Tom Hamilton, Joey Kramer). (See Brad Whitford, February 23.)

1960
Elvis Presley records a TV show with Frank Sinatra at the Fountainbleu Hotel in Miami Beach, Florida.

NUMBER ONE SONGS:

1977
Rich Girl by Hall & Oates (2)
1988
Man in the Mirror by Michael Jackson (2)

27

NUMBER ONE SONGS:

1965
Stop! In the Name of Love by The Supremes (2)

28

1946
John Evan is born in England. Keyboardist for the progressive rock group Jethro Tull (Ian Anderson, Mick Abrahams, Glenn Cornick, Clive Bunker), known for its flamboyant leader, Ian Anderson. Between 1969 and 1982, Tull had 16 Top 30 LPs, including *Aqualung, War Child, Living in the Past* and two No. 1 albums, *Thick as a Brick* and *A Passion Play.*

1974
Arthur "Big Boy" Crudup, influential bluesman who wrote classic rock songs such as *That's All Right, Mama; My Baby Left Me* and *Rock Me, Mama*, dies at age 69 in Nassawadox, Virginia.

1960
New York Rep. Emanuel Cellar says payola was the reason for the popularity of rock 'n' roll and asks for $1,000 fines for those who participated.

1983
Prince begins his five-month-long 1999 tour at the Universal Amphitheatre in Los Angeles.

NUMBER ONE SONGS:

1981
Rapture by Blondie (2)

29

1973
Dr. Hook and The Medicine Show appear on the cover of *Rolling Stone* magazine, fulfilling their wish in the group's hit *The Cover of Rolling Stone.*

1980
Dark Side of the Moon by Pink Floyd breaks Carole King's record with *Tapestry* as the longest-running LP chart hit when it goes to 303 weeks on the Billboard charts.

1990
The Recording Industry Association of America agrees to put new warning labels about potentially offensive lyrics on records, tapes and compact discs.

NUMBER ONE SONGS:

1975
Lady Marmalade by LaBelle (1)

30

1942
Graeme Edge is born in Staffordshire, England. Drummer for The Moody Blues (Denny Laine, Ray Thomas, Clint Warwick, Mike Pinder, later Justin Hayward, John Lodge), which popularized fusion of classical music with rock. The group had 12 Top 30 singles and 13 Top 30 LPs, including two No. 1 LPs, but is best known for its first LP, *Days of Future Passed*, which yielded the No. 2 hit *Nights in White Satin.*

1945
Eric Clapton is born in Ripley, England. Influential guitarist whose work with The Yardbirds, Cream, John Mayall and Derek & the Dominos set the standard for blues rock guitarists. His solo career has included 13 Top 35 LPs, including the No. 1 album *461 Ocean Boulevard*, and more than a dozen hit singles, including the No. 1 *I Shot the Sheriff.*

1948
Jim Dandy Mangrum is born in Black Oak, Arkansas. Lead singer for the 1970s southern heavy metal band Black Oak Arkansas (Ricky Reynolds, Jimmy Henderson, Stan Knight, Pat Daughterty, Wayne Evans), which had a No. 1 hit with *Jim Dandy to the Rescue.*

1962
(MC) Hammer is born Stanley Kirk Burrell in Oakland, California. Singer and dancer who became the first rap music performer to find crossover pop success, with his Top 10 hit *U Can't Touch This.*

NUMBER ONE SONGS:

1957
Party Doll by Buddy Knox and The Rhythm Orchids (1)
1963
He's So Fine by The Chiffons (4)
1974
Sunshine on My Shoulders by John Denver (1)
1985
One More Night by Phil Collins (2)

31

1937
Herb Alpert is born in Los Angeles. Trumpeter, songwriter, arranger, producer and record company executive (cofounder of A&M Records), he had 17 Top 40 singles hits, mostly as instrumentals, with his group The Tijuana Brass and as a solo artist, including two No. 1 songs, the vocal *This Guy's in Love with You* and the instrumental *Rise.* His 14 Top 30 albums include five No. 1 LPs: *Whipped Cream & Other Delights, Going Places, What Now My Love, Sounds Like* and *The Best of the Brass.*

NUMBER ONE SONGS:

1962
Don't Break the Heart That Loves You by Connie Francis (1)
1984
Footloose by Kenny Loggins (3)

1

1939
Rudolph Isley is born in Cincinnati, Ohio. Founding member, with brothers Ronald and O'Kelly, of the R&B-soul group The Isley Brothers. The group had 11 Top 40 singles between 1962 and 1980, including the Top 10 hits *It's Your Thing, That Lady (Part 1)* and *Fight the Power—Part 1*, and a dozen LPs, including the No. 1 *The Heat Is On.* Inducted into the Rock and Roll Hall of Fame in 1992.

1956
Producer Hal Wallis holds a screen test for Elvis Presley and offers him a three-film contract for $450,000.

1970
The film *Woodstock* opens in Hollywood.

1972
The Mar Y Sol festival takes place in Vega Baja, Puerto Rico. Performers include The Allman Brothers Band; Black Sabbath; B. B. King; Emerson, Lake & Palmer and others.

AN ILLUSTRATED RECORD OF ROCK 'N' ROLL

2

1939

Marvin Gaye is born in Washington, D.C. One of the Motown label's earliest hitmakers, he had 40 chart hits as a solo artist or in duets with Diana Ross, Tammi Terrell, Mary Wells and Kim Weston. His solo No. 1 hits were *I Heard It Through the Grapevine, Let's Get It On* and *Got to Give It Up Part 1*. He had four Top 10 hits with Tammi Terrell—*Your Precious Love, Ain't Nothing Like the Real Thing, If I Could Build My Whole World Around You* and *You're All I Need to Get By*. He died April 1, 1984, in Los Angeles at age 44 after his father shot him during an argument. Inducted into the Rock and Roll Hall of Fame January 21, 1987.

1941

Leon Russell is born in Lawton, Oklahoma. Highly regarded session man who also has had a performing career. Best known for his work with a wide variety of top musicians, including Joe Cocker, Phil Spector, The Rolling Stones and Bob Dylan, he has had nine Top 40 LPs and two Top 15 singles, *Tight Rope* and *Lady Blue*.

1967

The Beatles complete recording for the landmark album *Sgt. Pepper's Lonely Hearts Club Band.*

3

1941

Jan Berry is born in Los Angeles. Half of the vocal group Jan & Dean, with Dean Torrence, which created the 1960s "surfing sound" with 14 Top 40 singles, including the No. 1 *Surf City* and the Top 10 singles *Dead Man's Curve* and *The Little Old Lady (from Pasadena)*. On April 12, 1966, Berry was almost killed in an automobile accident, cutting short the duo's recording career.

1943

Richard Manuel is born in Stratford, Ontario. Pianist and vocalist for The Band (Levon Helm, Rick Danko, Garth Hudson, Robbie Robertson), which gained fame as backup group for Ronnie Hawkins and Bob Dylan before establishing its own name with *Music from Big Pink*. The first of

eight Top 30 albums, it produced two Top 40 singles, *Up on Cripple Creek* and *Don't Do It*. The group's final concert, with an all-star cast on Thanksgiving 1976, was filmed and released as *The Last Waltz*.

1944

Tony Orlando is born Michael Anthony Orlando Cassavitis in New York City. Leader of the pop vocal group Tony Orlando and Dawn (Telma Louise Hopkins, Joyce Elaine Vincent-Wilson), which had 14 Top 40 singles in the 1970s, including three No. 1 hits: *Knock Three Times, Tie a Yellow Ribbon Round the Ole Oak Tree* and *He Don't Love You (Like I Love You)*.

1948

Berry Oakley is born in Chicago. Bassist for The Allman Brothers Band (Duane Allman, Greg Allman, Dickey Betts, Jai Johanny Johanson, Butch Trucks), which influenced southern rock bands throughout the 1970s and 1980s with its blend of blues, country, gospel and R&B, highlighted by lengthy jams. The group had eight Top 40 albums in the 1970s, including the No. 1 *Brothers and Sisters*, which produced a No. 2 single, *Ramblin' Man*. Oakley died at age 24 in a motorcycle accident November 11, 1972.

1956

Elvis Presley sings *Heartbreak Hotel* and *Blue Suede Shoes* on Milton Berle's television show from the flight deck of the USS *Hancock*, giving him his first major national exposure.

NUMBER ONE SONGS:

1961
Blue Moon by The Marcels (3)
1971
Just My Imagination (Running Away with Me) by The Temptations (2)
1976
Disco Lady by Johnnie Taylor (4)

4

1915

Muddy Waters is born McKinley Morganfield in Rolling Fork, Mississippi. His electric guitar blues style was influential in defining the Chicago blues of the 1950s. He had R&B hits with songs such as *Rollin' Stone, I Just Wanna Make Love to You, I'm Your Hoochie-Coochie Man*

and *Got My Mojo Working*. Inducted into the Rock and Roll Hall of Fame January 21, 1987.

1941

Major Lance is born in Chicago. Pioneering soul singer who helped create the Chicago Sound with six Top 40 singles, including *The Monkey Time*, which kicked off the dance craze The Monkey, and *Um, Um, Um, Um, Um, Um*.

1964

Beatlemania peaks as The Beatles hold the top five positions on the Hot 100 of Billboard's hit list with *Can't Buy Me Love, Twist and Shout, She Loves You, I Want to Hold Your Hand* and *Please Please Me*. They also break Elvis Presley's record of having nine records in the Hot 100 when they reach 10 on March 28, go to 12 on April 4 and peak at 14 on March 11. *Can't Buy Me Love* will remain at No. 1 for five weeks.

1968

James Brown goes on national television in the U.S. in an appeal for calm after the assassination of Martin Luther King, Jr. Later, B. B. King, Jimi Hendrix and Buddy Guy perform at a club to collect money for the Southern Christian Leadership Conference in memory of Dr. King.

NUMBER ONE SONGS:

1964
Can't Buy Me Love by The Beatles (5)
1987
Nothing's Gonna Stop Us Now by Starship (2)

5

1958

Irving Feld's Greatest Show of Stars tour begins in Norfolk, Virginia, featuring The Everly Brothers, Paul Anka, Sam Cooke and Frankie Avalon.

1971

After receiving complaints about lyrics, The Federal Communications Commission issues a notice to radio stations requiring them to screen records before playing them on the air.

NUMBER ONE SONGS:

1975
Lovin' You by Minnie Riperton (1)

6

1945

Bob Marley is born in Rhoden Hall, Jamaica. Influential singer-songwriter who spread Jamaican reggae music throughout the world with his band, The Wailers (Peter Tosh, Aston "Family Man" Barrett, Bunny Livingston, Carlton Barrett), which had two Top 20 albums in the 1970s, *Rastaman Vibration* and *Exodus*. He died May 11, 1981, in Miami at age 36 of cancer.

1960

The Everly Brothers, backed by The Crickets, open their first tour of England at New Victoria Theatre in London.

1974

Ladies and Gentlemen: The Rolling Stones opens in New York City, marking the first time a film uses quadraphonic sound.

NUMBER ONE SONGS:

1974
Hooked on a Feeling by Blue Swede (1)

7

1943

Spencer Dryden is born in New York City. Drummer who replaced Skip Spence in Jefferson Airplane (Marty Balin, Jorma Kaukonen, Paul Kantner, Signe Anderson, Bob Harvey, later Jack Casady, Grace Slick, Papa John Creach, John Barbata, Aynsley Dunbar, among others) when the group had its first success with the Top 10 singles *Somebody to Love* and *White Rabbit*. (See Marty Balin, January 30; Paul Kantner, March 12.)

1947

Patricia Bennett is born in the Bronx, New York. Member of the female vocal group The Chiffons (Barbara Lee, Sylvia Peterson, Judy Craig), which had three Top 10 hits between 1963 and 1966: *One Fine Day, Sweet Talkin' Guy* and the No. 1 *He's So Fine*.

1949

John Oates is born in New York City. Guitarist and vocalist who is half of the R&B duo Hall & Oates, with Daryl Hall, which produced nearly two dozen hit singles in the 1970s and '80s, including six top hits—*Rich Girl, Kiss on My List, Private Eyes, I Can't Go for That (No Can Do), Maneater* and *Out of Touch*—from a dozen Top 35 albums.

1956
CBS radio network begins the national broadcast of *Alan Freed's Rock 'n' Roll Dance Party.*

1962
Johnny Angel by Shelley Fabares (2)
1973
The Night the Lights Went Out in Georgia by Vicki Lawrence (2)
1990
Love Will Lead You Back by Taylor Dayne (1)

8

1947
Steve Howe is born in London. Guitarist who replaced Peter Banks in Yes (Jon Anderson, Chris Squire, Tony Kaye, Bill Bruford, later Rick Wakeman). (See Chris Squire, March 4.)

1963
Julian Lennon is born in Liverpool, England. The son of John Lennon, he became the first offspring of The Beatles to have a music career. His debut album, *Valotte,* resulted in three Top 40 hits in 1984 and 1985, including two Top 10 singles, *Valotte* and *Too Late for Goodbyes.*

1989
Roy Orbison is the first performer since Elvis Presley to have two albums in the Top 5: the No. 4 *Mystery Girl* and No. 5 *Traveling Wilburys, Vol. 1.*

1989
The Look by Roxette (1)

MUDDY WATERS, 1969

AN ILLUSTRATED RECORD OF ROCK 'N' ROLL

ELTON JOHN, 1972

9

1932
Carl Perkins is born near Lake City, Tennessee. One of the original rockabilly artists on the Sun Records label. Best known for writing the classic rock song *Blue Suede Shoes*, the first song that was a simultaneous hit on the pop, country and R&B charts. Inducted into the Rock and Roll Hall of Fame January 21, 1987.

NUMBER ONE SONGS

1966
(You're My) Soul and Inspiration by The Righteous Brothers (3)
1977
Dancing Queen by Abba (1)
1988
Get Outta My Dreams, Get Into My Car by Billy Ocean (2)

10

1957
Ricky Nelson sings the Fats Domino song *I'm Walkin'* on *The Adventures of Ozzie and Harriet*, resulting in an overwhelming response by teenagers and launching his recording career.

1962
Stu Sutcliffe, the original bass player for The Beatles, dies in Hamburg, West Germany, of a brain hemorrhage at age 22.

NUMBER ONE SONGS

1965
I'm Telling You Now by Freddie & The Dreamers (2)

11

1961
Bob Dylan performs for the first time, at Gerde's Folk City in Greenwich Village, when he opens for John Lee Hooker.

NUMBER ONE SONGS

1970
Let It Be by The Beatles (2)
1981
Kiss on My List by Hall & Oates (3)

12

1944
John Kay is born Joachin F. Krauledat in Tilsit, Germany. Lead singer for Steppenwolf (Michael Monarch, Goldy McJohn, Rushton Moreve, Jerry Edmonton), the hard-rock group that had seven Top 40 hits in the late '60s and early '70s but is best known for its No. 2 single *Born to Be Wild*.

1950
David Cassidy is born in New York City. Singer and guitarist who led the made-for-TV family group The Partridge Family (Shirley Jones, Danny Bonaduce, Brian Foster, Suzanne Crough, Susan Dey) to seven Top 40 hits, including the No. 1 single *I Think I Love You*. Cassidy's solo career produced the No. 9 hit *Cherish*.

1954

Bill Haley & The Comets record *Rock Around the Clock* at Pythian Temple studios in New York City. A little more than a year later, in July 1955, it becomes the first rock 'n' roll song to reach No. 1 on the Billboard charts.

1955

The Brooklyn Paramount Theater is the setting for the opening of Alan Freed's Rock 'n' Roll Easter Jubilee, a week-long music showcase. Performers include The Penguins, B. B. King, The Clovers, LaVern Baker and The Count Basie Orchestra. The shows eventually draw 97,000 people.

1961

Ray Charles takes four Grammy Awards — two for *Georgia on My Mind* and one each for the album *The Genius of Ray Charles* and the single *Let the Good Times Roll*.

1966

Jan Berry of Jan and Dean nearly dies following an automobile accident in Los Angeles.

NUMBER ONE SONGS:

1969
Aquarius/Let the Sunshine In by The 5th Dimension (6)
1975
Philadelphia Freedom by The Elton John Band (2)

13

1940

Lester Chambers is born in Mississippi. One of the four Chambers Brothers (George, Willie, Joe), the pioneering and innovative funk/psychedelic band that had the Top 40 hits *I Can't Turn You Loose* and *Time Has Come Today* in the late 1960s.

1944

Jack Casady is born in Washington, D.C. Bass player who was a member of Jefferson Airplane when the group had its first success with the Top 10 singles *Somebody to Love* and *White Rabbit*. Formed the blues-based Hot Tuna with Jorma Kaukonen as an acoustic band and later went electric. (See Marty Balin, January 30.)

1946

Al Green is born in Forest City, Arkansas. Pioneering R&B vocalist who helped establish the popularity of soul-R&B with mass audiences. He had 13 Top 40 hits in five years during the early 1970s, including the No. 1 *Let's Stay Together*.

NUMBER ONE SONGS

1957
All Shook Up by Elvis Presley (9)
1959
Come Softly to Me by the Fleetwoods (4)

1968
Honey by Bobby Goldsboro (5)
1974
Bennie and the Jets by Elton John (1)
1985
We Are the World by USA for Africa (4)

14

1945

Ritchie Blackmore is born in Weston-super-Mare, England. Guitarist who founded Deep Purple (Rod Evans, Nick Semper, Jon Lord, Ian Paice), which had single hits with *Smoke on the Water* and *Hush* from eight Top 35 LPs, and Rainbow, which produced three LPs and the Top 40 single *Stone Cold*.

1956

Please, Please, Please becomes the first R&B chart hit for James Brown.

NUMBER ONE SONGS

1979
What a Fool Believes by The Doobie Brothers (1)
1990
I'll Be Your Everything by Tommy Page (1)

15

1894

Bessie Smith is born in Chattanooga, Tennessee. Pioneering and influential blues singer who established R&B as a popular form of music, later influencing rock singers such as Janis Joplin. She died September 26, 1937, in an automobile accident in Memphis. Inducted into the Rock and Roll Hall of Fame January 18, 1989.

1928

Tony Williams is born in Elizabeth, New Jersey. Lead singer for the vocal group The Platters (David Lynch, Paul Robi, Herb Reed, Alex Hodge, later Zola Taylor), which had 22 Top 40 chart hits over a 20-year period, including *(You've Got) The Magic Touch, Harbor Lights, Only You (and You Alone)* and the No. 1 songs *The Great Pretender, My Prayer, Twilight Time* and *Smoke Gets in Your Eyes*. Inducted into the Rock and Roll Hall of Fame with The Platters in 1990.

1944

Dave Edmunds is born in Cardiff, Wales. Multitalented guitarist, singer and arranger who championed American rockabilly in England's pubs. His LPs have introduced writers such as Elvis Costello and Graham Parker. He had a No. 4 hit as a solo with *I Hear You Knocking*.

1956

Alan Freed defends rock 'n' roll on national television during an interview with Eric Sevareid on *CBS Sunday News*.

1960

Only the Lonely by Roy Orbison is released.

NUMBER ONE SONGS

1967
Somethin' Stupid by Nancy and Frank Sinatra (4)
1972
The First Time Ever I Saw Your Face by Roberta Flack (6)
1989
She Drives Me Crazy by Fine Young Cannibals (1)

AN ILLUSTRATED RECORD OF ROCK 'N' ROLL

16

1939
Dusty Springfield is born Mary O'Brien in London, England. Singer and guitarist who was one of the first female British rockers. She had 10 Top 40 hits and is best known for the Top 15 singles *I Only Want to Be with You, Wishin' and Hopin', You Don't Have to Say You Love Me* and *Son of a Preacher Man.*

1941
Bobby Vinton is born in Cannonsburg, Pennsylvania. Versatile singer-songwriter-arranger who found success as a pop balladeer. He had 30 Top 40 singles, including the No. 1 hits *Roses Are Red (My Love), Blue Velvet, There! I've Said It Again* and *Mr. Lonely.*

1945
Stefan Grossman is born in New York City. Blues guitarist who has performed with a variety of musicians but is best known as a teacher of blues guitar techniques, influencing thousands of musicians.

1956
Blue Days, Black Nights, Buddy Holly's first single record, is released.

NUMBER ONE SONGS

1977
Don't Give Up on Us by David Soul (1)

17

1960
Eddie Cochran dies at age 21 after an automobile accident on his way to London. Gene Vincent is also injured in the crash, but he survives.

1969
The Band performs its first concert, at Winterland in San Francisco.

1970
Paul McCartney releases his first solo LP, *McCartney.*

NUMBER ONE SONGS

1971
Joy to the World by Three Dog Night (6)

18

1983
Marvin Gaye begins what will be his final concert tour.

NUMBER ONE SONGS

1987
I Knew You Were Waiting (for Me) by Aretha Franklin and George Michael (2)

19

1928
Alexis Korner is born in Paris. Influential blues musician who revived the blues in both England and the U.S. in the 1960s by working with musicians in his bands, such as Charlie Watts, Ginger Baker, Jack Bruce, Long John Baldry, Mick Jagger, Robert Plant and Steve Marriott.

1944
Mark Volman is born in Los Angeles. Singer and guitarist with The Turtles (Howard Kaylan, Al Nichol, Chuck Portz, Donald Ray Murray), the 1960s pop group that had nine Top 30 hits, including the No. 1 single *Happy Together.* Later formed Flo & Eddy with Kaylan.

1946
Alan Price is born in County Durham, England. Keyboardist for The Animals (Eric Burdon, Chas Chandler, John Steel, Hilton Valentine). (See John Steel, February 4.)

NUMBER ONE SONGS

1980
Call Me by Blondie (6)
1986
Kiss by Prince & The Revolution (2)

20

1939
Johnny Tillotson is born in Jacksonville, Florida. Early country-rock performer who had 14 Top 40 singles, including the Top 5 hits *Poetry in Motion* and *It Keeps Right on a-Hurtin'.*

1968
Deep Purple performs its first concert, at Tastrup, Denmark, outside of Copenhagen.

NUMBER ONE SONGS

1974
TSOP (The Sound of Philadelphia) by MFSB with The Three Degrees (2)

21

NUMBER ONE SONGS

1956
Heartbreak Hotel by Elvis Presley (8)
1958
Twilight Time by The Platters (1)
1962
Good Luck Charm by Elvis Presley (2)
1979
Knock on Wood by Amii Stewart (1)
1984
Against All Odds (Take a Look at Me Now) by Phil Collins (3)
1990
Nothing Compares 2 U by Sinead O'Connor (4)

22

1950
Peter Frampton is born in Beckenham, England. Singer-songwriter-guitarist who played with several British groups before finding success as a solo performer with the No. 1 concert LP *Frampton Comes Alive!,* which became one of the best-selling albums of all time.

1959
Alan Freed's *Go Johnny Go,* one of the earliest rock 'n' roll films, premieres in the U.S. One of the highlights is Jackie Wilson singing *You Better Know It.*

NUMBER ONE SONGS

1989
Like a Prayer by Madonna (3)

AN ILLUSTRATED RECORD OF ROCK 'N' ROLL

23

1936
Roy Orbison is born in Vernon, Texas. An original rockabilly artist on Sun Records, his haunting voice and songwriting launched 22 Top 40 hits, including two No. 1 songs, *Running Scared* and *Oh, Pretty Woman.* His popularity and influence in England was initially greater than it was in the U.S. in the early 1960s. His career was reviving in the late 1980s when he joined the all-star group The Traveling Wilburys, which included George Harrison, Bob Dylan, Tom Petty and Jeff Lynne. He died of a heart attack in Hendersonville, Tennessee, December 7, 1988. Inducted into the Rock and Roll Hall of Fame January 21, 1987.

1954
The Crows' single *Gee* enters the Top 20, marking the first time a black group crosses over to the pop charts.

NUMBER ONE SONGS:

1977
Don't Leave Me This Way by Thelma Houston (1)
1983
Come on Eileen by Dexys Midnight Runners (1)
1988
Where Do Broken Hearts Go by Whitney Houston (2)

24

1957
Verve Records releases Ricky Nelson's first single, *A Teenager's Romance/I'm Walkin'*, which becomes the first of his 35 Top 40 hits.

1977
Santana and Joan Baez perform a free concert at Soledad Prison in California.

NUMBER ONE SONGS:

1961
Runaway by Del Shannon (4)
1965
Game of Love by Wayne Fontana & The Mindbenders (1)

25

1933
Jerry Leiber is born in Baltimore, Maryland. Along with Mike Stoller, wrote classic rock 'n' roll songs in the 1950s and '60s, such as *Kansas City, Hound Dog, Yakety-Yak, On Broadway* and *Young Blood*, which have been recorded by major rock performers from Elvis Presley and The Drifters to The Beatles and The Rolling Stones. Inducted into the Rock and Roll Hall of Fame January 21, 1987.

NUMBER ONE SONGS:

1960
Stuck on You by Elvis Presley (4)
1970
ABC by The Jackson 5 (2)

26

1886
Ma Rainey is born in Columbus, Georgia. Early blues singer whose style influenced Bessie Smith, a member of Rainey's Georgia Jazz Band. She died December 22, 1939, in Rome, Georgia. Inducted into the Rock and Roll Hall of Fame in 1990.

1938
Duane Eddy is born in Corning, New York. Guitarist who popularized the "twanging" guitar sound through 15 Top 40 instrumental hits, such as *Rebel-Rouser, Peter Gunn* and *The Ballad of Paladin,* influencing guitarists in the 1960s, such as George Harrison.

1942
Bobby Rydell is born Robert Ridarelli in Philadelphia. Drummer and singer who rode the pop wave in the late '50s and early '60s with 18 Top 25 singles, including the Top 10 hits *We Got Love, Wild One, Volare* and *Forget Him.*

1964
The Rolling Stones release their first album, *The Rolling Stones.*

1977
The disco club Studio 54 opens in New York City.

NUMBER ONE SONGS:

1975
(Hey Won't You Play) Another Somebody Done Somebody Wrong Song by B. J. Thomas (1)

27

1963
I Will Follow Him by Little Peggy March (3)

NUMBER ONE SONGS:

28

1968
The rock musical *Hair* opens at the Biltmore Theater on Broadway in New York City.

1980
Tommy Caldwell, bass player for The Marshall Tucker Band, dies at age 30 after an automobile accident near Spartanburg, South Carolina.

NUMBER ONE SONGS:

1979
Heart of Glass by Blondie (1)

29

1928
Carl Gardner is born in Texas. Tenor for The Coasters (Leon Hughes, Billy Guy, Bobby Nunn), vocal group that had a No. 1 hit with *Yakety Yak* and Top 10 chart success with *Charlie Brown* and *Along Came Jones.* Inducted into the Rock and Roll Hall of Fame January 21, 1987.

1947
Tommy James is born Thomas Gregory Jackson in Dayton, Ohio. Lead singer for Tommy James and the Shondells (Joseph Kessler, Ronald Rosman, Michael Vale, Vincent Pietropaoli, George Magura), the late-'60s pop group that had 14 Top 40 singles, including the No. 1 hits *Hanky Panky* and *Crimson and Clover* and the hit songs *I Think We're Alone Now* and *Mony Mony.*

THE ROLLING STONES, 1972

AN ILLUSTRATED RECORD OF ROCK 'N' ROLL

30

1896
The Rev. Gary Davis is born in Laurens, South Carolina. Influential blues and folk guitar stylist whose finger-picking style was important to performers such as Taj Mahal, Ry Cooder and Jorma Kaukonen. He died of a heart attack May 5, 1972, in Hammonton, New Jersey.

1927
Johnny Horton is born in Tyler, Texas. Pioneered in crossing over from country music to pop chart success when he had the No. 1 hit *The Battle of New Orleans* and later *Sink the Bismarck* and *North to Alaska.*

1933
Willie Nelson is born in Abbott, Texas. Singer-songwriter who made his early reputation as a session guitarist and who, through his songwriting and performing, has influenced many of today's country-rock performers. His solo work has included crossing over from country into the pop charts with the singles *Always on My Mind* and *On the Road Again.*

1943
Bobby Vee is born Robert Belline in Fargo, North Dakota. Teen idol of the 1960s who had the No. 1 hit *Take Good Care of My Baby* as one of his 14 Top 40 singles.

1983
Chicago blues pioneer Muddy Waters, a member of the Rock and Roll Hall of Fame, dies of a heart attack at age 68 in Chicago.

NUMBER ONE SONGS:

1965
Good Lovin' by The Young Rascals (1)
1977
Southern Nights by Glen Campbell (1)
1983
Beat It by Michael Jackson (3)

1

1911
Ralph Bass is born. Record company executive and producer who signed James Brown to King Records, where he made many of his greatest hits. Bass later moved to Chess Records, where he helped develop other black artists. Inducted into the Rock and Roll Hall of Fame in 1991.

1930
Little Walter is born Marion Walter Jacobs in Marksville, Louisiana. Influential blues musician who was one of the first to use a microphone to amplify the sound of the harmonica, making it sound like a horn and establishing the moaning blues harmonica style. He died February 15, 1968, in Chicago.

1939
Judy Collins is born in Seattle. Folksinger who influenced the folk-rock movement in the 1960s through her covers of songs by emerging writers such as Joni Mitchell, Sandy Denny, Leonard Cohen and Randy Newman. She had five Top 40 chart hits and eight top LPs, but she is best known for *Both Sides Now.*

1944
Rita Coolidge is born in Nashville. Singer who began as a backup vocalist for Delaney and Bonnie and Joe Cocker's Mad Dogs and Englishmen before establishing a solo career. She had six chart hits, including the No. 2 *(Your Love Has Lifted Me) Higher and Higher.*

1966
The Beatles make their last public appearance in England, at *The New Musical Express* poll winners' concert.

1967
Elvis Presley marries Priscilla Beaulieu before 100 guests at the Aladdin Hotel in Las Vegas.

NUMBER ONE SONGS:

1965
Mrs. Brown You've Got a Lovely Daughter by Herman's Hermits (3)
1976
Let Your Love Flow by The Bellamy Brothers (1)

2

1935
Link Wray is born in Fort Bragg, North Carolina. Pioneering rock guitarist who was the first to use a distorted fuzz-tone sound (on his Top 20 hit *Rumble* in 1958). He also had a hit with *Raw-Hide.*

1945
Randy Cain is born in Philadelphia. Vocalist for The Delfonics (Wilbert Hart, William Hart, Ritchie Daniels), the 1960s Philadelphia vocal group that set the standards for sophisticated black pop. Recorded six Top 40 hits, including *La - La Means I Love You* and *Didn't I (Blow Your Mind This Time).*

1946
Leslie Gore is born in New York City. Vocalist who had 11 Top 35 hits in the 1960s, including *Judy's Turn to Cry, She's a Fool, You Don't Own Me* and the No. 1 *It's My Party.*

NUMBER ONE SONGS:

1981
Morning Train (Nine to Five) by Sheena Easton (2)
1987
(I Just) Died in Your Arms by Cutting Crew (2)

3

1919
Pete Seeger is born in New York City. Musicologist, folksinger and composer who has influenced countless folk, pop and country-rock performers through his touring and performing over more than 45 years, first with Woody Guthrie, then with The Weavers (Lee Hays, Ronnie Gilbert, Fred Hellerman) and later with Arlo Guthrie, as well as through his solo work.

1933
James Brown is born near Augusta, Georgia. The self-proclaimed "Soul Brother No. 1" was the most successful black male singer of the 1960s and '70s with 44 top chart hits, such as *Papa's Got a Brand New Bag, I Got You (Feel Good), Say It Loud—I'm Black and I'm Proud* and *Make It Funky (Part 1),* influencing vocalists who followed. Inducted into the Rock and Roll Hall of Fame January 20, 1986.

1937
Frankie Valli is born Francis Casteluccio in Newark, New Jersey. Vocalist and founding member of the white doo-wop group The Four Seasons (Bob Gaudio, Tommy DeVito, Nick Massi), which had 30 Top 40 hits, including four No. 1 songs (*Sherry, Big Girls Don't Cry, Rag Doll* and *Walk Like a Man*) between 1962 and 1976. Valli went on to a solo career that included nine Top 40 hits, including two No. 1 songs: *My Eyes Adored You* and *Grease.* Inducted into the Rock and Roll Hall of Fame in 1990 as part of the group.

1950
Mary Hopkin is born in Pontardawe, South Wales. Singer who was one of the first performers signed to The Beatles' Apple label. Paul McCartney produced her No. 2 hit *Those Were the Days.*

NUMBER ONE SONGS:

1975
He Don't Love You (Like I Love You) by Tony Orlando & Dawn (3)
1986
Addicted to Love by Robert Palmer (1)

4

1931
Ed Cassidy is born in Chicago. Drummer for the rock fusion group Spirit (Jay Ferguson, John Locke, Mark Andes, Randy California), which had the Top 25 single *I Got a Line on You* in 1969 but is best known for its continual touring over the years.

1959
The National Academy of Recording Arts and Sciences presents the first Grammy Awards, in Los Angeles. The Best Contemporary Performance Award, which later will become the rock category, is presented to Nat King Cole for *Midnight Flyer.*

NUMBER ONE SONGS:

1974
The Loco-Motion by Grand Funk (2)

JAMES BROWN, 1969

5

1938
Johnnie Taylor is born in Crawfordsville, Arkansas. Vocalist who replaced Sam Cooke as lead singer in the gospel group The Soul Stirrers (Robert Harris, Jesse Farley, S. R. Crain, T. L. Brewster, Jimmy Outler, Willie Rogers). His subsequent solo career brought 11 chart hits, including the No. 5 *Who's Making Love* and the No. 1 *Disco Lady*. Inducted into the Rock and Roll Hall of Fame with The Soul Stirrers January 18, 1989.

1958
Johnny B. Goode by Chuck Berry enters Billboard's Top 40 chart, where it stays for 11 weeks, reaching No. 8.

1968
Buffalo Springfield breaks up after performing for the last time in Los Angeles, resulting in the formation of Crosby, Stills & Nash and Poco and the beginning of Neil Young's solo career.

NUMBER ONE SONGS:

1962
Soldier Boy by The Shirelles (3)
1979
Reunited by Peaches & Herb (4)
1984
Hello by Lionel Richie (2)

6

1939
Herbie Cox is born in New York City. Lead singer for The Cleftones (Berman Patterson, Warren Corbin, Charles James, William McClain, later Gene Pearson), the vocal group of the late 1950s and early 1960s that had a Top 20 hit with *Heart and Soul*.

1966
Pet Sounds by The Beach Boys, considered Brian Wilson's greatest record, is released. Wilson developed the album after hearing The Beatles' *Rubber Soul*. *Pet Sounds* included *Wouldn't It Be Nice* and *Sloop John B*.

May

7

1939
Johnny Maestro is born John Mastrangelo in Brooklyn, New York. Lead singer for The Crests (Tommy Gough, Jay Carter, Harold Torres) and The Brooklyn Bridge (Fred Ferrara, Mike Gregorio, Les Cauchi, Tom Sullivan, Carolyn Woods, Jim Rosica, Jim Macioce, Artie Cantanzarita, Shelly Davies, Joe Ruvio). The Crests had five Top 30 hits but are best known for the No. 2 *16 Candles*. The Brooklyn Bridge had a No. 10 hit with *Worst That Could Happen*.

1946
Bill Kreutzmann is born in Palo Alto, California. Drummer for The Grateful Dead (Jerry Garcia, Bob Weir, Pigpen McKernan, Phil Lesh, later Mickey Hart, Keith Godchaux). (See Phil Lesh, March 15.)

1951
Janis Ian is born Janis Eddy Fink in New York City. Singer-songwriter who came to national prominence as a teenager in 1967 with a song about interracial dating, *Society's Child (Baby I've Been Thinking)*, which was a top 15 hit. She later reemerged with *At Seventeen*, a Top 5 single.

1968
Aretha in Paris LP is recorded by Aretha Franklin at the Olympia Theatre in Paris during Franklin's first tour of Europe. The album reaches No. 13 during its nine weeks on the charts.

NUMBER ONE SONGS:

1966
Monday, Monday by The Mamas & The Papas (3)
1977
Hotel California by The Eagles (1)
1988
Wishing Well by Terence Trent D'Arby (1)

8

1911
Robert Johnson is born in Hazelhurst, Mississippi. One of the pioneering and most influential of the Mississippi Delta blues masters, he provided a model for the later styles of Muddy Waters, Robert Lockwood, Jr. and Elmore James.

Among the songs he is credited with writing are *Sweet Home Chicago, Ramblin' on My Mind* and *Crossroads*. He died August 16, 1938, in Greenwood, Mississippi. Inducted into the Rock and Roll Hall of Fame January 20, 1986.

1940
Ricky Nelson is born Eric Hillard Nelson in Teaneck, New Jersey. Pioneering singer-songwriter who was among the first rockers to use television to promote his records. Between 1957 and 1964 he had 33 chart hits, including 16 Top 10 singles, such as *A Teenager's Romance, Stood Up, Hello Mary Lou* and *For You,* and the No. 1 hits *Travelin' Man* and *Poor Little Fool.* He later moved into country-rock and had a Top 10 single with *Garden Party.* He died at age 45 December 31, 1985, in a plane crash in DeKalb, Texas. Inducted into the Rock and Roll Hall of Fame January 21, 1987.

1941
John Fred is born in Baton Rouge, Louisiana. Vocalist for John Fred and His Playboy Band (Charlie Spinosa, Ronnie Goodson, Andrew Bernard, James O'Rourke, Harold Cowart, Joe Micelli, Tommy Dee), a one-hit wonder band that had a No. 1 single, *Judy in Disguise (with Glasses).*

1943
Paul Samwell-Smith is born in London. Bassist for The Yardbirds (Keith Relf, Chris Dreja, Jim McCarty, Anthony Topham, later Eric Clapton, Jeff Beck, Jimmy Page), the pioneering band that set the style for blues-based guitar rock and was the link between the British R&B and Psychedelic eras that led to heavy metal when Page formed the New Yardbirds, which later became Led Zeppelin. The Yardbirds had limited chart success, with six Top 30 singles, including *For Your Love* and *I'm a Man*. Inducted into the Rock and Roll Hall of Fame in 1992.

1949
Billy Joel is born William Martin Joel in Hicksville, Long Island, New York. Pianist, singer and songwriter who became one of the most successful performers of the 1970s and 1980s with the release of the No. 2 LP *The Stranger*, which he followed with two top albums, *52nd Street* and *Glass Houses*. He has had almost 30 Top 35 singles, including three No. 1 hits: *It's*

RICKY NELSON, 1974

Still Rock and Roll to Me, Tell Her About It and *We Didn't Start the Fire.*

1976
Welcome Back by John Sebastian (1)
1982
Chariots of Fire by Vangelis (1)

9

1937
David Prater is born in Ocilla, Georgia. One-half of the vocal duo Sam & Dave, with Samuel Moore, which was the most successful black vocal twosome of the 1960s with songs like *Hold On! I'm A Comin', Soul Man* and *I Thank You.* Inducted into the Rock and Roll Hall of Fame in 1992.

1944
Richie Furay is born in Dayton, Ohio. Guitarist and vocalist who was a founding member of Buffalo Springfield (Neil Young, Stephen Stills, Dewey Martin, Bruce Palmer, Jim Messina). He formed the country-rock band Poco with Messina after the breakup of Springfield. Poco had three Top 40 albums, which resulted in two Top 20 singles, *Crazy Love* and *Heart of the Night.*

1945
Steve Katz is born in Brooklyn, New York. Guitarist and vocalist who was a founding member of two influential groups—Blood Sweat & Tears (Al Kooper, Fred Lipsius, Jim Fielder, Bobby Colomby, Dick Halligan, Randy Brecker, Jerry Weiss), which helped pioneer jazz-rock, and The Blues Project (Danny Kalb, Andy Kulberg, Tommy Flanders, Al Kooper), a band that kicked off the blues revival in the late 1960s.

1964
Chuck Berry begins his first tour of England at Finsbury Park Astoria in London. Also on the tour are Carl Perkins, The Animals and The Nashville Teens.

1964
Hello, Dolly! by Louis Armstrong (1)
1970
American Woman by The Guess Who (3)

10

1941
Danny Rapp is born in Philadelphia. Lead vocalist for Danny and The Juniors (Joe Terranova , Frank Mattei, Dave White), the Philadelphia vocal quartet that produced four Top 40 singles between 1957 and 1960, including the No. 1 *At the Hop* and the anthem *Rock and Roll Is Here to Stay.* He was found shot to death April 5, 1983, in Parker, Arizona.

1946
Donovan Leitch is born in Glasgow, Scotland. Known by his first name, Donovan was the archetypical flower child of the 1960s and had 12 hit singles, including *Hurdy Gurdy Man, Mellow Yellow, Catch the Wind* and the No. 1 *Sunshine Superman.*

1947
Dave Mason is born in Worcester, England. Singer, songwriter and guitarist who was a founding member of the influential British band Traffic (Steve Winwood, Chris Wood, Jim Capaldi, later Rich Grech, Jim Gordon, Reebop Kwaku Baah), which is best known for the FM radio staple *John Barleycorn Must Die.* He wrote *Feelin' Alright* for the band. His solo career included four hit LPs and the Top 15 single *We Just Disagree.*

1960
New York District Attorney Frank Hogan files bribery charges against Alan Freed as part of the payola investigation.

1986
West End Girls by Pet Shop Boys (1)

11

1941
Eric Burdon is born in Newcastle-upon-Tyne, England. Lead singer for The Animals (Alan Price, Chas Chandler, John Steel, Hilton Valentine). His solo career after The Animals included the No. 2 hit *Spill the Wine,* as well as *Sky Pilot* and *San Franciscan Nights.* (See John Steel, February 4.)

1943
John Chadwick is born in Liverpool, England. Bassist for Gerry and the Pacemakers (Gerry Marsden, Les Maguire, Freddie Marsden), which was the second band to work with Brian Epstein as manager and George Martin as producer. The group had seven Top 30 singles, including *Don't Let the Sun Catch You Crying, Ferry Across the Mersey* and *How Do You Do It?*

1957
The Everly Brothers perform for the first time, on the *Grand Ole Opry* show in Nashville.

1959
The Happy Organ by Dave Cortez (1)
1985
Crazy for You by Madonna (1)

12

1945
Jayotis Washington is born in Detroit. Tenor vocalist for The Persuasions (Jerry Lawson, Joseph Jesse Russell, Herbert Rhoad, Jimmy Hayes, Willie Daniels). (See Jerry Lawson, January 23.)

1948
Steve Winwood is born in Birmingham, England. Keyboardist and singer who began with the Spencer Davis Group (Davis, Pete York, Muff Winwood) and then founded Traffic (Dave Mason, Chris Wood, Jim Capaldi, later Rich Grech, Jim Gordon, Reebop Kwaku Baah) before going solo and having a No. 1 single with *Higher Love.*

1955
Most of Elvis Presley's clothes are ripped from his body after a show in Jacksonville, Florida, the first such incident he experienced.

1971
Mick Jagger marries Bianca Rosa Perez-Mora in St. Tropez, France.

1958
All I Have to Do Is Dream by The Everly Brothers (5)

13

1941
Ritchie Valens is born Richard Valenzuela in Pacoima, California. Pioneering singer-songwriter who influenced Latin rock 'n' roll performers such as Chris Montez and Los Lobos during his brief career in the late 1950s. Valens had two Top 25 hits, *Donna* and *La Bamba.* He died at age 18 February 3, 1959, in the same plane crash that killed Buddy Holly and the Big Bopper, near Mason City, Iowa.

1943
Mary Wells is born in Detroit. One of the first stars of the Motown label, she had 10 top hits between 1961 and 1965, including *The One Who Really Loves You, Two Lovers* and the No. 1 *My Guy.*

1950
Peter Gabriel is born in London. Vocalist who began as lead singer with Genesis (Tony Banks, Michael Rutherford, Anthony Phillips, Chris Stewart, later Phil Collins), the art-rock band that influenced the style of Kansas and Styx and found pop success after he left. His solo career includes four LPs, including the No. 2 hit *So,* which provided his No. 1 single *Sledgehammer.*

1950
Stevie Wonder is born Steveland Morris in Saginaw, Michigan. Multitalented musician, singer and composer who has influenced pop music for more than 30 years through his writing and performing, which has resulted in 16 Grammy Awards and more than 40 hit singles, including *I Was Made to Love Her; For Once in My Life; My Cherie Amour; Living for the City; Signed, Sealed, Delivered I'm Yours* and the No. 1 hits *Fingertips Part 2, Superstition, You Are the Sunshine of My Life, You Haven't Done Nothin, I Wish, Sir Duke, I Just Called to Say I Love You, Part-Time Lover* and a duet with Paul McCartney, *Ebony and Ivory.* Inducted into the Rock and Roll Hall of Fame January 18, 1989.

1967
The Happening by The Supremes (1)
1978
If I Can't Have You by Yvonne Elliman (1)
1989
I'll Be There for You by Bon Jovi (1)

May

AN ILLUSTRATED RECORD OF ROCK 'N' ROLL

14

1936
Bobby Darin is born Walden Robert Cassotto in New York City. Singer-songwriter who was one of the early teen pop idols in the 1950s when he had a top hit with *Splish Splash*. He had 20 more top hits, including *Queen of the Hop*, *Dream Lover*, *You Must Have Been a Beautiful Baby*, *Things* and the No. 1 *Mack the Knife*. Darin died during heart surgery December 20, 1973, in Los Angeles. Inducted into the Rock and Roll Hall of Fame in 1990.

1943
Jack Bruce is born in Lanarkshire, Scotland. Bassist and singer-songwriter who joined with Eric Clapton and Ginger Baker to form the power trio Cream, which released only four albums while it was together, including the No. 1 *Wheels of Fire*. The group's two Top 10 singles were *Sunshine of Your Love* and *White Room*. Bruce pursued a solo career, later forming another power trio with Corky Laing and Leslie West.

1945
Gene Cornish is born in Ottawa, Ontario. Guitarist for The Young Rascals (Eddie Brigati, Dino Dinelli, Felix Cavaliere), later The Rascals, which had 13 Top 40 singles between 1966 and 1969, including three No. 1 hits—*Good Lovin'*, *Groovin'* and *People Got to Be Free*. The group's greatest hits LP, *Time Peace*, reached No. 1.

1976
Keith Relf, vocalist for The Yardbirds, dies at age 33 of electrocution in England.

NUMBER ONE SONGS:

1977
When I Need You by Leo Sayer (1)
1988
Anything for You by Gloria Estefan & The Miami Sound Machine (2)

15

1948
Brian Eno is born Brian Peter George St. John de Baptiste de la Salle Eno in Woodbridge, England. Art-rock conceptualist and producer who has worked with Roxy Music, Robert Fripp, John Cale, David Bowie, Talking Heads, Devo and David Byrne.

NUMBER ONE SONGS:

1976
Boogie Fever by The Sylvers (1)
1982
Ebony and Ivory by Paul McCartney and Stevie Wonder (7)

16

1944
Billy Cobham is born in Panama. Drummer who has performed in groups and as a solo during a diverse career. He has performed with Quincy Jones, James Brown, Carlos Santana, Miles Davis, Sam & Dave, Carly Simon, George Duke, Larry Coryell, John McLaughlin and Mose Allison, among others. He has had three Top 40 LPs: *Spectrum*, *Crosswinds* and *Total Eclipse*.

1947
Barbara Lee is born in the Bronx, New York. Member of the female vocal group The Chiffons (Patricia Bennett, Sylvia Peterson, Judy Craig), which had three Top 10 hits between 1963 and 1966: *One Fine Day*, *Sweet Talkin' Guy* and the No. 1 *He's So Fine*.

1983
NBC television airs the *Motown 25th Anniversary Special*, which features the greatest Motown performers and is highlighted by the reunions of Smokey Robinson and The Miracles and The Jackson 5.

NUMBER ONE SONGS:

1963
My Guy by Mary Wells (2)
1981
Bette Davis Eyes by Kim Carnes (9)
1987
With or Without You by U2 (3)

17

1942
Taj Mahal is born Henry Saint Clair Fredericks in New York City. A multi-instrumentalist and ethnomusicologist, he has built his career by specializing in the performance and recording of the style of rural black music, particularly blues.

1963
Bob Dylan and Joan Baez meet for the first time, at the Monterey Folk Festival.

NUMBER ONE SONGS:

1986
Greatest Love of All by Whitney Houston (3)

18

1911
"Big" Joe Turner is born in Kansas City, Missouri. One of rock 'n' roll's forefathers, his R&B hits in the early 1950s have become classic rock songs, including *Sweet Sixteen*, *Chains of Love* and *Shake, Rattle and Roll*. Inducted into the Rock and Roll Hall of Fame January 21, 1987.

1949
Rick Wakeman is born in London. Keyboardist for Yes (Chris Squire, Jon Anderson, Peter Banks, Tony Kaye, Bill Bruford, later Steve Howe). Wakeman joined and left the band several times to pursue solo activities, having his greatest success in 1974 with the LP *Journey to the Center of the Earth*. (See Chris Squire, March 4.)

1963
Roy Orbison, The Beatles and Gerry & The Pacemakers open a tour of England at the Adelphi Cinema in Slough, marking the first time The Beatles are headliners.

1978
The Buddy Holly Story, starring Gary Busey, opens in Dallas.

NUMBER ONE SONGS:

1959
Kansas City by Wilbert Harrison (2)
1963
If You Wanna Be Happy by Jimmy Soul (2)

17 (continued)

1968
Tighten Up by Archie Bell & The Drells (2)
1974
The Streak by Ray Stevens (3)
1985
Don't You (Forget About Me) by Simple Minds (1)

19

1945
Pete Townshend is born in London. Guitarist, singer and songwriter for The Who (Roger Daltrey, John Entwistle, Keith Moon, later Kenny Jones). Inducted into the Rock and Roll Hall of Fame in 1990. (See Roger Daltrey, March 1.)

NUMBER ONE SONGS:

1973
You Are the Sunshine of My Life by Stevie Wonder (1)
1990
Vogue by Madonna (4)

20

1944
Joe Cocker is born John Robert Cocker in Sheffield, England. Raspy-voiced white soul singer who had success in the early and mid 1970s with the No. 2 LP *Mad Dogs & Englishmen*. He has had Three Top 10 singles, *The Letter*, *You Are So Beautiful* and the No. 1 *Up Where We Belong*, a duet with Jennifer Warnes.

1946
Cher is born Cherilyn Sarkasian LaPier in El Centro, California. Formed the duo Sonny and Cher with her husband, Sonny Bono, in the mid 1960s and had 10 Top 35 singles, including the No. 1 hit *I Got You Babe*. They had a network television series from 1971 to 1975 before their divorce ended their success and Cher went on to a solo career as a singer and actor. Her solo career includes more than a dozen Top 35 singles, including three No. 1 hits: *Gypsys, Tramps & Thieves*; *Half-Breed* and *Dark Lady*.

NUMBER ONE SONGS:

1967
Groovin' by The Young Rascals (4)
1978
With a Little Luck by Wings (2)
1989
Forever Your Girl by Paula Abdul (2)

AN ILLUSTRATED RECORD OF ROCK 'N' ROLL

21

1941
Ronald Isley (The Isley Brothers) is born in Cincinnati, Ohio. Inducted into the Rock and Roll Hall of Fame in 1992. (See Rudolph Isley, April 1.)

NUMBER ONE SONGS:

1977
Sir Duke by Stevie Wonder (3)
1983
Let's Dance by David Bowie (1)

22

1950
Bernie Taupin is born in Sleaford, England. Lyricist who teamed with Elton John to create some of the biggest hits of the 1970s, including 15 Top 10 hits, among them *Your Song, Rocket Man, Honkey Cat, Daniel* and *The Bitch Is Back*.

1955
A Fats Domino concert scheduled for the Ritz Ballroom in Bridgeport, Connecticut, is cancelled after police cite a "near riot" at a dance in New Haven.

1958
Jerry Lee Lewis arrives in England with his 13-year-old bride, his cousin Myra Brown, and the British press jumps on the story, resulting in the cancellation of all but three of his scheduled 37 concerts in England.

1966
The New Jersey band The Castilles records *That's What You Get*, resulting in one of the earliest recordings made by Bruce Springsteen.

1974
Rock critic Jon Landeau sees Bruce Springsteen perform twice in Boston, later writing "I saw rock and roll future and its name is Bruce Springsteen," thus launching Springsteen's popular and critical acclaim.

NUMBER ONE SONGS:

1965
Ticket to Ride by The Beatles (1)
1976
Silly Love Songs by Wings (5)

23

NUMBER ONE SONGS:

1960
Cathy's Clown by The Everly Brothers (5)

24

1941
Bob Dylan is born Robert Allen Zimmerman in Duluth, Minnesota. Singer-songwriter who is one of the most important and influential musicians of his generation. Each of his albums brought new ideas and expanded the range of pop music, with his lyrics sounding the signal for the activism of the 1960s. Although he had modest success on the singles charts, his more than 25 albums resulted in landmark shifts in music. His best-selling LPs include *Highway 61 Revisited, John Wesley Harding, Nashville Skyline, Slow Train Coming* and the No. 1 hits *Planet Waves, Blood on the Tracks* and *Desire*. In the late 1980s, Dylan became a member of The Traveling Wilburys (Roy Orbison, Tom Petty, George Harrison, Jeff Lynne). Inducted into the Rock and Roll Hall of Fame January 20, 1988.

1963
Slide guitar innovator Elmore James, a member of the Rock and Roll Hall of Fame, dies in Chicago at age 45 of a heart attack.

NUMBER ONE SONGS:

1969
Get Back by The Beatles (5)

25

1926
Miles Davis is born in Alton, Illinois. Trumpeter, composer and producer whose work moved jazz in different directions and who had major influence on rock music with, among other things, the fusion of jazz and rock. He performed with Charlie Parker, Billy Eckstine, Charles Mingus, Max Roach, Gerry Mulligan, John Lewis, John Coltrane, Herbie Hancock, Ron Carter, Chick Corea, Harvey Brooks and John McLaughlin over the years. His landmark rock-style album is *Bitches Brew*. He died September 28, 1991, at age 65.

NUMBER ONE SONGS:

1985
Everything She Wants by Wham! (2)

26

1933
Jimmie Rogers dies in New York City at age 46. Considered the "Father of Modern Country Music," he was a member of the Rock and Roll Hall of Fame. His style later influenced country and blues musicians who, in turn, were important to early rockabilly performers.

1942
Levon Helm is born in Marvell, Arkansas. Drummer and vocalist for The Band (Richard Manuel, Rick Danko, Garth Hudson, Robbie Robertson). (See Richard Manuel, April 3.)

1978
Bob Marley and The Wailers play at The Roxy in Los Angeles in what is considered by *Rolling Stone* magazine "the single greatest performance" by the band.

NUMBER ONE SONGS:

1962
Stranger on the Shore by Mr. Acker Bilk (1)
1973
Frankenstein by The Edgar Winter Group (1)
1984
Let's Hear It for the Boy by Deneice Williams (2)

27

1957
The Crickets' *That'll Be the Day*, written by Buddy Holly, is released, becoming the group's first Top 10 hit and the only No. 1 hit for Holly.

NUMBER ONE SONGS:

1972
Oh Girl by The Chi-Lites (1)

STEVIE WONDER, 1974

AN ILLUSTRATED RECORD OF ROCK 'N' ROLL

DEBBY and PAT BOONE, 1978

28

1910
Aaron Thibeaux "T-Bone" Walker is born in Los Angeles. Blues guitarist who influenced the styles of B. B. King and other electric R&B pioneers, including the innovator of the electric guitar, Charlie Christianson. Chuck Berry guitar riffs can be traced to Walker's gritty chord style. His best-known record is *Call It Stormy Monday*. He died March 16, 1975, in Los Angeles at age 64. Inducted into the Rock and Roll Hall of Fame January 21, 1987.

1944
Gladys Knight is born in Atlanta. Lead vocalist for Gladys Knight and The Pips (Merald Knight, Brenda Knight, William Guest, Elenor Guest), a family of musicians that had 24 singles hits over a 15-year period, such as *I Heard It Through the Grapevine*, *If I Were Your Woman*, *Neither One of Us (Wants to Be the First to Say Goodbye)*, *The Best Thing That Ever Happened to Me* and the No. 1 *Midnight Train to Georgia*.

1945
John Fogerty is born in Berkeley, California. Multi-instrumentalist, vocalist and founder, with his brother Tom, of the R&B-based rock group Creedence Clearwater Revival (Stu Cook, Doug Clifford), which had seven Top 15 albums, including the No. 1 hits *Green River* and *Cosmo's Factory*, and 14 Top 30 singles, including *Proud Mary*, *Bad Moon Rising* and *Travelin' Band/Who'll Stop the Rain*. He revived a solo career in the mid 1980s with the Top 10 hit *The Old Man Down the Road*.

1977
Bruce Springsteen regains the right to record and perform when he settles a lawsuit with his former manager, Mike Appel.

NUMBER ONE SONGS:

1966
When a Man Loves a Woman by Percy Sledge (2)
1988
One More Try by George Michael (3)

29

1957
An R&B festival takes place at Herndon Stadium in Atlanta, where performers include B. B. King, The Drifters, Ray Charles, Jimmy Reed and Ruth Brown.

NUMBER ONE SONGS:

1961
Travelin' Man by Ricky Nelson (2)
1965
Help Me, Rhonda by The Beach Boys (2)

1971
Brown Sugar by The Rolling Stones (2)
1976
Love Hangover by Diana Ross (2)

30

NUMBER ONE SONGS:

1964
Love Me Do by The Beatles (1)

1970
Everything Is Beautiful by Ray Stevens (2)

31

1938
Peter Yarrow is born in New York City. Singer-songwriter and guitarist who, with Noel Paul Stookey and Mary Travers, formed the influential folk group Peter, Paul

and Mary. The group helped popularize Bob Dylan's songs and had 11 Top 25 albums, including the No. 1 LPs *Peter, Paul & Mary* and *In the Wind*, and 12 Top 40 singles, including *If I Had a Hammer, Puff the Magic Dragon, Blowin' in the Wind* and the No. 1 *Leaving on a Jet Plane*.

1948
John Bonham is born in Redditch, England. Drummer for the pioneering heavy metal band Led Zeppelin (John Paul Jones, Robert Plant, Jimmy Page). The group had 10 Top 10 albums, including six No. 1 albums, among them *Houses of the Holy* and *Physical Graffiti*. The band's best-known song, *Stairway to Heaven*, from *Led Zeppelin IV*, was never released as a single. Bonham died September 25, 1980, in Windsor, England, at age 32.

1976
The Who concert at the Charlton Football Club soccer stadium in London is recorded at 120 decibels at 55 yards away from the stage, causing the *Guinness Book of Records* to proclaim The Who as the loudest band in the world.

NUMBER ONE SONGS:

1975
Before the Next Teardrop Falls by Freddy Fender (1)
1980
Funkytown by Lipps, Inc. (4)

1

1934
Pat Boone is born in Jacksonville, Florida. One of pop music's biggest hitmakers, second only to Elvis Presley in the 1950s. Between 1955 and 1962, he had 38 Top 40 singles, many of them covers of songs by black musicians, including his first No. 1 single, Fats Domino's *Ain't That a Shame*. His other top hits include *I Almost Lost My Mind, Don't Forbid Me, Love Letters in the Sand, April Love* and *Moody River*. His daughter Debby recorded one of the all-time best-selling records in 1977, *You Light Up My Life*.

1947
Ron Wood is born in Hillington, Middlesex, England. Guitarist who

began with The Jeff Beck Group (Jeff Beck, Rod Stewart, Aynsley Dunbar), was a founding member, with Rod Stewart, of Faces (Ronnie Lane, Ian McLagan, Kenny Jones) and joined The Rolling Stones (Mick Jagger, Keith Richards, Charlie Watts, Bill Wyman) in 1975, where he has remained for more than 15 years. Toured briefly with Stone Keith Richards and Stanley Clarke as The New Barbarians. He has been part of the Stones' LPs since the No. 1 *Black and Blue* in 1976, including the No. 1 albums *Some Girls, Emotional Rescue* and *Tattoo You*. Inducted into the Rock and Roll Hall of Fame in 1989.

1959
BBC television premieres *Juke Box Jury*, where a panel of celebrities predict whether new records will become hits.

1967
Sgt. Pepper's Lonely Hearts Club Band by The Beatles is released. The album, which spent 15 weeks at No. 1, is considered the group's masterpiece. It was a landmark in recording technique because at the time only four-track tape recorders existed and most of the album's songs were multilayered recordings. It was the first theme-concept LP, which opened the pop music spectrum, paving the way for The Who's rock opera, *Tommy*. At the time, it was also the most expensive record ever made, at a cost of $75,000.

1991
David Ruffin, lead singer for The Temptations and a member of the Rock and Roll Hall of Fame, dies at age 50 in Philadelphia from a drug overdose.

NUMBER ONE SONGS:

1959
The Battle of New Orleans by Johnny Horton (9)
1963
It's My Party by Lesley Gore (2)
1968
Mrs. Robinson by Simon & Garfunkel (3)

2

1941
William Guest is born in Atlanta. Vocalist for Gladys Knight and The Pips (Merald Knight, Brenda Knight, Gladys Knight, Elenor Guest). (See Gladys Knight, May 28.)

1941
Charlie Watts is born in Islington, England. Drummer and founding member of The Rolling Stones (Mick Jagger, Keith Richards, Bill Wyman, Brian Jones). The R&B-based rock 'n' roll group has had more than 40 top LPs and more than 30 Top 40 singles, including the No. 1 hits *(I Can't Get No) Satisfaction, Get off of My Cloud, Paint It Black, Ruby Tuesday, Honky Tonk Women, Brown Sugar, Angie* and *Miss You*. The group's top LPs include *Out of Our Heads, Sticky Fingers, Goats Head Soup, It's Only Rock 'n' Roll, Black and Blue, Some Girls, Emotional Rescue* and *Tattoo You*. Inducted into the Rock and Roll Hall of Fame in 1989.

1964
The Rolling Stones begin their first tour of the U.S. in Lynn, Massachusetts.

1972
Dion & The Belmonts reunite for a performance during Richard Nader's Rock and Roll Revival #9 at Madison Square Garden in New York City.

NUMBER ONE SONGS:

1962
I Can't Stop Loving You by Ray Charles (5)

1973
My Love by Paul McCartney & Wings (4)

1979
Hot Stuff by Donna Summer (3)

3

1942
Curtis Mayfield is born in Chicago. Singer, songwriter and producer who began his career as cofounder, with Jerry Butler, of The Impressions (Arthur Brooks, Richard Brooks, Sam Gooden). The group had 16 Top 35 hits, including *It's All Right, Keep on Pushing* and *Amen*. His solo career included five Top 40 singles, including *Freddie's Dead* and *Superfly*, from the No. 1 LP *Superfly* (the soundtrack from the film). The

Impressions were inducted into the Rock and Roll Hall of Fame in 1991.

1943
Michael Clarke is born in New York City. Drummer for the pioneering folk-rock band The Byrds (Roger McGuinn, Chris Hillman, Gene Clark, David Crosby). The group's early use of harmonies influenced many later bands. The Byrds had seven Top 40 singles, including two No. 1 hits, *Mr. Tambourine Man* and *Turn! Turn! Turn!* Inducted into the Rock and Roll Hall of Fame with The Byrds in 1991.

1946
John Paul Jones is born John Baldwin in Sidcup, England. Bass player for the pioneering heavy metal band Led Zeppelin (Jimmy Page, Robert Plant, John Bonham). The group had 10 Top 10 albums, including six No. 1 albums, among them *Houses of the Holy* and *Physical Graffiti*. The band's best-known song, *Stairway to Heaven*, from *Led Zeppelin IV*, was never released as a single.

1950
Suzi Quatro is born in Detroit. Pioneer of female rockers who influenced later rockers such as Joan Jett. Between 1973 and 1980 she made five albums and released a *Greatest Hits* LP, which included her only Top 10 hit, *Stumblin' In*, a duet with Chris Norman. During her heyday she played Leather Tuscadero on the TV series *Happy Days*.

1964
The Rolling Stones make their debut on U.S. television, on *The Les Crane Show*.

1975
Ralph J. Gleason, music critic and cofounder of *Rolling Stone* magazine, dies of a heart attack in Berkeley, California, at age 58.

NUMBER ONE SONGS:

1957
Love Letters in the Sand by Pat Boone (7)
1967
Respect by Aretha Franklin (2)
1972
I'll Take You There by The Staple Singers (1)
1978
Too Much, Too Little, Too Late by Johnny Mathis & Deneice Williams (1)
1989
Rock On by Michael Damian (1)

JACKIE WILSON, 1969

June

4

1945
Michelle Phillips is born Holly Michelle Gilliam in Long Beach, California. Vocalist with the folk-rock group The Mamas & The Papas (John Phillips, Dennis Doherty, Cass Elliot), which had nine singles hits within two years in the mid 1960s, including *Words of Love, I Saw Her Again, California Dreamin'* and the No. 1 *Monday, Monday*, before breaking up.

1945
Gordon Waller is born in Braemar, Scotland. With Peter Asher, formed the mid-1960s pop duo Peter & Gordon, which had 10 Top 35 singles, including *Lady Godiva, I Go to Pieces* and the No. 1 *A World Without Love*.

5

1986
Fats Domino and Friends cable television special is recorded for Home Box Office. The friends include Jerry Lee Lewis, Ray Charles and Ron Wood.

NUMBER ONE SONGS:

1961
Running Scared by Roy Orbison (1)

6

1939
Gary U.S. Bonds is born Gary Anderson in Jacksonville, Florida. Rough-voiced early-1960s rocker who had five Top 10 singles, including the No. 1 *Quarter to Three*. He resurfaced 20 years later with *This Little Girl* and *Out of Work* with help from his admirer, Bruce Springsteen.

1962
The Beatles audition for George Martin at the EMI Studios in St. Johns Wood, London. They play some original compositions, including *Love Me Do, P.S. I Love You, Ask Me Why* and *Hello Little Girl*.

NUMBER ONE SONGS:

1964
Chapel of Love by The Dixie Cups (3)
1987
You Keep Me Hangin' On by Kim Wilde (1)

7

1970
The Who play the rock opera *Tommy* for the first of two shows at the Metropolitan Opera House in New York City.

1979
President Jimmy Carter hosts Chuck Berry at a special performance at the White House in Washington, D.C.

NUMBER ONE SONGS:

1975
Thank God I'm a Country Boy by John Denver (1)
1986
Live to Tell by Madonna (1)

8

1940
Nancy Sinatra is born in Jersey City, New Jersey. The daughter of the original pop superstar, Frank Sinatra, she had 10 Top 40 songs, including her solo No. 1 hit *These Boots Are Made for Walkin'* and a No. 1 with Dad, *Somethin' Stupid*, in the mid 1960s.

1944
Boz Scaggs is born William Royce Scaggs in Ohio. Singer-songwriter who was an original member of the early Steve Miller Band (Steve Miller, Jim Peterman, Lonnie Turner, Tim Davis). He had brief solo success with the No. 2 album *Silk Degrees*, which yielded two Top 15 singles, *Lido Shuffle* and *Lowdown*.

NUMBER ONE SONGS:

1974
Band on the Run by Paul McCartney & Wings (1)
1985
Everybody Wants to Rule the World by Tears For Fears (2)

9

1929
Johnny Ace is born John Alexander, Jr. in Memphis. Popular 1950s balladeer who had a hit with *Pledging My Love* but is best known for his death by playing Russian roulette December 24, 1954.

1934
Jackie Wilson is born in Detroit, Michigan. One of the most distinctive vocal stylists of the 1950s and '60s, he had 24 Top 40 hits, including *Lonely Teardrops, Night, Alone at Last, My Empty Arms, Baby Workout* and *(Your Love Keeps Lifting Me) Higher and Higher*. He died January 21, 1984, in Mount Holly, New Jersey, at age 50, never having regained consciousness after suffering a heart attack while performing in September 1975. Inducted into the Rock and Roll Hall of Fame January 21, 1987.

1958
Yakety Yak by The Coasters enters the Billboard charts, where it will reach No. 1.

1969
The Rolling Stones announce that Brian Jones has quit the band and will be replaced by Mick Taylor.

1972
John Hammond signs Bruce Springsteen to CBS Records.

1972
Elvis Presley performs in New York City for the first time, at Madison Square Garden.

NUMBER ONE SONGS:

1958
The Purple People Eater by Sheb Wooley (6)
1979
Love You Inside Out by The Bee Gees (1)
1984
Time After Time by Cyndi Lauper (2)
1990
Hold On by Wilson Phillips (2)

10

1910
Howlin' Wolf is born Chester Arthur Burnett in West Point, Mississippi. Influential Delta bluesman whose electric guitar and deep-throated vocals helped shape rock 'n' roll. His covers of songs written by Willie Dixon have been used by Jeff Beck, The Yardbirds, Little Feat, Led Zeppelin, Electric Flag, The Doors, The Rolling Stones and many others. He died January 10, 1976, at age 65 in Hines, Illinois. Inducted into the Rock and Roll Hall of Fame in 1991.

1941
Shirley Owens Alston is born in Passaic, New Jersey. Lead singer with The Shirelles (Micki Harris, Doris Coley Kenner, Beverly Lee), the pioneering female vocal group that was one of the first to write its own hit songs. Between 1960 and 1963, the group had a dozen Top 40 hits, including *Mama Said, Dedicated to the One I Love* and the No. 1 singles *Will You Love Me Tomorrow* and *Soldier Boy*.

1982
Micki Harris of The Shirelles dies of a heart attack in Los Angeles at age 42.

NUMBER ONE SONGS:

1972
The Candy Man by Sammy Davis, Jr. (3)
1978
You're the One That I Want by John Travolta and Olivia Newton-John (1)
1989
Wind Beneath My Wings by Bette Midler (1)

June

11

1940
Joey Dee is born Joseph Dinicola in Passaic, New Jersey. Lead singer for Joey Dee and the Starlighters (Carlton Latimor, Willie Davis, Larry Vernieri, David Brigati), the house band at the Peppermint Lounge in New York City, which spun off the Twist craze set in motion by Chubby Checker by creating the No. 1 hit *Peppermint Twist*. The group had four other Top 40 singles, including the Top 10 hit *Shout, Part 1*.

NUMBER ONE SONGS:

1966
Paint It Black by The Rolling Stones (2)
1977
I'm Your Boogie Man by KC & The Sunshine Band (1)

12

1942
Len Barry is born Leonard Borisoff in Philadelphia. Lead singer for The Dovells (Arnie Satin, Jerry Summers, Mike Dennis, Danny Brooks), the doo-wop group that had five dance hits, including *You Can't Sit Down* and *Bristol Stomp*. His solo career included the No. 2 hit *1-2-3*.

1965
The Beatles are made Members of the Order of the British Empire by Queen Elizabeth.

NUMBER ONE SONGS:

1965
Back in My Arms Again by The Supremes (1)
1971
Want Ads by The Honey Cone (1)

13

1940
Bobby Freeman is born in San Francisco. R&B vocalist who first made *Do You Want to Dance* a Top 10 hit. He also had success with *C'mon and Swim*, *Betty Lou Got a New Pair of Shoes* and *(I Do the) Shimmy Shimmy*.

1969
Soul Bowl '69 takes place at the Astrodome in Houston, Texas, with featured performers Sam & Dave, Ray Charles, The Staple Singers and Aretha Franklin.

1972
Clyde McPhatter, founder and lead singer of The Drifters and a member of the Rock and Roll Hall of Fame, dies of heart failure at age 38 in New York City.

NUMBER ONE SONGS:

1970
The Long and Winding Road by The Beatles (2)
1987
Always by Atlantic Starr (1)

14

1945
Rod Argent is born in St. Albans, England. Keyboardist and vocalist for The Zombies (Colin Blunstone, Paul Atkinson, Hugh Grundy, Paul Arnold), part of the British Invasion, which produced three Top 10 hits: *She's Not There*, *Tell Her No* and *Time of the Season*. He later formed his own group, Argent (Jim Rodford, Robert Henrit, Russ Ballard), and had a hit with *Hold Your Head Up*.

NUMBER ONE SONGS:

1975
Sister Golden Hair by America (1)
1986
On My Own by Patti LaBelle & Michael McDonald (3)

15

1937
Waylon Jennings is born in Littlefield, Texas. Guitarist, singer-songwriter and pioneer, with Willie Nelson, of the outlaw country movement, which revived the honky-tonk country sound and influenced country-rockers. Worked with Buddy Holly as a bass player. Jennings was going to fly with Holly the night Holly was killed, but he offered his seat to the Big Bopper. His solo work has been primarily in country, but he has had two crossover hits, *Luckenbach, Texas* and *Theme from the Dukes of Hazzard (Good Ol' Boys)*.

1941
Harry Nilsson is born Harry Edward Nelson III in Brooklyn, New York. Singer-songwriter who sang *Everybody's Talkin'*, the theme song from the film *Midnight Cowboy*, the first of his eight Top 40 songs, which included *I Guess the Lord Must Be in New York City*, *Coconut* and the No. 1 hit *Without You*.

1956
John Lennon meets Paul McCartney at a picnic at Woolton Parish Church in Liverpool, where Lennon's band, The Quarrymen, is performing.

1957
Whole Lotta Shakin' Going On by Jerry Lee Lewis enters the Billboard charts, where it stays for 20 weeks, going as high as No. 3.

1965
Bob Dylan records *Like a Rolling Stone* in New York City with Al Kooper on organ and Mike Bloomfield on guitar.

NUMBER ONE SONGS:

1963
Sukiyaki by Kyu Sakamoto (3)
1974
Billy, Don't Be a Hero by Bo Donaldson & The Heywoods (2)

16

1941
Lamont Dozier is born in Detroit. One-third of the team of (Brian) Holland-Dozier-(Eddie) Holland, which wrote and produced most of Motown's biggest hits in the 1960s. Inducted into the Rock and Roll Hall of Fame in 1990. (See Brian Holland, February 15.)

1967
The Monterey Pop Festival opens a three-day series of concerts at the Monterey Fairgrounds in California. Janis Joplin and Otis Redding give landmark performances. Jimi Hendrix ends his set by setting fire to his Stratocaster guitar. The success of the festival opens the era of large-scale rock concerts, which culminates at Woodstock.

1980
The Blues Brothers film opens in Chicago, starring John Belushi and Dan Aykroyd and featuring performances by Ray Charles, Aretha Franklin, John Lee Hooker, Cab Calloway and James Brown.

NUMBER ONE SONGS:

1956
The Wayward Wind by Gogi Grant (8) (knocks *Heartbreak Hotel* by Elvis Presley from No. 1)
1990
It Must Have Been Love by Roxette (2)

17

1944
Chris Spedding is born in Sheffield, England. Highly respected session guitarist who has worked with Dusty Springfield, David Essex, Lulu, Gilbert O'Sullivan, Bill Bruford, Roy Harper, Bryan Ferry, Robert Gordon, Alan Price, Paul Jones and many other British musicians, helping shape the sound of British music.

1954
The first edition of the U.K. weekly music magazine *Record Mirror* is published. *Record Mirror* was the first music publication to write about The Beatles and to run a Top 50 singles chart.

NUMBER ONE SONGS:

1978
Shadow Dancing by Andy Gibb (7)
1989
I'll Be Loving You (Forever) by The New Kids on the Block (1)

BOB DYLAN, 1972

June

18

1942

Paul McCartney is born in Liverpool, England. Founder, with John Lennon, of The Beatles (George Harrison, Ringo Starr), the most influential band in rock 'n' roll history. The group expanded the possibilities of writing, recording and sound and was the first band to perform almost exclusively its own compositions. The all-time greatest recording group, they had 21 No. 1 hits, including I Want to Hold Your Hand, Love Me Do, Help!, Yesterday, Paperback Writer and Hey Jude, and 15 No. 1 albums, including Rubber Soul, Revolver, Sgt. Pepper's Lonely Hearts Club Band and Let It Be, in the decade of the 1960s. McCartney's solo career has been the most successful of the group, with seven No. 1 hits among his 31 Top 40 singles. Also had No.1 hit singles with Michael Jackson (Say Say Say) and Stevie Wonder (Ebony and Ivory) He has had seven No. 1 LPs either as a solo or with his band, Wings, including Band on the Run, Wings at the Speed of Sound and Tug of War. Inducted into the Rock and Roll Hall of Fame with The Beatles January 20, 1988.

NUMBER ONE SONGS:

1977
Dreams by Fleetwood Mac (1)
1988
Together Forever by Rick Astley (1)

19

1936

Tommy DeVito is born in Bellville, New Jersey. Guitarist for The Four Seasons (Frankie Valli, Bob Gaudio, Nick Massi). Inducted into the Rock and Roll Hall of Fame in 1990 as part of the group. (See Frankie Valli, May 3.)

1942

Spanky McFarlane is born Elaine McFarlane in Peoria, Illinois. Lead singer for Spanky and Our Gang (Malcolm Hale, Kenny Hodges, Nigel Pickering, Lefty Baker, Eustace Britchforth, John Seiter), the folk-pop band that had a Top 10 hit with Sunday Will Never Be the Same. McFarlane joined the reunited The Mamas & The Papas, replacing Cass Elliot.

1951

Ann Wilson is born in San Diego. Lead singer for Heart (Nancy Wilson, Roger Fisher, Howard Leese, Steve Fossen, Michael Derosier), the group that demonstrated that women could lead a heavy metal band with more than a dozen Top 35 singles, including Magic Man, Barracuda, Tell It Like It Is, What About Love and the No. 1 These Dreams, and the No. 1 LP Heart.

NUMBER ONE SONGS:

1961
Moody River by Pat Boone (1)
1965
I Can't Help Myself by The Four Tops (2)
1971
It's Too Late by Carole King (5)

20

1924

Chet Atkins is born in Luttrell, Tennessee. Innovative and influential country guitarist and record company executive who, as a producer and session player at RCA Records in Nashville in the 1950s, helped launch the recording careers of Elvis Presley, the Everly Brothers and Roy Orbison.

1936

Billy Guy is born in Los Angeles. Baritone for The Coasters (Carl Gardner, Leon Hughes, Bobby Nunn), vocal group that had a No. 1 hit with Yakety Yak and Top 10 chart success with Charlie Brown and Along Came Jones. Inducted into the Rock and Roll Hall of Fame with The Coasters January 21, 1987.

1942

Brian Wilson is born in Hawthorne, California. Composer, producer, bass player and vocalist who was the innovative force behind The Beach Boys (Dennis Wilson, Carl Wilson, Mike Love, Alan Jardine). Inducted into the Rock and Roll Hall of Fame with The Beach Boys January 20, 1988. (See Mike Love, March 15.)

1949

Lionel Richie is born in Tuskegee, Alabama. Singer, songwriter and keyboardist for The Commodores (William King, Milan Williams, Thomas McClary, Walter Orange, Ronald La Praed), one of the most successful soul groups of the 1970s with his Just to Be Close to You, Easy, Lady and Still. His successful solo career has included 11 Top 10 hits, including four No. 1 songs: Truly, All Night Long (All Night), Hello and Say You, Say Me.

NUMBER ONE SONGS:

1981
Stars on 45 by Stars on 45 (1)
1987
Head to Toe by Lisa Lisa & Cult Jam (1)

21

1944

Ray Davies is born in London. Guitarist, vocalist and leader of The Kinks (Dave Davies, Mick Avory, Pete Quaife), the British Invasion band that had 12 Top 40 singles hits and as many albums over nearly 20 years. The group's most popular songs were You Really Got Me, Lola, All Day and All of the Night, Tired of Waiting for You and Come Dancing.

1948

Records made of vinyl, which were made at the Columbia Records plant in Bridgeport, Connecticut, are played in public for the first time, at the Waldorf Astoria Hotel in New York City.

NUMBER ONE SONGS:

1975
Love Will Keep Us Together by The Captain & Tennille (4)

22

1944

Peter Asher is born in London. With Gordon Waller, formed the mid-1960s pop duo Peter & Gordon, which had 10 Top 35 singles, including Lady Godiva, I Go to Pieces and the No. 1 A World Without Love. Following the breakup of the group, Asher became a manager and record producer, working with James Taylor and Linda Ronstadt, among others.

1945

Howard Kaylan is born in New York City. Singer with The Turtles (Mark Volman, Al Nichol, Chuck Portz, Donald Ray Murray), the 1960s pop group that had nine Top 30 hits, including the No. 1 single Happy Together. Later formed Flo & Eddy with Volman.

1948

Todd Rundgren is born in Upper Darby, Pennsylvania. Multitalented musician and producer who was instrumental in the formation of Nazz (Robert Antoni, Carson Van Osten, Thom Mooney) and Utopia (Mark Klingman, Ralph Shuckett, Roger Powell, John Siegler, John Wilcox, Kevin Elliman). As a performer, his best-known hit was the No. 5 Hello It's Me. He is also credited as a pioneer of rock videos.

1968

The Jeff Beck Group performs its first U.S. concert, at the Fillmore East in New York City, with Rod Stewart as lead singer.

NUMBER ONE SONGS:

1968
This Guy's in Love with You by Herb Alpert (4)
1985
Heaven by Bryan Adams (2)

23

1983

The Kool Jazz Festival in New York City is highlighted by a jam session that includes B. B. King, Ray Charles and Miles Davis.

NUMBER ONE SONGS:

1984
The Reflex by Duran Duran (2)

24

1942

Mick Fleetwood is born in London. Drummer with Fleetwood Mac (Peter Green, John McVie, Jeremy Spencer, later Christine Perfect McVie, Bob Welch, Stevie Nicks, Lindsey Buckingham), one of the longest-running British bands, whose only remaining original members are Fleetwood and bass player John McVie. The group began its greatest success in the mid 1970s when it launched six Top 40 LPs (including the three No. 1 albums Rumours, Fleetwood Mac and Mirage) and had 13 Top 25 singles, including the No. 1 Dreams.

1944
Jeff Beck is born in Surrey, England. Innovative rock guitarist whose work influenced most forms of rock, from blues to heavy metal. He first worked with many prominent musicians, including the members of his first Jeff Beck Group (Rod Stewart, Ron Wood, Aynsley Dunbar). Beck replaced Eric Clapton in The Yardbirds, the pioneering band that set the style for blues-based guitar rock and was the link between the British R&B and Psychelic eras. Beck was inducted into the Rock and Roll Hall of Fame as a member of The Yardbirds in 1992.

1964
A 70-foot billboard in Times Square announces the opening of Sam Cooke's two-week performance at the Copacabana nightclub in New York City.

1966
The Beatles begin their final world tour with a concert at Circus-Krone-Bau in Munich.

NUMBER ONE SONGS:

1989
Satisfied by Richard Marx (1)

THE BEACH BOYS
*at the closing of the
Fillmore East, 1971*

AN ILLUSTRATED RECORD OF ROCK 'N' ROLL

25

1935
Eddie Floyd is born in Montgomery, Alabama. Singer-songwriter who began with the R&B vocal group The Falcons (Joe Stubbs, Bonny Rice, Willie Schoefield, Lance Finnie), which had a hit with *You're So Fine*, before going solo and having hits with *Knock on Wood* and *Bring It on Home to Me*.

1945
Carly Simon is born in New York City. Singer-songwriter who found success in the 1970s with the No. 1 album *No Secrets*, which produced the top single *You're So Vain*. She has had nine other Top 40 singles, including the Top 10 hits *Nobody Does It Better*, *You Belong to Me* and the duet *Mockingbird*, with James Taylor, to whom she was married from 1972 to 1981.

1967
The Beatles record *All You Need Is Love* and later broadcast it live around the world as part of the *Our World* program. The single spends nine weeks on the Billboard charts, peaking at No. 1 on August 19, 1967.

NUMBER ONE SONGS:

1966
Paperback Writer by The Beatles (2)
1977
Got to Give It Up (Part 1) by Marvin Gaye (1)
1988
Foolish Beat by Debbie Gibson (1)

26

1977
Elvis Presley gives his final concert, at Market Square Arena in Indianapolis, Indiana.

NUMBER ONE SONGS:

1961
Quarter to Three by Gary U.S. Bonds (2)
1965
Mr. Tambourine Man by The Byrds (1)

27

1925
Jerome "Doc" Pomus is born in Brooklyn, New York. Innovative songwriter who, with Mort Shuman, wrote many classic rock hits for performers such as The Coasters, Dion & The Belmonts, Jay & The Americans and Gary U.S. Bonds. Among his songs were *Young Blood*, *Save the Last Dance for Me*, *Surrender*, *A Teenager in Love*, *Suspicion* and *This Magic Moment*. He died March 14, 1991, in New York City at age 66 of lung cancer. Inducted into the Rock and Roll Hall of Fame in 1992.

1968
Elvis Presley begins working on the NBC television special *Elvis*, which will mark his return to his roots of rock 'n' roll performing.

1971
The Fillmore East in New York City closes with performances by The Allman Brothers Band, The J. Geils Band, Albert King, The Beach Boys, Edgar Winter's White Trash, Ric Derringer and Country Joe McDonald. The Allman Brothers' set became the *Live at the Fillmore East* LP.

NUMBER ONE SONGS:

1960
Everybody's Somebody's Fool by Connie Francis (2)
1964
A World Without Love by Peter & Gordon (1)
1970
The Love You Save by The Jackson 5 (2)
1987
I Wanna Dance with Somebody (Who Loves Me) by Whitney Houston (2)

28

NUMBER ONE SONGS:

1969
Love Theme from Romeo and Juliet by Henry Mancini (2)
1980
Coming Up (Live at Glasgow) by Paul McCartney & Wings (3)

29

1945
Little Eva is born Eva Narcissus Boyd in Bell Haven, North Carolina. Vocalist who was the baby-sitter for Carole King and Gerry Goffin when she was asked to record their newly written song *The Loco-Motion*, which became a No. 1 hit.

1979
Lowell George, founder of Little Feat, dies of a heart attack at age 34 in Arlington, Virginia.

NUMBER ONE SONGS:

1974
Sundown by Gordon Lightfoot (1)

30

1943
Florence Ballard is born in Detroit. Founding member of The Supremes (Diana Ross, Mary Wilson). She died of a heart attack February 21, 1976, in Detroit. Inducted into the Rock and Roll Hall of Fame January 20, 1988. (See Mary Wilson, March 6.)

1956
Chuck Berry's classic *Roll Over Beethoven* enters the Billboard Top 40 charts. It goes to No. 29 for a week.

1983
The Everly Brothers announce plans for a reunion concert, ending 10 years of estrangement.

NUMBER ONE SONGS:

1973
Give Me Love (Give Me Peace on Earth) by George Harrison (1)
1979
Ring My Bell by Anita Ward (2)

1

1939
Delaney Bramlett is born in Pontotoc County, Mississippi. Vocalist and guitarist who performed with his wife as Delaney and Bonnie, attracting sidemen such as Eric Clapton, Leon Russell, Dave Mason and George Harrison. The duo's best-selling album was *Delaney & Bonnie & Friends on Tour with Eric Clapton* in 1970.

1967
The Rock Music Championship in Lambertville, New Jersey, draws 2,000 bands.

NUMBER ONE SONGS:

1967
Windy by The Association (4)
1972
Song Sung Blue by Neil Diamond (1)
1989
Baby Don't Forget My Number by Milli Vanilli (1)

July

2

1956
Elvis Presley records *Hound Dog* and *Don't Be Cruel* at RCA Studios in New York City, using The Jordanaires as back-up vocalists for the first time. *Don't Be Cruel* goes on to become the all-time No. 1 single, staying at the top of the charts for 11 weeks in 1956.

1981
The Brendan Byrne Arena in the New Jersey Meadowlands opens with the first of six shows by Bruce Springsteen.

NUMBER ONE SONGS:

1966
Strangers in the Night by Frank Sinatra (1)
1977
Gonna Fly Now by Bill Conti (1)
1988
Dirty Diana by Michael Jackson (1)

3

1954
Alan Freed announces that he will leave Cleveland for WINS radio in New York City.

1957
Atlantic Records releases Ray Charles's first album, *Ray Charles*.

1969
Brian Jones, who has just left The Rolling Stones, is found dead at age 27 in his swimming pool in London due to "misadventure," according to the coroner's report, the result of drugs and alcohol.

1969
The Newport Jazz Festival includes rock bands for the first time, opening the summer of rock festivals. Opening night performers include George Benson, Kenny Burrell, Sun Ra, Phil Woods, Anita O'Day, Jeremy Steig, Bill Evans, Young-Holt Unlimited, Freddie Hubbard and Sonny Murray. Rock performances begin the next day.

1970
The Atlanta Pop Festival attracts 200,000 people to Bryon, Georgia, to hear Jimi Hendrix, B. B. King, Jethro Tull, Johnny Winter and other performers.

1971
Jim Morrison of The Doors dies of a heart attack in Paris at age 28.

1976
Brian Wilson performs with The Beach Boys for the first time in seven years, at Anaheim Stadium in California.

NUMBER ONE SONGS:

1982
Don't You Want Me by The Human League (3)

4

1900
Louis Armstrong's traditional birthdate (actually born August 4, 1901, in New Orleans). Trumpeter, vocalist, composer and jazz legend who influenced countless horn players in R&B, jazz and rock. He had three Top 30 chart hits: *Mack The Knife*, *Blueberry Hill* and the No. 1 *Hello Dolly*. He died July 6, 1971, in Corona, New York. Inducted into the Rock and Roll Hall of Fame in 1990.

1938
Bill Withers is born in Slab Fork, West Virginia. Singer-songwriter and guitarist who had five Top 30 hits in the 1970s, including the Top 10 singles *Ain't No Sunshine* and *Use Me* and the No. 1 *Lean on Me*.

1944
Harvey Brooks is born Harvey Goldstein in New York City. Bass player who gained his reputation as a session player for Bob Dylan, Eric Anderson, Judy Collins and Phil Ochs. Original member of the first rock-jazz-R&B ensemble, Electric Flag (Mike Bloomfield, Buddy Miles, Barry Goldberg, Nick Gravenities, Peter Strazza, Marcus Doubleday, Herbie Rich), which set the stage for Blood, Sweat & Tears and Chicago. His major credits include work on the Mike Bloomfield-Stephen Stills-Al Kooper LP *Super Session* and The Doors' *Soft Parade*. In 1989 he served as the music consultant for the first rock 'n' roll museum exhibition, Rock 'n' Roll Art & Artifacts, at the Museum of Art, Science & Industry in Bridgeport, Connecticut.

1948
Jeremy Spencer is born in West Hartlepool, England. Guitarist and vocalist for the original Fleetwood Mac (Peter Green, Mick Fleetwood,

John McVie), he left the group in 1971 to become a member of the Children of God, a religious group in Los Angeles.

1969
The first rock performers at the Newport Jazz Festival include Jeff Beck, Blood Sweat & Tears, Ten Years After and Jethro Tull.

1970
The syndicated radio show *American Top Forty*, hosted by Casey Kasem, debuts with seven radio stations.

1971
The Fillmore West in San Francisco closes with performances by Tower of Power, Santana, Creedence Clearwater Revival, Mike Bloomfield, Van Morrison, Jorma Kaukonen, Jack Casady, Lydia Pense, John Cippolina and Linda Tillory.

NUMBER ONE SONGS:

1964
I Get Around by The Beach Boys (2)

5

1944
Robbie Robertson is born in Toronto. Vocalist and guitarist for The Band (Levon Helm, Richard Manuel, Garth Hudson, Rick Danko). (See Richard Manuel, April 3.)

1954
Elvis Presley has his first formal session at Sun Records. While on a break from recording, he plays an up-tempo version of Arthur Crudup's *That's All Right, Mama* with guitarist Scotty Moore and bass player Bill Black.

1957
The Great National Skiffle Contest is held in the U.K. Skiffle, a precursor to rock in England, influenced many British musicians, including John Lennon and Eric Clapton.

1969
Sly & The Family Stone, John Mayall, Gary Burton, Mothers of Invention and Miles Davis perform at the Newport Jazz Festival.

NUMBER ONE SONGS:

1986
There'll Be Sad Songs (to Make You Cry) by Billy Ocean (1)

6

1925
Bill Haley is born in Highland Park, Michigan. One of the early rockabilly performers, his only No. 1 hit, *Rock Around the Clock*, was an important landmark in spreading rock 'n' roll to the masses when it opened the film *Blackboard Jungle*. One of the 1950s' biggest hitmakers, Haley and his group, The Comets, sold close to 60 million records, including the Top 10 hits *Burn That Candle* and *See You Later Alligator*. He died February 2, 1981, in Harlingen, Texas. Inducted into the Rock and Roll Hall of Fame January 21, 1987.

1940
Gene Chandler is born Eugene Dixon in Chicago. Vocalist and producer who had a No. 1 hit with *Duke of Earl*, he later became a record executive with Mr. Chand Records and Chi-Sound Records.

1961
The first edition of the music paper *Mersey Beat* is published in Liverpool by Bill Harry.

1964
The Beatles' film *A Hard Day's Night* has its world premiere in London, attended by Princess Margaret and Lord Snowden.

1969
Led Zeppelin, James Brown and Johnny Winter perform at the Newport Jazz Festival.

1971
Louis Armstrong dies at age 70 in Corona, New York. Jazz legend who influenced countless horn players in R&B, jazz and rock and was a member of the Rock and Roll Hall of Fame.

1985
Aretha Franklin returns to the Top 10 for the first time in 12 years with the entry of *Freeway of Love* into the charts, where it will stay for 13 weeks, peaking at No. 3.

NUMBER ONE SONGS:

1963
Easier Said Than Done by The Essex (2)
1985
Sussudio by Phil Collins (1)

7

1940
Ringo Starr is born Richard Starkey in Liverpool, England. Drummer for The Beatles (John Lennon, Paul McCartney, George Harrison), the most influential band in rock 'n' roll history. As a solo performer, he has had two No. 1 singles, *Photograph* and *You're Sixteen*, as part of 10 Top 40 hits. He also has had two Top 10 albums, *Ringo* and *Goodnight Vienna*. Inducted into the Rock and Roll Hall of Fame as a member of The Beatles January 20, 1988. (See Paul McCartney, June 18.)

NUMBER ONE SONGS:

1962
The Stripper by David Rose (1)
1973
Will It Go Round in Circles by Billy Preston (2)

1974
Rock the Boat by The Hues Corporation (1)
1984
When Doves Cry by Prince (5)

8

1908
Louis Jordan is born in Brinkley, Arkansas. Vocalist and saxophone player who developed the shuffle-boogie rhythm style of playing, fusing jazz with R&B. He died February 4, 1975, at age 66. Inducted into the Rock and Roll Hall of Fame January 21, 1987.

1944
Jai Johanny "Jaimoe" Johanson is born John Lee Johnson in Ocean Springs, Mississippi. Drummer for The Allman Brothers Band (Duane Allman, Greg Allman, Berry Oakley, Dickey Betts, Butch Trucks), which influenced southern rock bands throughout the 1970s and 1980s with its blend of blues, country, gospel and R&B, highlighted by lengthy jams. The group had eight Top 40 albums in the 1970s, including the No. 1 *Brothers and Sisters*, which produced a No. 2 single, *Ramblin' Man*.

1970
The Everly Brothers Show begins as

an 11-week replacement for *The Johnny Cash Show* on ABC television.

NUMBER ONE SONGS:

1957
(Let Me Be Your) Teddy Bear by Elvis Presley (7)
1972
Lean on Me by Bill Withers (3)
1989
Good Thing by Fine Young Cannibals (1)

JEFF BECK, 1969
at the Newport Jazz Festival

THE BYRDS, 1971
Chris Hillman, Gene Clark,
Michael Clarke, Roger McGuinn

9

1953
Ruth Brown, The Clovers and Wynonie Harris kick off Alan Freed's The Biggest Rhythm and Blues Show tour in Revere, Massachusetts. Also on the bill: The Lester Young Combo, Buddy Johnson's Orchestra and former heavyweight boxing champion Joe Louis and his band.

1955
Rock Around the Clock by Bill Haley & The Comets becomes the first rock 'n' roll song to reach No. 1 on the Billboard charts, marking the true beginning of the rock 'n' roll era.

1956
Dick Clark hosts the *Bandstand* show, on WFIL in Philadelphia, for the first time.

NUMBER ONE SONGS:

1977
Undercover Angel by Alan O'Day (1)
1983
Every Breath You Take by The Police (8)
1988
The Flame by Cheap Trick (2)

10

1947
Arlo Guthrie is born in Coney Island, New York. Singer, songwriter and guitarist who is best known for his 1960s period satire *Alice's Restaurant* and the Top 40 single *The City of New Orleans*. The son of Woody Guthrie, he continued the tradition of folksingers like his father and Pete Seeger who became activists, later influencing rock 'n' roll performers, including Jackson Browne, Bruce Springsteen, Bob Geldof and others, who put on large-scale benefit concerts such as Live Aid and Farm Aid.

1954
At 9:30 p.m., WHBQ (Memphis) disc jockey Dewey Phillips plays Elvis Presley's first record, *That's All Right, Mama*, on station WHBQ for the first time anywhere, resulting in requests for repeat playing.

1979
Chuck Berry is sentenced to a jail term

of four months on charges of income tax evasion stemming from 1973.

NUMBER ONE SONGS:

1961
Tossin' and Turnin' by Bobby Lewis (7)
1965
(I Can't Get No) Satisfaction by The Rolling Stones (4)
1976
Afternoon Delight by Starland Vocal Band (2)

11

1938
Terry Garthwaite is born in Berkeley, California. Guitarist and founder of Joy of Cooking (Toni Brown, Ron Wilson, Fritz Kasten, David Garthwaite), one of the early rock groups led by women.

1951
Alan Freed begins his new R&B program on radio station WJW in Cleveland, the early predecessor to his rock 'n' roll shows.

NUMBER ONE SONGS:

1960
Alley-Oop by The Hollywood Argyles (1)
1970
Mama Told Me (Not to Come) by Three Dog Night (2)
1987
Alone by Heart (3)

12

1943
Christine Perfect McVie is born in Birmingham, England. Keyboardist and singer-songwriter with Fleetwood Mac (Peter Green, John McVie, Mick Fleetwood, Jeremy Spencer, later Bob Welch, Stevie Nicks, Lindsey Buckingham). (See Mick Fleetwood, June 24.)

1954
Elvis Presley signs his first record contract, with Sam Phillips and Sun Records.

1957
The Everly Brothers, Frankie Lymon, Connie Francis and Buddy Knox headline Alan Freed's new television

show, *Friday Night Rock 'n' Roll*, on ABC television.

1962
The substitute band for Alexis Korner's Blues Incorporated at the Marquee in London includes Brian Jones, Keith Richards and Mick Jagger, an early version of The Rolling Stones.

1979
Minnie Riperton dies of cancer in Los Angeles at age 32.

NUMBER ONE SONGS:

1969
In the Year 2525 (Exordium & Terminus) by Zager & Evans (6)
1986
Holding Back the Years by Simply Red (1)

13

1942
Roger McGuinn is born in Chicago. Guitarist and singer-songwriter for the pioneering folk-rock band The Byrds (Chris Hillman, Michael Clarke, Gene Clark, David Crosby). He had a modest solo career after The Byrds and later joined with Clark and Hillman briefly. Inducted into the Rock and Roll Hall of Fame with The Byrds in 1991. (See Michael Clarke, June 3.)

1985
The Live Aid concerts take place at Wembly Stadium in London and at JFK Stadium in Philadelphia to benefit USA for Africa. Phil Collins performs at both shows, flying from London to Philadelphia via Concorde jet. Performers include The Who, Paul McCartney, The Beach Boys, Bryan Ferry, Madonna, Dire Straits, Elton John and David Bowie, among others.

NUMBER ONE SONGS:

1959
Lonely Boy by Paul Anka (4)
1974
Rock Your Baby by George McCrae (2)
1985
A View to a Kill by Duran Duran (2)

14

1887
North American Phonograph Company becomes the first record company.

1912
Woody Guthrie is born Woodrow Wilson Guthrie in Okemah, Oklahoma. Influential folksinger and songwriter, a contemporary of Leadbelly and Pete Seeger, he re-established folk as a means of social protest and commentary with songs like *This Land Is Your Land* and *Pastures of Plenty*. His work directly influenced Bob Dylan's writing, which helped kick off 1960s activism. His son, Arlo, continues in his tradition. He died October 3, 1967, in New York City at age 55 of Huntington's chorea. Inducted into the Rock and Roll Hall of Fame January 20, 1988.

1973
The Everly Brothers announce their breakup onstage at the John Wayne Theater in Hollywood, after Phil Everly smashes his guitar and leaves the stage.

NUMBER ONE SONGS:

1962
Roses Are Red (My Love) by Bobby Vinton (4)
1979
Bad Girls by Donna Summer (5)

15

1946
Linda Ronstadt is born in Tucson, Arizona. Vocalist who began with the Stone Poneys (Bob Kimmel, Kenny Edwards) and has had a successful career covering songs written by a variety of writers, including Maria Muldauer, Karla Bonoff, Buddy Holly, Emmy Lou Harris, Smokey Robinson and others. She has had more than 20 Top 40 chart hits, including *Heat Wave, Blue Bayou, It's So Easy, Hurt So Bad* and the No. 1 *You're No Good*. Her albums include three No. 1 hits, *Heart Like a Wheel, Simple Dreams* and *Living in the USA*. In recent years, she has recorded albums of big band, opera and Spanish music.

NUMBER ONE SONGS:

1989
If You Don't Know Me by Now by Simply Red (1)

CARLOS SANTANA, 1970

AN ILLUSTRATED RECORD OF ROCK 'N' ROLL

16

1972
Smokey Robinson gives his last performance with The Miracles in Washington, D.C., at the end of a six-month farewell tour of the U.S. before starting a solo career.

1981
Harry Chapin dies at age 39 after an automobile accident in Jericho, New York.

NUMBER ONE SONGS:

1966
Hanky Panky by Tommy James & The Shondells (2)

17

1942
Spencer Davis is born in Birmingham, England. Guitarist, vocalist and producer who formed the Spencer Davis Group (Pete York, Steve Winwood, Muff Winwood, later Nigel Olsson, Dee Murray), which had two Top 10 singles hits, *Gimme Some Lovin'* and *I'm a Man*.

NUMBER ONE SONGS:

1960
I'm Sorry by Brenda Lee (3)
1975
Listen to What the Man Said by Wings (1)

18

1939
Brian Auger is born in London. Keyboard player and songwriter who was a pioneer in jazz-rock fusion with his group Steampacket (Long John Baldry, Rod Stewart, Rick Brown, Mickey Waller, Julie Driscoll) in the early 1960s and 1970s.

1939
Dion DiMucci is born in the Bronx, New York. Lead singer for Dion & The Belmonts (Fred Milano, Carlo Mastangelo, Angelo D'Aleo), the vocal group that had seven Top 40 singles in the late 1950s, including *I Wonder Why*, *A Teenager in Love* and *Where or When*. In his solo career he had 14 top singles, including *The Wanderer*; *Ruby Baby*; *Donna the Prima Donna*; *Drip Drop*; *Abraham, Martin and John*

and the No. 1 *Runaround Sue*. Inducted into the Rock and Roll Hall of Fame January 18, 1989.

1941
Martha Reeves is born in Detroit. Lead vocalist for Martha and the Vandellas (Annette Sterling, Rosalind Ashford), one of Motown's best-selling female groups, which had a dozen Top 40 dance records in the 1960s, including *Heat Wave, Dancing in the Street, Nowhere to Run* and *Jimmy Mack*.

1970
The Randall Island (N.Y.) Rock Festival includes Little Richard, Jethro Tull, Grand Funk Railroad, Steppenwolf and other groups.

NUMBER ONE SONGS:

1964
Rag Doll by The Four Seasons (2)

19

1947
Bernie Leadon is born in Minneapolis. Guitarist, mandolin and banjo player, vocalist and founding member of The Eagles (Don Henley, Glenn Frey, Randy Meisner, later Don Felder). (See Randy Meisner, March 8.)

1981
Odessa, Texas, celebrates Roy Orbison Day, where Orbison plays for the first time in 15 years.

NUMBER ONE SONGS:

1980
It's Still Rock and Roll to Me by Billy Joel (2)
1986
Invisible Touch by Genesis (1)

20

1940
Billboard magazine begins its pop music chart listings.

1945
John Lodge is born in Birmingham, England. Bassist and vocalist who replaced Clint Warwick in The Moody Blues (Ray Thomas, Mike Pinder, Graeme Edge, later Justin Hayward). Lodge formed the Blue Jays with Hayward during one of the group's

separations. (See Graeme Edge, March 30.)

1947
Carlos Santana is born in Autlan de Navarro, Mexico. Innovative guitarist who has led several bands with his name. His groups' fusion of rock, Afro-Latin rhythms and jazzy vocals have produced 10 Top 40 hits, including *Evil Ways*, *Black Magic Woman* and *Oye Como Va* in the 1970s and 1980s.

1959
What'd I Say (Part 1) by Ray Charles enters the Billboard charts, where it stays for 11 weeks, reaching No. 6.

1975
Miami Steve Van Zandt performs as a member of Bruce Springsteen's E Street Band for the first time, in Providence, Rhode Island.

NUMBER ONE SONGS:

1963
Surf City by Jan & Dean (2)

1968
Grazing in the Grass by Hugh Masekela (2)

21

1947
Cat Stevens is born Steven Georgiou in London. Singer-songwriter who had 11 Top 40 singles and nine Top 35 albums in the 1970s before becoming a Muslim and leaving music. His best-known songs are *Peace Train*, *Morning Has Broken*, *Oh Very Young* and *Moon Shadow*, and his No. 1 LP was *Catch Bull at Four*.

1983
Diana Ross's free concert in Central Park in New York City is stopped after heavy rains interrupt it. Later, rampaging gangs of youths result in a ban on such concerts until 1991, when Paul Simon performs.

1990
Pink Floyd performs *The Wall* at the Berlin Wall before 150,000 people to celebrate the fall of the Iron Curtain. Other performers include Sinead O'Conner, Bryan Adams, Phil Collins, Van Morrison, Joni Mitchell and Cyndi Lauper.

NUMBER ONE SONGS:

1958
Hard Headed Woman by Elvis Presley (2)
1973
Bad, Bad Leroy Brown by Jim Croce (2)
1990
She Ain't Worth It by Glenn Medeiros and Bobby Brown (2)

22

1940
George Clinton is born in Kannapolis, North Carolina. Pioneering soul-funk songwriter, singer and producer who began with The Parliaments (Audrey Boykins, Eugene Boykins, Glen Carlos, Charles Davis, Herbie Jenkins, later Robert Lambert, Danny Mitchell, Grady Thomas), which had a Top 20 hit with *(I Wanna) Testify*. His later band, the Funkadelics, merged with The Parliaments to create influential funk LPs such as *Mothership Connection*, *The Clones of Dr. Funkenstein* and *One Nation Under a Groove*, all of which set the stage for the 1980s emergence of rap.

1944
Estelle Bennett is born in New York City. Member of the mid-'60s vocal trio The Ronettes (Ronnie Sepctor, Nedra Talley), which had five Top 40 singles produced by Phil Spector, including the No. 2 hit *Be My Baby* in 1963.

1947
Don Henley is born in Gilmer, Texas. Drummer, vocalist, songwriter and founding member of The Eagles (Bernie Leadon, Glenn Frey, Randy Meisner, later Don Felder). His solo career includes three Top 40 LPs—*I Can't Stand Still, Building the Perfect Beast* and *The End of the Innocence*—which produced several hit singles, including *Dirty Laundry, All She Wants to Do Is Dance* and *The End of the Innocence*. (See Randy Meisner, March 8.)

NUMBER ONE SONGS:

1989
Toy Soldiers by Martika (2)

MICK JAGGER, 1969

July

23

1945
Dino Dinelli is born in New York City. Drummer for The Young Rascals, later The Rascals (Eddie Brigati, Gene Cornish, Felix Cavaliere), which had 13 Top 40 singles between 1966 and 1969, including three No. 1 hits—*Good Lovin'*, *Groovin'* and *People Got to Be Free*. The group's greatest hits LP, *Time Peace*, reached No. 1.

1965
The Beatles release the single *Help!*, the title track to the group's second film, which becomes a No. 1 hit.

NUMBER ONE SONGS:

1977
Looks Like We Made It by Barry Manilow (1)
1988
Hold on to The Nights by Richard Marx (1)

24

NUMBER ONE SONGS:

1971
Indian Reservation by The Raiders (1)
1976
Kiss and Say Goodbye by The Manhattans (2)
1982
Eye of the Tiger by Survivor (6)

25

1943
Jim McCarty is born in Liverpool, England. Drummer for The Yardbirds (Keith Relf, Chris Dreja, Paul Samwell-Smith, Anthony Topham, later Eric Clapton, Jeff Beck, Jimmy Page). Inducted into the Rock and Roll Hall of Fame in 1992. (See Paul Samwell-Smith, May 8.)

1965
The Newport Folk Festival is highlighted by the first electric set played by Bob Dylan, who is booed by the audience.

NUMBER ONE SONGS:

1970
(They Long to Be) Close to You by The Carpenters (4)
1981
The One That You Love by Air Supply (1)

26

1943
Mick Jagger is born in Dartford, England. Lead singer, songwriter, producer and founding member of The Rolling Stones (Keith Richards, Charlie Watts, Bill Wyman, Brian Jones). Inducted into the Rock and Roll Hall of Fame in 1989. (See Charlie Watts, June 2.)

1968
Elvis Presley begins a four-week series of concerts at the Showroom of the International Hotel in Las Vegas, marking his first live performance since 1961.

NUMBER ONE SONGS:

1975
The Hustle by Van McCoy (1)
1986
Sledgehammer by Peter Gabriel (1)

27

1944
Bobbie Gentry is born Bobbie Lee Street in Chickasaw County, Mississippi. Singer who had a No. 1 hit with *Ode to Billie Joe* in 1967.

1969
Neil Young plays for the first time with Crosby, Stills & Nash, at the Fillmore East in New York City.

1976
John Lennon gets his green card, allowing him to stay in the United States.

NUMBER ONE SONGS:

1974
Annie's Song by John Denver (2)
1985
Everytime You Go Away by Paul Young (1)

28

1945
Richard Wright is born in London. Keyboardist and vocalist for the innovative rock group Pink Floyd (Syd Barrett, Nick Mason, Roger Waters, later David Gilmour). The group produced seven Top 40 albums, including one of the all-time best-selling LPs, the No. 1 *The Dark Side of the Moon*, which sold more than 10 million copies. Also had No. 1 LPs with *Wish You Were Here* in 1975 and *The Wall* in 1979 and a No. 1 single in 1980 with *Another Brick in The Wall (Part II)*.

1957
Jerry Lee Lewis appears on American television for the first time, singing *Whole Lotta Shakin' Goin' On* on *The Steve Allen Show*.

1973
Watkins Glen Summer Jam draws 600,000 to Watkins Glen, New York, to hear groups such as The Allman Brothers Band, The Band and The Grateful Dead.

NUMBER ONE SONGS:

1956
I Want You, I Need You, I Love You by Elvis Presley (1)
1958
Patricia by Prez Prado (1)

29

1916
Charlie Christian is born in Dallas. Influential and pioneering guitarist who is a jazz immortal. He was the first player to make electric guitar an important element in jazz, which influenced everyone who came later, including Wes Montgomery, George Benson, Barney Kessel, Sal Salvador and Jim Hall in the 1950s and the rock guitarists they have inspired. He died March 2, 1942, in New York City at age 25 of pneumonia. Inducted into the Rock and Roll Hall of Fame in 1990.

1962
WRVR-FM in New York City broadcasts Bob Dylan's first radio performance as part of the 21-hour *Hootenanny Saturday Night Special*.

1966
Bob Dylan is seriously injured in a mortorcycle accident near Woodstock, New York. It is more than a year before he begins to record again.

1974
Cass Elliot of The Mamas & The Papas dies in London at age 30, reportedly from choking on a sandwich.

NUMBER ONE SONGS:

1967
Light My Fire by The Doors (3)
1972
Alone Again (Naturally) by Gilbert O'Sullivan (6)

AN ILLUSTRATED RECORD OF ROCK 'N' ROLL

30

1941

Paul Anka is born in Ottawa, Alberta. Singer-songwriter who was one of the early teen idols with more than 20 hit singles in the 1950s and '60s, including *Put Your Head On My Shoulder, Puppy Love* and the No. 1 hits *Lonely Boy* and *Diana*. He continued to have hits through the 1980s with songs such as *Times of Your Life, Dance On Little Girl* and the No. 1 *(You're) Having My Baby*. His composing talent has resulted in film scores and hit singles, incuding Frank Sinatra's *My Way*, the theme for *The Tonight Show* and the score for *The Longest Day*.

NUMBER ONE SONGS:

1966
Wild Thing by The Troggs (2)
1977
I Just Want to Be Your Everything by Andy Gibb (4)
1988
Roll With It by Steve Winwood (4)

31

1923

Ahmet Ertegun is born in Istanbul, Turkey. Record company executive who began Atlantic Records as a jazz label and developed R&B and rock acts to make it one of the most diverse and talent-studded recording companies in history, signing such performers as Phil Collins, Roberta Flack, Foreigner, The Drifters, Bette Midler, Aretha Franklin, Genesis and Led Zeppelin. Inducted into the Rock and Roll Hall of Fame in 1987.

1956
Jukebox operators in Asbury Park, New Jersey, ban rock 'n' roll records.

1966
Cream performs its first concert, at the Jazz & Blues Festival in Windsor, England, under the band members' individual names.

NUMBER ONE SONGS:

1971
You've Got a Friend by James Taylor (1)

1

1942

Jerry Garcia is born in San Francisco. Guitarist, vocalist and leader of The Grateful Dead (Phil Lesh, Bob Weir, Pigpen McKernan, Bill Kreutzmann, later Mickey Hart, Keith Godchaux), one of the longest-running groups in history. An improvisational group from the beginning, the Dead displayed a diversity of musical influences even when they were a psychedelic band. Until *Touch of Grey*, the band never had a Top 40 single, but it had 10 Top 30 LPs over the years due to the loyal tour following of its fans, known as Deadheads. Garcia has also toured with his own Jerry Garcia Band and done session work with a variety of artists over the years.

1960

Aretha Franklin records her first secular tracks in a New York City recording studio. She sings *Right Now, Over the Rainbow, Love Is the Only Thing* and *Today I Sing the Blues*. Later, she is signed to CBS/Columbia by John Hammond.

1969

The three-day Atlantic City Pop Festival attracts 110,000 people as it begins at the Atlantic City (New Jersey) Race Track. Performers include Iron Butterfly; Johnny Winter; Crosby, Stills & Nash; Chicago; Procol Harum; Joni Mitchell; Mother Earth; Santana Blues Band and Booker T & The M.G.s.

1971

The Concert for Bangladesh at Madison Square Garden in New York City raises more than $243,000 for the impoverished nations of East and West Pakistan. The concert, organized by Ravi Shankar and George Harrison, features performances by Eric Clapton, Ringo Starr, Bob Dylan, Billy Preston and Leon Russell and is later released as an album, which reaches No. 2 on the LP charts.

1971

The Sonny and Cher Comedy Hour premieres on CBS television, where it will have a run of six years.

1981

Music Television (MTV), the first 24-hour video music network, goes on the air to cable television systems. The first video played is *Video Killed the Radio Star* by The Buggles. MTV soon becomes an important factor in defining the cutting edge of rock music. Later, a soft-rock sister network, Video Hits One (VH-1), aimed at more adult viewers, is also launched.

NUMBER ONE SONGS:

1964
A Hard Day's Night by The Beatles (2)
1981
Jessie's Girl by Rick Springfield (2)
1987
Shakedown by Bob Seger (1)

2

1943

Garth Hudson is born in London, Ontario. Organist and saxophonist for The Band (Richard Manuel, Rick Danko, Levon Helm, Robbie Robertson), which gained fame as backup group for Ronnie Hawkins and Bob Dylan before establishing its own name with *Music from Big Pink*. The first of eight Top 30 albums, it produced two Top 40 singles, *Up on Cripple Creek* and *Don't Do It*. The group's final concert, with an all-star cast on Thanksgiving 1976, was filmed and released as *The Last Waltz*.

1969

Performers on the second day of the Atlantic City Pop Festival include Jefferson Airplane, Creedence Clearwater Revival, Crazy World of Arthur Brown, Tim Buckley, B. B. King, Butterfield Blues Band, The Byrds, Hugh Masekela, Lighthouse and American Dream.

NUMBER ONE SONGS:

1975
One of These Nights by The Eagles (1)
1980
Magic by Olivia Newton-John (4)
1986
Glory of Love by Peter Cetera (2)

3

1963

The Beatles give their final performance at The Cavern Club in Liverpool, England.

1969

Performers on the final night of the Atlantic City Pop Festival include Janis Joplin, Canned Heat, Mothers of Invention, The Moody Blues, Three Dog Night, The Sir Douglas Quintet, The Buddy Rich Big Band and Dr. John, the Night Tripper.

NUMBER ONE SONGS:

1963
So Much in Love by The Tymes (1)
1968
Hello, I Love You by The Doors (2)
1985
Shout by Tears For Fears (3)

4

1956

Don't Be Cruel/Hound Dog by Elvis Presley enters Billboard's Top 40 chart, where it will become the longest-running No. 1 single, with 11 weeks at the top of the chart.

1957

The Everly Brothers sing *Bye, Bye Love* and *Wake Up Little Susie* on *The Ed Sullivan Show*.

1958

The Hot 100 is introduced as the new singles chart in *Billboard*.

1980

John Lennon and Yoko Ono begin recording for *Double Fantasy*, which will be Lennon's last LP, at the Hit Factory in New York City.

NUMBER ONE SONGS:

1956
My Prayer by The Platters (5)
1958
Poor Little Fool by Ricky Nelson (2)
1973
The Morning After by Maureen McGovern (2)
1990
Vision of Love by Mariah Carey (4)

5

1957

American Bandstand, hosted by Dick Clark, premieres on ABC television, beginning a run of more than 30 years as the top dance show on television. The show featured the Rate-a-Record segment, which

coined the phrase, "It's got a good beat, you can dance to it. . . ."

1990
The HBO broadcast of Madonna's *Blond Ambition* concert is the most widely viewed show in the cable channel's history.

NUMBER ONE SONGS:

1978
Miss You by The Rolling Stones (1)
1989
Batdance by Prince (1)

JERRY GARCIA, 1968
The Grateful Dead

August

6

1938
Isaac Hayes is born in Covington, Tennessee. Singer, songwriter, producer and arranger who helped create the Memphis soul sound at Stax Records. He had a No. 1 single with *Theme from Shaft* as one of eight Top 40 hits.

1954
The second annual Biggest Rhythm and Blues Show tour, produced by Alan Freed, begins in the Cleveland Arena, featuring The Drifters, LaVern Baker, The Spaniels, King Pleasure, The Comets, Erskine Hawkins and Rusty Bryant.

1970
An antiwar festival takes place at Shea Stadium in New York City, which includes performances by Steppenwolf, Paul Simon, Janis Joplin, Paul Butterfield and others.

7

NUMBER ONE SONGS:

1965
I'm Henry VIII, I Am by Herman's Hermits (1)
1971
How Can You Mend a Broken Heart by The Bee Gees (4)

1976
Don't Go Breaking My Heart by Elton John and Kiki Dee (4)

8

1933
Joe Tex is born Joseph Arrington, Jr. in Rogers, Texas. R&B and soul vocalist who had nine Top 40 hits between 1965 and 1977, including the Top 10 singles *Hold What You've Got, Skinny Legs and All* and *I Gotcha*. He died August 12, 1982, at age 49 of a heart attack in Navosta, Texas.

NUMBER ONE SONGS:

1960
Itsy Bitsy Teenie Weenie Yellow Polkadot Bikini by Brian Hyland (1)
1987
I Still Haven't Found What I'm Looking For by U2 (2)

9

1963
Whitney Houston is born in New Jersey. Vocalist who is the daughter of Cissy Houston and cousin of pop star Dionne Warwick, she became one of the best-selling artists of the 1980s with seven No. 1 singles: *Greatest Love of All, I Wanna Dance with Somebody (Who Loves Me), Didn't We Almost Have It All, How Will I Know, Where Do Broken Hearts Go, So Emotional* and *Saving All My Love for You.*

1973
Lillian Roxon, author of the first encyclopedia devoted to rock music, dies at age 40 from an asthma attack.

NUMBER ONE SONGS:

1975
Jive Talkin' by The Bee Gees (2)

10

1909
Leo Fender is born. Pioneering electronics inventor, his solid-body electric guitars changed the sound of music. His Telecaster and Stratocaster guitars became the standard for rock guitarists. He died March 21, 1991, at age 81. Inducted into the Rock and Roll Hall of Fame in 1992.

1940
Bobby Hatfield is born in Beaver Dam, Wisconsin. Half of the blue-eyed soul vocal duo The Righteous Brothers, with Bill Medley, which helped create Phil Spector's Wall of Sound (the heavy overdubbing of musicians) with the No. 1 hit *You've Lost That Lovin' Feelin'*. The Righteous Brothers had six other Top 20 singles in two years, including *Unchained Melody, Ebb Tide* and the No. 1 *(You're My Soul and) Inspiration* before breaking up. When they reunited in 1974, they had a Top 5 hit with *Rock and Roll Heaven.*

1943
Ronnie Spector is born Veronica Bennett in New York City. Lead singer of the mid-'60s vocal trio The Ronettes (Estelle Bennett, Nedra Talley), which had five Top 40 singles produced by Phil Spector, including the No. 2 hit *Be My Baby* in 1963. She was married to Spector from 1968 to 1974.

1947
Ian Anderson is born in Edinburgh, England. Lead singer, guitarist and flute player for Jethro Tull (Mick Abrahams, John Evan, Glenn Cornick, Clive Bunker), the progressive rock band that had six Top 10 albums in the 1970s, including *Aqualung, Living in the Past, War Child, Minstrel in the Gallery* and the No 1 LPs *Thick as a Brick* and *A Passion Play.*

NUMBER ONE SONGS:

1959
A Big Hunk o' Love by Elvis Presley (2)
1963
Fingertips—Part 2 by Little Stevie Wonder (3)
1974
Feel Like Makin' Love by Roberta Flack (1)

11

1949
Eric Carmen is born in Cleveland, Ohio. Lead singer, guitarist and bass player for The Raspberries (Wally Bryson, Jim Bonfanti, Dave Smalley), the 1970s pop group that had four Top 40 hits, including *Go All the Way* and *Overnight Sensation (Hit Record)*. His solo career included the No. 2 single *All By Myself* and five other Top 40 chart hits.

NUMBER ONE SONGS:

1962
Breaking Up Is Hard to Do by Neil Sedaka (2)
1984
Ghostbusters by Ray Parker, Jr. (3)

12

1966
The Beatles fly to Chicago to begin their final U.S. tour and hold a press conference. John Lennon apologizes for commenting in an interview that The Beatles were "now more popular than Christ."

1982
Soul singer Joe Tex dies at age 49 from a heart attack August 12, 1982, in Navosta, Texas.

NUMBER ONE SONGS:

1978
Three Times a Lady by The Commodores (2)
1989
Right Here Waiting by Richard Marx (3)

WOODSTOCK MUSIC
AND ART FESTIVAL, 1969

AN ILLUSTRATED RECORD OF ROCK 'N' ROLL

13

1965
Jefferson Airplane plays its first major show, at the opening of the Matrix Club, which becomes a prime club for San Francisco bands.

1975
Bruce Springsteen and the E Street Band open a five-night stand at The Bottom Line in New York City, in part to prove they are worthy of the hype started by Jon Landeau's memorable statement, "I saw rock and roll future and its name is Bruce Springsteen."

NUMBER ONE SONGS:

1966
Summer in the City by The Lovin' Spoonful (3)

14

1941
David Crosby is born David Van Cortland in Los Angeles. Singer, songwriter and guitarist for the pioneering folk-rock band The Byrds (Chris Hillman, Michael Clarke, Gene Clark, Roger McGuinn). The group's early use of harmonies influenced many later bands. The Byrds had seven Top 40 singles, including two No. 1 hits, *Mr. Tambourine Man* and *Turn! Turn! Turn!* In 1968 he formed Crosby, Stills & Nash with Stephen Stills and Graham Nash. CSN had six Top 30 hits in its early days and four more with Neil Young, including *Woodstock* and *Teach Your Children*. He also performed as a duo with Nash. Inducted into the Rock and Roll Hall of Fame with The Byrds in 1991.

NUMBER ONE SONGS:

1965
I Got You Babe by Sonny & Cher (3)

15

1925
Billy Pinkney is born in Sumter, South Carolina. Founding member of The Drifters (Clyde McPhatter, Andrew Thrasher, Gerhart Thrasher), vocal group that had 16 Top 40 hits between 1959 and 1964, including the No. 1 *Save the Last Dance*

for Me and the Top 10 singles *There Goes My Baby, Up on the Roof, On Broadway* and *Under the Boardwalk*.

1946
Jimmy Webb is born in Elk City, Oklahoma. Composer and pianist who wrote top chart hits such as *Galveston, By the Time I Get to Phoenix* and *Wichita Lineman* for Glen Campbell and *Up-Up and Away* for the 5th Dimension and had his greatest success with *MacArthur Park*, a No. 2 hit for Richard Harris in 1968 and a No. 1 hit for Donna Summer in 1979.

1958
Buddy Holly marries Maria Elena Santiago in Lubbock, Texas.

1965
The Beatles begin their U.S. tour at Shea Stadium in New York City.

1969
The three-day Woodstock Music and Art Festival begins on Max Yasgur's farm in Bethel, New York, attracting more than 400,000 people. It is one of the pivotal events of the 1960s, featuring major rock 'n' roll and folk performers, including Richie Havens, The Grateful Dead, Jimi Hendrix, The Who, Paul Butterfield Blues Band, Johnny Winter, Santana, Sha Na Na, Sly & The Family Stone, Joe Cocker, Arlo Guthrie and Jefferson Airplane. A documentary film and two Top 10 albums about Woodstock were later released.

NUMBER ONE SONGS:

1960
It's Now or Never by Elvis Presley (5)
1964
Everybody Loves Somebody by Dean Martin (1)
1981
Endless Love by Diana Ross and Lionel Richie (9)

16

1938
Robert Johnson, a pioneer of the Mississippi Delta blues style, which influenced Muddy Waters and Elmore James, and a member of the Rock and Roll Hall of Fame, dies in Greenwood, Mississippi, at age 27.

1958
Madonna is born Madonna Louise

Ciccone in Rochester, Michigan. Singer, songwriter, dancer, record producer and actor whose visual approach to performance helped establish MTV as an important influence on music. She has had more than a dozen top singles, including the No. 1 hits *Like a Virgin, Crazy for You, Live to Tell, Papa Don't Preach, Vogue* and *Like a Prayer*, and the top LPs *Like a Virgin* and *True Blue*.

1962
Drummer Pete Best is asked to leave The Beatles, to be replaced by Ringo Starr.

1977
Elvis Presley, member of the Rock and Roll Hall of Fame who changed the direction of popular music and established rock 'n' roll as an accepted art form, dies of a heart attack at age 42 in his home in the Graceland mansion in Memphis, Tennessee.

NUMBER ONE SONGS:

1986
Papa Don't Preach by Madonna (2)

17

NUMBER ONE SONGS:

1968
People Got to Be Free by The Rascals (5)
1974
The Night Chicago Died by Paper Lace (1)

18

1945
Nona Hendryx is born in Trenton, New Jersey. Vocalist with Labelle (Patti LaBelle, Sarah Dash, Cindy Birdsong)), which had a No. 1 single with *Lady Marmalade*.

1962
Ringo Starr replaces Pete Best as the drummer for The Beatles when the group goes into its first recording session for George Martin.

NUMBER ONE SONGS:

1956
Don't Be Cruel/Hound Dog by Elvis Presley (11)

1973
Touch Me in the Morning by Diana Ross (1)
1979
Good Times by Chic (1)

19

1939
Ginger Baker is born Peter Baker in Lewisham, England. Drummer who joined with Eric Clapton and Jack Bruce to form the power trio Cream, which released only four albums while it was together, including the No. 1 *Wheels of Fire*. The group's two Top 10 singles were *Sunshine of Your Love* and *White Room*. Baker later formed Blind Faith with Clapton and then went on to a solo career with Ginger Baker's Air Force and session work.

1940
Johnny Nash is born in Houston, Texas. Vocalist who had a No. 1 hit with *I Can See Clearly Now*, which helped bring reggae music to the U.S. He also had a No. 12 hit with Bob Marley's *Stir It Up* as one of his five Top 40 singles.

1943
Billy J. Kramer is born William Howard Ashton in Bootle, England. Lead singer for Billy J. Kramer & the Dakotas (Tony Mansfield, Mike Maxfield, Robin Macdonald, Raymond Jones), the English pop group managed by Brian Epstein and produced by George Martin that had four Top 30 hits, including *Little Children* and *Bad to Me*.

1964
The Beatles begin their first North American tour at the Cow Palace in San Francisco. The tour will cover 24 cities in the U.S. and Canada in 32 days.

NUMBER ONE SONGS:

1957
Tammy by Debbie Reynolds (5)
1958
Volare by Domenico Modugno (5)
1967
All You Need Is Love by The Beatles (1)

August

20

1948
Robert Plant is born in Bromwich, England. Lead singer for the pioneering heavy metal band Led Zeppelin (John Paul Jones, John Bonham, Jimmy Page). The group had 10 Top 10 albums, including six No. 1 albums, among them *Houses of the Holy* and *Physical Graffiti*. Plant's solo career included three Top 20 albums and three Top 40 singles, including *Little By Little*. He also recorded with Page, Jeff Beck and Nile Rodgers as The Honeydrippers, who had a No. 3 single with a remake of *Sea of Love*.

1955
Bo Diddley performs at the Apollo Theater in Harlem, New York City.

1955
Maybellene enters the Billboard charts to become Chuck Berry's first Top 10 hit, staying on for 11 weeks and reaching No. 5.

NUMBER ONE SONGS:

1977
Best of My Love by The Emotions (5)

21

1944
Jackie DeShannon is born in Hazel, Kentucky. Singer-songwriter who was successful as a composer of hits like *Dum Dum* (Brenda Lee), *When You Walk in the Room* (The Searchers) and *Day Dreamin' of You* (The Fashionettes) before having a brief performing career with the Top 10 hits *What the World Needs Now Is Love* and *Put a Little Love in Your Heart* .

22

1917
John Lee Hooker is born in Clarksdale, Mississippi. Influential electric blues guitarist and singer-songwriter who was an important link between blues and rock 'n' roll. His songs have been covered by performers from The Animals to George Thorogood. Inducted into the Rock and Roll Hall of Fame in 1991.

1953
Fats Domino and Joe Turner headline the Big Rhythm and Blues Show emceed by Alan Freed in the Cleveland Arena.

1956
Elvis Presley begins filming his first movie, originally titled *The Reno Brothers*, in Hollywood. Later it is retitled *Love Me Tender*.

1985
A television special featuring Rick Nelson and Fats Domino is filmed at the University Amphitheater in Los Angeles.

1988
The Public Broadcasting System in the United States premieres the one-hour documentary *Aretha Franklin: The Queen of Soul*.

NUMBER ONE SONGS:

1964
Where Did Our Love Go by The Supremes (2)
1970
Make It with You by Bread (1)
1987
Who's That Girl by Madonna (1)

23

1947
Keith Moon is born in London. Manic drummer for The Who (Pete Townshend, John Entwistle, Roger Daltrey, later Kenny Jones), which personified 1960s teenage rebellion in its music and its actions, becoming known for smashing its instruments after performing during the band's early days. The Who created the first rock opera, *Tommy*, one of its 12 Top 40 LPs, which also included *Who Are You* and the No. 2 *Quadrophenia*. The albums produced 16 Top 40 singles, with *I Can See for Miles* as a Top 10 hit. Moon died at age 31 from a drug overdose on September 7, 1978. Inducted into the Rock and Roll Hall of Fame in 1990.

NUMBER ONE SONGS:

1969
Honky Tonk Women by The Rolling Stones (4)
1975
Fallin' in Love by Hamilton, Joe Frank & Reynolds (1)

24

1942
Joe Chambers is born in Scott County, Mississippi. One of the four Chambers Brothers (George, Willie, Lester), the pioneering and innovative funk/psychedelic band that had the Top 40 hits *I Can't Turn You Loose* and *Time Has Come Today* in the late 1960s.

1956
Studio 5 on Great Newport Street in Soho opens as the first rock 'n' roll club in London.

1967
The Beatles listen to a public lecture by the Maharishi Mahesh Yogi at the Hilton Hotel in London.

1979
B. B. King performs a concert at the Roxy in Los Angeles to celebrate 30 years in the music business.

NUMBER ONE SONGS:

1959
The Three Bells by The Browns (4)

1974
(You're) Having My Baby by Paul Anka (3)
1985
The Power of Love by Huey Lewis & The News (2)

25

1958
Summertime Blues by Eddie Cochran enters the Billboard charts, where it remains for 12 weeks, reaching No. 8.

1970
Elton John makes his American concert debut, at The Troubadour in Los Angeles, playing the piano like no one since Jerry Lee Lewis.

NUMBER ONE SONGS:

1958
Little Star by The Elegants (1)
1962
The Loco-Motion by Little Eva (1)
1973
Brother Louie by The Stories (2)
1979
My Sharona by The Knack (6)

26

NUMBER ONE SONGS:

1967
Ode to Billie Joe by Bobbie Gentry (4)
1972
Brandy (You're a Fine Girl) by Looking Glass (1)
1978
Grease by Frankie Valli (2)

August / September

27

1965
Elvis Presley hosts The Beatles at his home in Bel Air, California, during the Fab Four's U.S. tour. They play music and talk through the night.

1967
Brian Epstein, who as manager of The Beatles helped engineer the band's success, dies of a drug overdose at age 33 in London while The Beatles are meeting with the Maharishi Mahesh Yogi in North Wales.

NUMBER ONE SONGS:

1988
Monkey by George Michael (2)

28

NUMBER ONE SONGS:

1961
Wooden Heart by Joe Dowell (1)

29

1958
Michael Jackson is born in Gary, Indiana. Singer-songwriter who began his career with his brothers as The Jackson 5 (Jackie, Tito, Jermaine, Marlon, later Randy Jackson), a group that was one of Motown's top hitmakers in the 1970s, before becoming one of the biggest solo artists in history. With the Jackson 5, he was the lead singer on more than 20 Top 40 singles, including four No. 1 hits: *I Want You Back, ABC, The Love You Save* and *I'll Be There.* As a solo, he has had more than 16 top singles, including the No. 1 songs *Ben, Don't Stop 'Til You Get Enough, Rock With You, Billie Jean* and *Beat It.* His LP *Thriller* is the best-selling album in history, with more than 40 million sold.

1965
The Beatles concert at the Hollywood Bowl in Hollywood is recorded by engineer Pete Abbott and producer George Martin. Together with a concert recorded at the same place on August 23, 1964, it is released in 1977 as *The Beatles at the Hollywood Bowl,* which will reach No. 2 on the Billboard album charts.

1966
The last formal concert by The Beatles takes place at Candlestick Park in San Francisco before 25,000 fans.

NUMBER ONE SONGS:

1970
War by Edwin Starr (3)
1987
La Bamba by Los Lobos (3)

30

1935
John Phillips is born in Parris Island, South Carolina. Singer-songwriter and founder of the folk-rock group The Mamas & The Papas (Michelle Phillips, Cass Elliot, Dennis Doherty), which had nine Top 30 singles hits, including *California Dreamin', I Saw Her Again, Words of Love, Dedicated to the One I Love, Creeque Alley* and the No. 1 *Monday, Monday.*

1969
International Pop Festival takes place at Dallas Speedway in Lewisville, Texas. Performers include B. B. King, Janis Joplin, Canned Heat, Santana, Led Zeppelin and others.

NUMBER ONE SONGS:

1975
Get Down Tonight by KC & The Sunshine Band (1)
1980
Sailing by Christopher Cross (1)
1986
Higher Love by Steve Winwood (1)

31

1945
Van Morrison is born in Belfast, Ireland. Singer-songwriter whose soul-influenced voice has been admired for many years. He had five Top 40 hits in the 1960s and '70s, including *Brown-Eyed Girl* and *Domino.*

NUMBER ONE SONGS:

1963
My Boyfriend's Back by The Angels (3)

1

1947
Barry Gibb is born in Isle of Man, Australia. Leader of The Bee Gees, which include his twin brothers Robin and Maurice, one of the most successful pop groups of the 1970s. The Gibbs have followed musical trends and hit it big with the disco craze in the '70s, when their soundtrack for the film *Saturday Night Fever* yielded three No. 1 hits en route to becoming the best-selling soundtrack LP in history. Between 1967 and 1983, the group had 28 Top 40 hits, including the No. 1 singles *How Can You Mend a Broken Heart, Jive Talkin', You Should Be Dancing, How Deep Is Your Love, Stayin' Alive, Night Fever, Too Much Heaven, Tragedy* and *Love You Inside Out.* Barry Gibb also had two Top 10 singles in duet with Barbra Streisand, *Guilty* and *What Kind of Fool.*

NUMBER ONE SONGS:

1962
Sheila by Tommy Roe (2)
1984
What's Love Got to Do with It by Tina Turner (3)
1990
If Wishes Came True by Sweet Sensation (1)

2

1967
(Your Love Keeps Lifting Me) Higher and Higher by Jackie Wilson enters the Billboard charts, where it stays for nine weeks, reaching No. 6.

NUMBER ONE SONGS:

1989
Cold Hearted by Paula Abdul (1)

STEVE WINWOOD, 1970

AN ILLUSTRATED RECORD OF ROCK 'N' ROLL

3

1942
Alan Jardine is born in Lima, Ohio. Vocalist and guitarist for The Beach Boys, (Dennis Wilson, Carl Wilson, Mike Love; Brian Wilson). Inducted into the Rock and Roll Hall of Fame with The Beach Boys January 20, 1988. (See Mike Love, March 15.)

1970
Alan Wilson, guitarist and vocalist for the blues-rock group Canned Heat, dies at age 27 of a drug overdose in Torrance, California.

NUMBER ONE SONGS:

1955
The Yellow Rose of Texas by Mitch Miller (6)
1966
Sunshine Superman by Donovan (1)

4

1942
Merald Knight is born in Atlanta. Vocalist for Gladys Knight and The Pips (Gladys Knight, Brenda Knight, William Guest, Elenor Guest), a family of musicians that had 24 singles hits over a 15-year period, including *I Heard It Through the Grapevine*, *If I Were Your Woman*, *Neither One of Us (Wants to Be the First to Say Goodbye)*, *The Best Thing That Ever Happened to Me* and the No. 1 *Midnight Train to Georgia*.

1962
The Beatles record their first U.K. single, *Love Me Do/ How Do You Do It*, at EMI Studios, Abbey Road in London.

NUMBER ONE SONGS:

1961
Michael by The Highwaymen (2)
1965
Help! by The Beatles (3)
1971
Uncle Albert/Admiral Halsey by Paul and Linda McCartney (1)
1976
You Should Be Dancing by The Bee Gees (1)
1982
Abracadabra by The Steve Miller Band (2)

5

1946
Freddie Mercury is born Frederick Bulsara in Zanzibar. Lead singer for Queen (Brian May, John Deacon, Roger Meadows-Taylor), the glitter-rock band that had 11 Top 25 albums, including *A Night at the Opera* and the No. 1 *The Game*, and a dozen Top 25 singles, including *We Are the Champions/ We Will Rock You*, *Bohemian Rhapsody* and the No. 1 hits *Crazy Little Thing Called Love* and *Another One Bites the Dust*. He died November 24, 1991, in Kensington, England, at age 45 of AIDS.

1946
Buddy Miles is born in Omaha, Nebraska. Drummer who is known for his work with Jimi Hendrix's Band of Gypsys (Billy Cox, Hendrix), Wilson Pickett and Electric Flag (Mike Bloomfield, Harvey Brooks, Barry Goldberg, Nick Gravenities, Peter Strazza, Marcus Doubleday, Herbie Rich). He later formed The Buddy Miles Band. He had two Top 35 albums in the early 1970s—a solo, *Them Changes*, and a concert LP, *Carlos Santana & Buddy Miles! Live!*

NUMBER ONE SONGS:

1964
The House of the Rising Sun by The Animals (3)

6

1925
Jimmy Reed is born in Dunleith, Mississippi. Influential blues musician who wrote and performed in the 1950s such hits as *Honest I Do* and *Baby What You Want Me to Do* on the R&B charts. He died August 29, 1976. Inducted into the Rock and Roll Hall of Fame in 1991.

1944
Roger Waters is born in Surrey, England. Bassist and vocalist for Pink Floyd (Richard Wright, Syd Barrett, Nick Mason, later David Guilmour). (See Richard Wright, July 28.)

NUMBER ONE SONGS:

1980
Upside Down by Diana Ross (4)

7

1936
Buddy Holly is born Charles Hardin Holley in Lubbock, Texas. One of rock 'n' roll's pioneers as a singer, songwriter and guitarist, he and his sidemen, The Crickets (originally Sonny Curtis, Don Guess, Jerry Allison, later Niki Sullivan, Larry Welborn, Joe Mauldin, Tommy Alsup, Glen Hardin, Jerry Naylor, Waylon Jennings), were one of the first groups to write their own material, use advanced recording techniques and establish the standard ensemble in rock as drums, bass and two guitars. The Crickets had a No. 1 single with *That'll Be the Day*, but Holly's songs such as *Rave On*, *Not Fade Away* and *Peggy Sue* influenced songwriters and musicians who followed. He died February 3, 1959, in a plane crash near Clear Lake, Iowa, with Ritchie Valens and the Big Bopper. Inducted into the Rock and Roll Hall of Fame January 20, 1986.

1954
Alan Freed begins broadcasting on WINS in New York City, playing *What a Dream* by Ruth Brown.

NUMBER ONE SONGS:

1985
St. Elmo's Fire (Man in Motion) by John Parr (2)

8

1897
Jimmie Rodgers is born in Meridian, Mississippi. The father of modern country music, he blended traditional hillbilly country sounds with black blues and folk styles, influencing later country and blues musicians such as Hank Williams, whose style gave birth to rockabilly, the first incarnation of rock 'n' roll. He died May 26, 1933, in New York City. Inducted into the Rock and Roll Hall of Fame January 20, 1986.

1942
Pigpen McKernan is born Ron McKernan in San Bruno, California. Keyboardist and harmonica player for The Grateful Dead (Phil Lesh, Bob Weir, Jerry Garcia, Bill Kreutzmann, later Mickey Hart, Keith Godchaux). McKernan died March 8, 1973, of liver failure in San Francisco. (See Jerry Garcia, August 1.)

1956
Jackie Wilson begins his solo career after leaving The Dominoes with the release of the single *Reet Petite (The Finest Girl You Ever Want to Meet)*.

NUMBER ONE SONGS:

1973
Let's Get It On by Marvin Gaye (2)
1990
Blaze of Glory by Jon Bon Jovi (1)

9

1941
Otis Redding is born in Dawson, Georgia. Singer-songwriter who was one of the greatest soul singers, he had hits with such songs as *Respect*, *The Happy Song* and *Papa's Got a Brand New Bag*, but he didn't live to see *(Sittin' on) The Dock of the Bay* become a No. 1 hit. He died December 10, 1967, in a plane crash near Madison, Wisconsin. Inducted into the Rock and Roll Hall of Fame January 18, 1989.

1946
Billy Preston is born in Houston. Keyboardist and vocalist who is best known for his session work and touring with such major performers as The Beatles, The Rolling Stones, Ray Charles and Little Richard. His performing career in the early 1970s resulted in four Top 5 singles: *Outa-Space*, *Space Race* and two No. 1 hits, *Will It Go Round in Circles* and *Nothing from Nothing*.

1956
Elvis Presley appears on *The Toast of the Town*, Ed Sullivan's show, for the first time. Approximately 54 million people watch the show.

NUMBER ONE SONGS:

1957
Diana by Paul Anka (1)
1975
Rhinestone Cowboy by Glen Campbell (2)
1978
Boogie Oogie Oogie by A Taste of Honey (3)
1989
Hangin' Tough by New Kids on the Block (1)

1986
Venus by Bananarama (1)

September

10

1945
Jose Feliciano is born in Lares, Puerto Rico. Guitarist, songwriter and singer, he was the first performer to win Grammy Awards in two language categories, English and Spanish. He is best known for his cover of The Doors' *Light My Fire* and the Top 25 single *Hi-Heel Sneakers*.

1970
The Federal Communications Commission issues a list to Sen. Frank Moss of songs that "appear to be eulogizing the use of narcotics," including three songs by The Beatles (*Happiness Is a Warm Gun*, *Everybody's Got Something to Hide Except Me and My Monkey* and *With a Little Help from My Friends*) and two songs by The Rolling Stones (*19th Nervous Breakdown* and *Let's Spend the Night Together*).

NUMBER ONE SONGS:

1966
You Can't Hurry Love by The Supremes (2)
1983
Maniac by Michael Sembello (2)
1988
Sweet Child o' Mine by Guns N' Roses (2)

11

1962
The Beatles re-record *Love Me Do* and record *P.S. I Love You* at EMI Studios, Abbey Road, London.

NUMBER ONE SONGS:

1971
Go Away Little Girl by Donny Osmond (3)
1976
(Shake, Shake, Shake) Shake Your Booty by KC & The Sunshine Band (1)
1982
Hard to Say I'm Sorry by Chicago (2)

12

1943
Maria Muldaur is born Maria Grazia Rosa Domenica d'Amato in New York City. Singer who began with the Jim Kweskin Jug Band (Jim Kweskin, Bill Keith, Mel Lyman, Fritz Richmond, Richard Greene, Geoff Muldaur) and established a solo career with two albums, *Maria Muldaur* and *Waitress in the Donut Shop*, and the Top 15 singles *Midnight at The Oasis* and *I'm a Woman*.

1952
Gerry Beckley is born in Texas. One of three guitarist-vocalists who made up the trio America (Dewey Bunnell, Dan Peek), which had 11 Top 35 singles, including *I Need You*, *Ventura Highway*, *Tin Man* and two No. 1 hits—*A Horse with No Name* and *Sister Golden Hair*—between 1972 and 1983.

13

1944
Peter Cetera is born in Chicago. Guitarist and vocalist for the jazz-rock group Chicago Transit Authority, later known as Chicago. The group had more than 30 Top 40 hits and 15 Top 25 LPs, including five No. 1 albums—*Chicago V* through *Chicago IX*. Cetera left the group after *Chicago 17*. His solo career includes the No. 1 hit *Glory of Love*, along with a No. 1 duet with Amy Grant, *The Next Time I Fall*.

1969
The Rock & Roll Revival at Varsity Stadium in Toronto is highlighted by a surprise performance by John Lennon and the Plastic Ono Band, which includes Eric Clapton, Klaus Voormann and Alan White.

NUMBER ONE SONGS:

1986
Take My Breath Away by Berlin (1)

14

1955
Little Richard records *Kansas City* and *Tutti Frutti* in New Orleans with The Crescent City Rhythm Section. *Tutti Frutti* will become his first hit record.

1968
Pete Townshend first discusses his ideas for a rock opera about a deaf, dumb and blind pinball player in a music magazine article.

NUMBER ONE SONGS:

1974
I Shot the Sheriff by Eric Clapton (1)

15

NUMBER ONE SONGS:

1962
Sherry by The Four Seasons (5)
1973
Delta Dawn by Helen Reddy (1)
1990
Release Me by Wilson Phillips (2)

16

1925
B. B. King is born Riley B. King near Indianola, Mississippi. Influential modern blues guitarist whose style was important in the development of many rock guitarists, including Eric Clapton and Mike Bloomfield. He has had half a dozen singles hits, including *The Thrill Is Gone*. Inducted into the Rock and Roll Hall of Fame January 21, 1987.

1948
Kenny Jones is born in London. Drummer for the original Faces (Rod Stewart, Ron Wood, Ronnie Lane, Ian McLagan). After Keith Moon died, Jones replaced him in The Who for a 1978 tour. (See Keith Moon, August 23.)

1964
Shindig premieres on ABC television with performances by The Everly Brothers, Sam Cooke and The Righteous Brothers.

1977
Marc Bolan, leader of T Rex, dies at age 25 in an automobile accident in London.

NUMBER ONE SONGS:

1972
Black & White by Three Dog Night (1)
1989
Don't Wanna Lose You by Gloria Estefan (1)

RAY CHARLES, 1973

AN ILLUSTRATED RECORD OF ROCK 'N' ROLL

17

1923

Hank Williams is born in Mount Olive, Alabama. The most important country music star of the modern era, his songs and singing style were cornerstones of rockabilly, one of the key elements in early rock 'n' roll development. Among his standard songs still heard today are *Your Cheatin' Heart* and *Hey, Good Lookin'*. He died of a heart attack at age 29, attributed to too much alcohol and drug consumption, on January 1, 1953, in Oak Hill, West Virginia. Inducted into the Rock and Roll Hall of Fame January 21, 1987.

1951

Jimmy Yancey, innovative pianist who developed the boogie-woogie style of playing and is a member of the Rock and Roll Hall of Fame, dies in Chicago at age 53.

NUMBER ONE SONGS:

1955

Ain't That a Shame by Pat Boone (2)

18

1940

Frankie Avalon is born Francis Avallone in Philadelphia. Singer who became a teen idol in the late 1950s with a string of singles hits, including *Ginger Bread*, *Bobby Sox to Stockings*, *Just Ask Your Heart* and the No. 1 hits *Venus* and *Why*.

1970

Jimi Hendrix, innovative guitarist and a member of the Rock and Roll Hall of Fame, dies at age 28 in London of a drug overdose.

NUMBER ONE SONGS:

1961

Take Good Care of My Baby by Bobby Vee (3)

1976

Play That Funky Music by Wild Cherry (3)

19

1931

Brook Benton is born Benjamin Franklin Peay in Camden, South Carolina. Singer-songwriter who had 22 Top 40 hit singles, including

---

the Top 10 songs *It's Just a Matter of Time*, *So Many Ways*, *Kiddio*, *The Boll Weevil Song*, *Hotel Happiness* and *Rainy Night in Georgia*.

1934

Brian Epstein is born in Liverpool, England. The record store owner turned manager who guided The Beatles through the most important phases of their early career and success, making them the top rock 'n' roll band of all time. He died August 27, 1967, in London at age 32, attributed to an accidental overdose of sleeping pills.

1940

Bill Medley is born in Santa Ana, California. Half of the vocal duo The Righteous Brothers (with Bobby Hatfield). Medley had a No. 1 hit with Jennifer Warnes in 1987 with *(I've Had) The Time of My Life*. (See Bobby Hatfield, August 10.)

1943

Cass Elliot is born in Baltimore. Began her career as a member of The Mugwumps (John Sebastian, Dennis Doherty) and became a vocalist with The Mamas & The Papas (Michelle Phillips, John Phillips, Dennis Doherty). She died July 29, 1974, in London, reportedly from choking on a sandwich. (See John Phillips, August 30.)

1945

David Bromberg is born in Philadelphia. Multi-instrumentalist and singer-songwriter who is a highly respected session guitarist and performer in almost every field of music, from jazz to bluegrass. He has played with musicians such as Tom Paxton, Bob Dylan, Carly Simon, Phoebe Snow and Chubby Checker.

1973

Graham Parsons, country-rock pioneer, dies at age 27 in Joshua Tree National Monument, California, of a drug overdose.

1976

Promoter Sid Bernstein takes out a full-page ad in *The New York Times* saying a Beatles concert could make $200 million.

NUMBER ONE SONGS:

1960

The Twist by Chubby Checker (1)

1970

Ain't No Mountain High Enough by Diana Ross (3)

1987

I Just Can't Stop Loving You by Michael Jackson and Siedah Garrett (1)

20

1973

Jim Croce dies at age 30 in a plane crash in Natchitoches, Louisiana.

1983

Jimmy Page, Eric Clapton and Jeff Beck perform *Layla* as the finale during a benefit concert at Royal Albert Hall in London for Ronnie Lane, the former bass player of Faces, who has multiple sclerosis. Also performing are Steve Winwood, Charlie Watts, Kenny Jones and Bill Wyman.

NUMBER ONE SONGS:

1969

Sugar, Sugar by The Archies (4)

1975

Fame by David Bowie (2)

1986

Stuck with You by Huey Lewis & The News (3)

21

NUMBER ONE SONGS:

1959

Sleep Walk by Santo & Johnny (2)

1963

Blue Velvet by Bobby Vinton (3)

1968

Harper Valley P.T.A. by Jeannie C. Riley (1)

1974

Can't Get Enough of Your Love, Babe by Barry White (1)

1985

Money for Nothing by Dire Straits (3)

22

1960

Joan Jett is born in Philadelphia. Singer and guitarist who has lived the life of the archetypical rocker, starting her career with the all-girl band The Runaways (Lita Ford, Jackie

---

Fox, Cherie Currie, Sandy West) before leading The Blackhearts (Ricky Byrd, Gary Ryan, Lee Crystal), which produced five Top 40 singles, including the No. 1 single *I Love Rock 'n' Roll*.

NUMBER ONE SONGS:

1984

Missing You by John Waite (1)

23

1930

Ray Charles is born Ray Charles Robinson in Albany, Georgia. Innovative vocalist, pianist and composer who fused gospel, blues, country and jazz to invent soul music and influence R&B, jazz, rock, country and pop performers. He has had more than 30 Top 40 singles, including *What'd I Say (Part 1)*, *Busted*, *Crying Time*, *You Are My Sunshine* and the No. 1 hits *Hit the Road Jack*, *I Can't Stop Loving You* and *Georgia on My Mind*. Inducted into the Rock and Roll Hall of Fame January 20, 1986.

1949

Bruce Springsteen is born in Freehold, New Jersey. Guitarist, singer and songwriter who established himself as America's blue-collar rock star in the 1970s and '80s with six Top 5 albums, including the No. 1 LPs *The River* and *Born in the U.S.A.*, and a dozen singles from those albums, including *Hungry Heart*, *Dancing in the Dark* and *Glory Days*. Also renowned as one of the most charismatic concert performers in rock.

1983

The Everly Brothers' reunion concert takes place before a sold-out audience at Royal Albert Hall in London.

NUMBER ONE SONGS:

1957

That'll Be the Day by The Crickets (1)

1967

The Letter by The Box Tops (4)

1972

Baby Don't Get Hooked on Me by Mac Davis (3)

1989

Girl I'm Gonna Miss You by Milli Vanilli (2)

AN ILLUSTRATED RECORD OF ROCK 'N' ROLL

24

1940
Barbara Allbut is born in Orange, New Jersey. Member of the vocal trio The Angels (her sister Phyllis Allbut [born on the same day in 1942], Linda Jansen, later Peggy Santigila McGannon), one of the successful early 1960s girl groups, best known for the No. 1 hit *My Boyfriend's Back.*

1942
Linda McCartney is born Linda Louise Eastman in Scarsdale, New York. Keyboardist and vocalist for Wings (Paul McCartney, Denny Laine, Denny Seiwell), the touring and recording band that her husband Paul McCartney established after he left The Beatles. She began her career as a successful photographer on the rock concert circuit. Wings produced five No. 1 LPs: *Red Rose Speedway, Band on the Run, Venus and Mars, Wings at the Speed of Sound* and *Wings over America,* which yielded a string of Top 40 singles, including the No. 1 hits *My Love, Band on the Run, Listen to What the Man Said, Silly Love Songs* and *With a Little Luck.*

1942
Gerry Marsden is born in Liverpool, England. Guitarist and singer for Gerry and the Pacemakers (Les Maguire, John Chadwick, Freddie Marsden), the second band to work with Brian Epstein as manager and George Martin as producer. The group had seven Top 30 singles, including *Don't Let the Sun Catch You Crying, Ferry Across the Mersey* and *How Do You Do It?*

NUMBER ONE SONGS:

1966
Cherish by The Association (3)
1988
Don't Worry Be Happy by Bobby McFerrin (2)

25

1939
Joseph Jesse Russell is born in Henderson, South Carolina. Tenor vocalist for the unique a cappella group The Persuasions (Jerry Lawson, Jayotis Washington, Herbert Rhoad, Jimmy Hayes, Willie Daniels),

who have performed in concert continuously since 1962 and as backup vocalists on recording sessions with artists such as Stevie Wonder, Phoebe Snow, Don McLean and many others.

1954
Elvis Presley makes his only appearance at the Grand Ole Opry, singing *Blue Moon of Kentucky,* and is advised to go back to driving a truck.

1965
ABC television premieres a Saturday morning cartoon series featuring The Beatles.

NUMBER ONE SONGS:

1965
Eve of Destruction by Barry McGuire (1)

26

1937
Bessie Smith, influential blues singer and a member of the Rock and Roll Hall of Fame, dies at age 43 in an automobile accident in Memphis, Tennessee.

1942
George Chambers is born in Scott County, Mississippi. One of the four Chambers Brothers (Joe, Willie, Lester), the pioneering and innovative funk/psychedelic band that had the Top 40 hits *I Can't Turn You Loose* and *Time Has Come Today* in the late 1960s.

1945
Bryan Ferry is born in Washington, England. Vocalist, keyboardist and leader of Roxy Music (Brian Eno, Graham Simpson, Andy Mackay, Dexter Lloyd, Roger Bunn, later Phil Manzanera), the English art-rock band of the 1970s. The group had three Top 40 LPs—*Country Life, Manifesto* and *Flesh + Blood*—and one single—*Love Is the Drug*—on the charts.

1948
Olivia Newton-John is born in Cambridge, England. Pop vocalist who has had more than 20 singles hits, including the No. 1 singles *I Honestly Love You, Have You Never Been Mellow, Magic* and *Physical,* from 14 Top 35 LPs, including the No. 1 hits *If You Love Me, Let Me Know, Have You Never Been Mellow* and *Grease.*

NUMBER ONE SONGS:

1960
My Heart Has a Mind of Its Own by Connie Francis (2)
1964
Oh, Pretty Woman by Roy Orbison (3)
1987
Didn't We Almost Have It All by Whitney Houston (2)

27

1954
Ground is broken for the Capitol Records Tower in Hollywood. Built to resemble a pile of records, it became a landmark.

NUMBER ONE SONGS:

1975
I'm Sorry by John Denver (1)

28

1938
Ben E. King is born Benjamin Earl Nelson in Henderson, North Carolina. Vocalist who began his career as the lead singer for the re-formed The Drifters (Charlie Thomas, Elsbeary Hobbs) in 1959, when the group started to have its greatest success with such hits as *There Goes My Baby* and *Save the Last Dance for Me.* He went on to a solo career with Top 30 hits such as *Spanish Harlem* and *Stand by Me.* Inducted into the Rock and Roll Hall of Fame with The Drifters January 20, 1988.

NUMBER ONE SONGS:

1974
Rock Me Gently by Andy Kim (1)

29

1935
Jerry Lee Lewis is born in Ferriday, Louisiana. Innovative vocalist and pianist who helped establish rock 'n' roll with his pounding piano style on such Top 10 hits as

Whole Lot of Shakin' Going On, Great Balls of Fire and *Breathless* before having his career cut short when it was discovered that he was married to his 13-year-old cousin. Inducted into the Rock and Roll Hall of Fame January 20, 1986.

1948
Mark Farner is born in Flint, Michigan. Guitarist and vocalist for Grand Funk Railroad (Mel Schacher, Don Brewer), America's most successful early heavy metal group, which produced nine Top 30 singles, including the No. 1 hits *We're An American Band* and *The Loco-Motion.*

1963
The Everly Brothers begin a tour of England at New Victoria Theatre in London with The Rolling Stones, Bo Diddley and Little Richard. The tour is the first for the Stones.

1975
Jackie Wilson has a heart attack while performing at the Latin Casino in Camden, New Jersey, suffering debilitating aftereffects from which he eventually will die.

NUMBER ONE SONGS:

1958
It's All in the Game by Tommy Edwards (6)
1968
Hey Jude by The Beatles (9)
1973
We're an American Band by Grand Funk Railroad (1)
1984
Let's Go Crazy by Prince & The Revolution (2)

30

1942
Dewey Martin is born in Chesterville, Canada. Drummer and vocalist for Buffalo Springfield (Neil Young, Stephen Stills, Richie Furay, Bruce Palmer, Jim Messina), the pioneering country-rock group that eventually led to the formation of Crosby, Stills & Nash and Poco and influenced the California rock scene. Buffalo Springfield had only one hit, *For What It's Worth.*

1946
Sylvia Peterson is born in the Bronx, New York. Member of the female

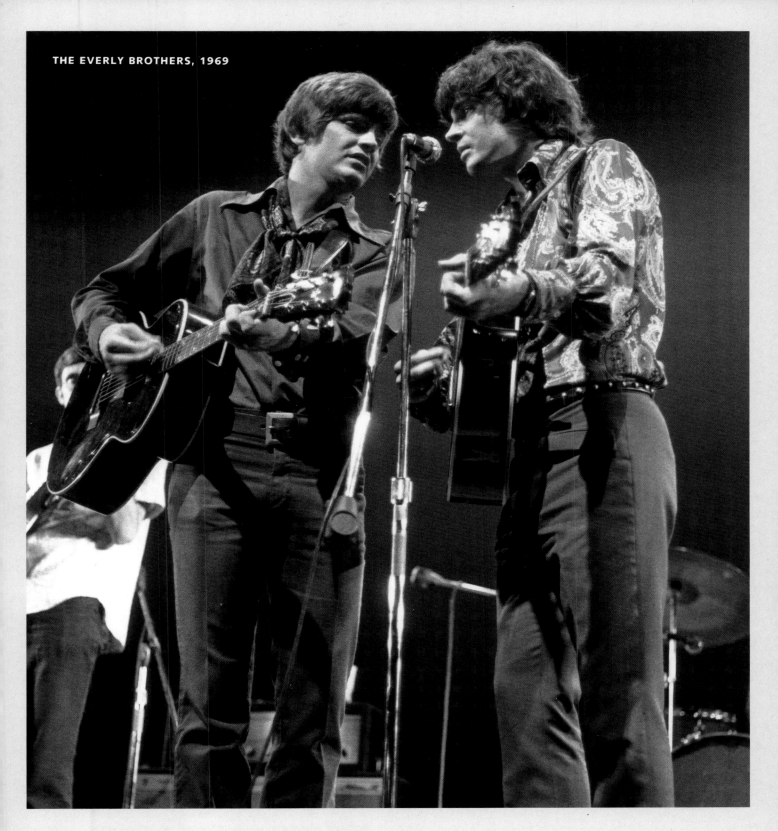

THE EVERLY BROTHERS, 1969

vocal group The Chiffons (Patricia Bennett, Barbara Lee, Judy Craig), which had three Top 10 hits between 1963 and 1966: *One Fine Day, Sweet Talkin' Guy* and the No. 1 *He's So Fine*.

1987
The Roy Orbison Cinemax cable special *Black & White Night* is filmed at the Coconut Grove in the Ambassador Hotel in Los Angeles. Orbison's band includes Bruce Springsteen, Elvis Costello, Tom Waits, J. D. Souther, Jackson Browne, Bonnie Raitt, k. d. lang and Jennifer Warnes.

NUMBER ONE SONGS:

1978
Kiss You All Over by Exile (4)

October

1

NUMBER ONE SONGS:

1977
Star Wars Theme/Cantina Band by Meco (2)
1983
Total Eclipse of the Heart by Bonnie Tyler (4)

2

1945
Don McLean is born in New Rochelle, New York. Singer-songwriter who had modest chart success in the early 1970s with the epic No. 1 hit *American Pie,* which memorialized Buddy Holly's death as "the day the music died." He had six other hits, including a No. 5 remake of Roy Orbison's *Crying.* He was also the inspiration for Roberta Flack's hit single *Killing Me Softly with His Song.*

1951
Sting is born Gordon Sumner in Wallsend, England. Singer, song-writer and bass player for The Police (Andy Summers, Stewart Copeland), which produced six Top 25 albums in the 1980s, including the No. 1 *Synchronicity.* The albums yielded six Top 10 singles, including the No. 1 *Every Breath You Take.*

1976
John Belushi does his Joe Cocker imitation with Cocker in a duet of *Feelin' Alright* on Saturday Night Live.

NUMBER ONE SONGS:

1965
Hang on Sloopy by The McCoys (1)
1971
Maggie May by Rod Stewart (5)
1982
Jack & Diane by John Cougar (4)

3

1938
Eddie Cochran is born in Oklahoma City. Early rockabilly guitarist best known for writing and performing the original version of *Summertime Blues,* his only Top 10 hit. He died at age 21 on April 17, 1960, following an automobile accident in London. Inducted into the Rock and Roll Hall of Fame January 21, 1987.

1941
Chubby Checker is born Ernest Evans in Philadelphia. Singer-dancer who popularized the Twist craze in the early 1960s. He had 21 Top 40 singles, including *Popeye the Hitchhiker, The Hucklebuck, Hooka Tooka* and the No. 1 singles *The Twist* and *Pony Time.*

1967
Woody Guthrie, influential folk-singer-songwriter and member of the Rock and Roll Hall of Fame, dies of Huntington's chorea at age 52 in New York City.

4

1942
Helen Reddy is born in Melbourne, Australia. Singer who charted 14 singles hits in the 1970s, including three No. 1 singles, *I Am Woman, Delta Dawn* and *Angie Baby.* Also served as host for the NBC television late-night rock show *Midnight Special.*

1944
Patti LaBelle is born Patricia Louise Holt in Philadelphia. Lead singer for Patti LaBelle & The Blue Belles, later known as LaBelle (Nona Hendryx, Sarah Dash, Cindy Birdsong), an early 1960s vocal group that had modest chart success until 1975, when it produced the No. 1 hit *Lady Marmalade.* She also had a No. 1 duet with Michael McDonald in 1986 with *On My Own.*

1970
Janis Joplin dies of a heroin overdose at age 27 in Hollywood.

NUMBER ONE SONGS:

1980
Another One Bites the Dust by Queen (3)

5

1943
Steve Miller is born in Milwaukee, Wisconsin. Singer-songwriter and guitarist who specialized in blues rock early in his career before having success on the pop charts with nine Top 25 hits, including three No. 1 songs—*The Joker, Rock'n Me* and *Abracadabra*—from 10 Top 40 albums, including *Fly Like an Eagle* and *Book of Dreams.*

1954
Bob Geldof is born in Dublin, Ireland. Vocalist for The Boomtown Rats (Johnnie Fingers, Gerry Cott, Pete Briquette). Geldof was the organizer of the Band Aid and Live Aid benefit performances to aid Africa.

1962
Love Me Do, the first single by The Beatles, is released in England.

NUMBER ONE SONGS:

1959
Mack the Knife by Bobby Darin (9)
1974
I Honestly Love You by Olivia Newton-John (2)

6

NUMBER ONE SONGS:

1973
Half-Breed by Cher (2)
1979
Sad Eyes by Robert John (1)

7

1951
John Cougar Mellencamp is born in Seymour, Indiana. Singer, songwriter and guitarist who became known as a champion of the blue-collar worker in his writing during the 1980s. He has had 14 Top 30 singles, including *Hurt So Good, Pink Houses, R.O.C.K. in the U.S.A., Authority Song* and the No. 1 *Jack & Diane,* from his top albums, which include *Uh-Huh, Scarecrow* and the No. 1 *American Fool.*

1967
Aretha Franklin's cover of Carole King's *(You Make Me Feel Like) A Natural Woman* enters the Billboard charts, where it will go to No. 8.

NUMBER ONE SONGS:

1989
Miss You Much by Janet Jackson (4)

PATTI LABELLE, 1976

October

8

1957
Jerry Lee Lewis records *Great Balls of Fire* at Sun Records in Memphis.

1973
Elvis and Priscilla Presley get divorced in Santa Monica, California.

NUMBER ONE SONGS:

1955
Love Is a Many-Splendored Thing by The Four Aces (6)
1988
Love Bites by Def Leppard (1)

9

1940
John Lennon is born in Liverpool, England. Founder, with Paul McCartney, of The Beatles (Ringo Starr, George Harrison). His solo career included two No. 1 hits, *Whatever Gets You Thru the Night* and *(Just Like) Starting Over*, as part of his 14 Top 40 hits. He died December 8, 1980, at age 40 when he was shot by Mark David Chapman in front of his home in New York City. Inducted into the Rock and Roll Hall of Fame with The Beatles January 20, 1988. (See Paul McCartney, June 18.)

1944
John Entwistle is born in London. Bassist for The Who (Pete Townshend, Keith Moon, Roger Daltrey, later Kenny Jones). The Who created the first rock opera, *Tommy*, one of its 12 Top 40 LPs, which also included *Who Are You* and the No. 2 *Quadrophenia*. The albums produced 16 Top 40 singles, with *I Can See for Miles* as a Top 10 hit. Inducted into the Rock and Roll Hall of Fame in 1990.

1944
Peter Tosh is born Winston Hubert MacIntosh in Westmoreland, Jamaica. Singer-songwriter who helped spread Jamaican reggae music throughout the world as part of Bob Marley & The Wailers (Aston "Family Man" Barrett, Bunny Livingston, Carlton Barrett), which had two Top 20 albums in the 1970s, *Rastaman Vibration* and *Exodus*. His solo career included several albums in the late 1970s and early 1980s.

10

1956
Blueberry Hill by Fats Domino enters the Billboard charts, where it will stay for 21 weeks, reaching No. 2.

1958
David Lee Roth is born in Bloomington, Indiana. Lead singer for the influential heavy metal band Van Halen (Alex Van Halen, Michael Anthony, Eddie Van Halen, later Sammy Hagar), which has had more than 10 Top 40 hits showcasing Eddie Van Halen's distinctive guitar work, including the No. 1 hit *Jump*, from the band's LPs, among them *1984* and *Women and Children First*. His post-Van Halen solo career includes three Top 20 hits: *California Girls*, *Just a Gigolo/I Ain't Got Nobody* and *Yankee Rose*.

NUMBER ONE SONGS:

1960
Mr. Custer by Larry Verne (1)
1987
Here I Go Again by Whitesnake (1)

11

1949
Daryl Hall is born in Pottstown, Pennsylvania. Half of the R&B duo Hall & Oates, with John Oates, which produced nearly two dozen hit singles in the 1970s and '80s, including six top hits—*Rich Girl, Kiss on My List, Private Eyes, I Can't Go for That (No Can Do), Maneater* and *Out of Touch*—from a dozen Top 35 albums.

1962
Love Me Do by The Beatles becomes the group's first single to enter the British singles charts, where it peaks at No. 17.

NUMBER ONE SONGS:

1975
Bad Blood by Neil Sedaka (3)
1986
When I Think of You by Janet Jackson (2)

12

1935
Samuel Moore is born in Miami. One-half of the vocal duo Sam & Dave, with David Prater, which was the most successful black vocal twosome of the 1960s with songs like *Hold On! I'm A Comin'*, *Soul Man* and *I Thank You*. Inducted into the Rock and Roll Hall of Fame in 1992.

1957
While on tour in Sydney, Australia, Little Richard renounces rock 'n' roll and says he will enter the seminary.

1966
Jimi Hendrix forms the Jimi Hendrix Experience in London with drummer Mitch Mitchell and bass player Noel Redding.

1970
The Fillmore East in New York City holds the Rock Relics Auction Show, raising $13,000 to benefit the peace movement.

1971
Gene Vincent, pioneering rock 'n' roll performer, dies from a bleeding ulcer at age 36 in Los Angeles.

NUMBER ONE SONGS:

1963
Sugar Shack by Jimmy Gilmer & The Fireballs (5)
1985
Oh Sheila by Ready for the World (1)

13

1942
Paul Simon is born in Newark, New Jersey. Singer-songwriter who with Art Garfunkel formed the popular 1960s folk-rock duo Simon & Garfunkel, which had 15 top 30 singles, including Three No. 1 hits (*The Sounds of Silence*, *Mrs. Robinson* and *Bridge Over Troubled Water*) and eight Top 30 LPs, including three consecutive No. 1 albums (*The Graduate, Bookends* and *Bridge Over Troubled Water*). His solo career has demonstrated his diversity as a writer and includes more than 10 Top 40 singles and nine hit albums, including *Still Crazy After All These Years, Graceland* and *Rhythm of the Saints*. Inducted into the Rock and Roll Hall of Fame in 1990.

1963
The Beatles perform as the featured act at the London Palladium, which is televised to an estimated 15 million people. This performance and the response it garners are considered the beginning of Beatlemania.

NUMBER ONE SONGS:

1979
Don't Stop 'Til You Get Enough by Michael Jackson (1)
1984
I Just Called to Say I Love You by Stevie Wonder (3)

14

1940
Cliff Richard is born Harry Roger Webb in Lucknow, India. One of England's most popular singers, he had eight Top 35 hits in the U.S., including the Top 10 singles *Devil Woman, We Don't Talk Anymore* and *Dreaming*.

1946
Justin Hayward is born in Swindon, Wiltshire, England. Guitarist and vocalist for The Moody Blues (Ray Thomas, Mike Pinder, Denny Laine, Clint Warwick, Graeme Edge, later John Lodge), which popularized fusion of classical music with rock. The group had 13 Top 30 LPs and 12 Top 30 singles, including two No. 1

13 (center top)

1948
Jackson Browne is born in Heidelberg, West Germany. Singer-songwriter whose introverted style has influenced other writers and singers. His early writing was recorded by Linda Ronstadt, Tom Rush, The Byrds and Bonnie Raitt before his performing career yielded 11 Top 40 singles and six Top 25 LPs, including *The Pretender, Running on Empty, Lawyers in Love* and the No. 1 *Hold Out*.

NUMBER ONE SONGS:

1961
Hit the Road Jack by Ray Charles (2)
1965
Yesterday by The Beatles (4)
1976
A Fifth of Beethoven by Walter Murphy & The Big Apple Band (1)

JOHN LENNON, 1972

LPs, but is best known for its first LP, *Days of Future Passed*, which yielded the No. 2 hit *Nights in White Satin*. Hayward formed the Blue Jays with Lodge during one of the group's separations.

1955
Buddy Holly, playing with Bob Montgomery as Buddy and Bob, performs as an opening act for Bill Haley & The Comets on Lubbock, Texas, radio station KDAV.

NUMBER ONE SONGS:

1957
Wake Up Little Susie by The Everly Brothers (4)
1972
Ben by Michael Jackson (1)

October

15

1937
Barry McGuire is born in Oklahoma City, Oklahoma. Singer-songwriter who was a one-hit wonder with the protest song *Eve of Destruction*, a No. 1 song in 1965.

1946
Richard Carpenter is born in New Haven, Connecticut. Singer-songwriter who with his sister, Karen, formed the 1970s pop duo The Carpenters, which had 20 Top 35 singles, including the No. 1 songs *(They Long to Be) Close to You*, *Top of the World* and *Please Mr. Postman* and the No. 2 hits *We've Only Just Begun*, *Superstar*, *Hurting Each Other* and *Yesterday Once More*.

1955
At a concert in Lubbock, Texas, Buddy Holly and Bob Montgomery open for Elvis Presley.

1971
Rick Nelson is booed during an oldies show at Madison Square Garden in New York City when he performs new material along with his old hits, sparking his response, *Garden Party*, which will become his last Top 10 hit.

NUMBER ONE SONGS:

1966
Reach Out I'll Be There by The Four Tops (2)

1977
You Light Up My Life by Debby Boone (10)

1988
Red Red Wine by UB40 (1)

16

1942
Bob Weir is born Robert Hall in San Francisco. Guitarist and vocalist for The Grateful Dead (Phil Lesh, Jerry Garcia, Pigpen McKernan, Bill Kreutzmann, later Mickey Hart, Keith Godchaux). (See Jerry Garcia, August 1.)

1951
Little Richard has his first recording session for RCA Records in Atlanta.

1969
Leonard Chess, pioneering record company executive and a member of the Rock and Roll Hall of Fame, dies at age 52.

1986
Keith Richards of The Rolling Stones leads a 60th birthday celebration for Chuck Berry at the Fox Theater in St. Louis. The event is filmed and later released as a documentary on Berry.

NUMBER ONE SONGS:

1976
Disco Duck (Part 1) by Rick Dees & His Cast of Idiots (1)

17

1942
Gary Puckett is born in Hibbing, Minnesota. Lead singer for Gary Puckett and The Union Gap (Dwight Bement, Kerry Chater, Mutha Withem, Paul Wheatbread), the pop group that performed in Civil War uniforms in the late 1960s singing half a dozen Top 15 hits, including *Young Girl*, *Over You*, *Lady Willpower* and *Woman, Woman*.

NUMBER ONE SONGS:

1960
Save the Last Dance for Me by The Drifters (3)
1964
Do Wah Diddy Diddy by Manfred Mann (2)

1970
I'll Be There by The Jackson 5 (5)
1981
Arthur's Theme (Best That You Can Do) by Christopher Cross (3)
1987
Lost in Emotion by Lisa Lisa & Cult Jam (1)

18

1926
Chuck Berry is born in San Jose, California. Pioneer of the double-stop guitar lick that became a staple of rock 'n' roll, his style has influenced many rock guitarists and songwriters who came after him. He had only one No. 1 hit, *My Ding-A-Ling* in 1972, but he wrote or recorded Top 40 hits with such classics as *Maybellene*, *Roll Over Beethoven*, *Sweet Little Sixteen* and *Johnny B. Goode*. Inducted into the Rock and Roll Hall of Fame January 20, 1986.

1967
How I Won the War, a film starring John Lennon, premieres in London.

NUMBER ONE SONGS:

1969
I Can't Get Next to You by The Temptations (2)

19

NUMBER ONE SONGS:

1974
Nothing from Nothing by Billy Preston (1)
1985
Take On Me by a-ha (1)

20

1953
Tom Petty is born in Gainesville, Florida. Singer, songwriter and guitarist whose work with his band The Heartbreakers (Mike Campbell, Howard Epstein, Benmount Tench, Stan Lyncy) showcased his songwriting talent on albums like *Dam the Torpedoes*, *Hard Promises* and *Southern Accents*. His solo work includes the top-selling LP *Full Moon Fever*. In the late 1980s, he became part of the all-star group The Traveling Wilburys (Bob Dylan, George Harrison, Jeff Lynne, Roy Orbison).

1977
Ronnie Van Zant, Steve Gaines and Cassie Gaines of Lynyrd Skynyrd die in a plane crash in Gillsburg, Mississippi.

NUMBER ONE SONGS:

1962
Monster Mash by Bobby "Boris" Pucket & The Crypt-Kickers (2)
1973
Angie by The Rolling Stones (1)

21

1940
Manfred Mann is born Michael Lubowitz in Johannesburg, South Africa. Keyboard player who led Manfred Mann (Paul Jones, Mike Hugg, Michael Vickers, Tom McGuiness), the 1960s group that had several pop chart successes in England before having a pair of Top 10 hits in the U.S.—*Mighty Quinn (Quinn the Eskimo)* and the No. 1 *Do Wah Diddy Diddy*. In the 1970s, with a harder sound, Manfred Mann's Earth Band had a No. 1 with *Blinded by the Light*.

1941
Steve Cropper is born in Willow Springs, Missouri. Guitarist, producer and songwriter whose R&B guitar style was the foundation for the Stax-Volt sound in the 1960s when he was a member of Booker T & The MGs and played on such hits as *In the Midnight Hour* (Wilson Pickett), *Soul Man* (Sam & Dave) and *Knock on Wood* (Eddie Floyd).

1958
Buddy Holly records with a string section, the Dick Jacobs Orchestra, for the first time, in New York City during his last recording session, which includes *It Doesn't Matter Anymore* and *True Love Ways*.

1985
Carl Perkins and Friends television special is taped at Limehouse Studios in London to mark the 30th anniversary of *Blue Suede Shoes*. His friends include George Harrison, Ringo Starr, Dave Edmunds, Eric Clapton and members of The Stray Cats.

NUMBER ONE SONGS:

1957
Jailhouse Rock by Elvis Presley (7)
1967
To Sir with Love by Lulu (5)
1972
My Ding-A-Ling by Chuck Berry (2)

1979
Rise by Herb Alpert (2)

CHUCK BERRY, 1969

October

22

1945
Leslie West is born Leslie Weinstein in New York City. Heavyweight guitarist and vocalist for the power trio Mountain (Felix Pappalardi, N. D. Smart, later Steve Knight, Corky Laing), which had a cult following and one top hit, *Mississippi Queen*. West later formed a power trio with Laing and Jack Bruce.

1946
Eddie Brigati is born in New York City. Vocalist for The Young Rascals, later The Rascals (Dino Dinelli, Gene Cornish and Felix Cavaliere), which had 13 Top 40 singles between 1966 and 1969, including three No. 1 hits—*Good Lovin'*, *Groovin'* and *People Got to Be Free*. The group's greatest hits LP, *Time Peace*, reached No. 1.

1964
An audition tape by the London band The High Numbers is rejected by EMI Records. The band is renamed The Who and goes on to success.

NUMBER ONE SONGS:

1988
Groovy Kind of Love by Phil Collins (2)

23

1940
Ellie Greenwich is born on Long Island, New York. Songwriter who collaborated with Jeff Barry, her then-husband, to create the 1960s hits *Leader of the Pack*; *Hanky Panky*; *River Deep, Mountain High*; *Chapel of Love*; *Be My Baby*; *Then He Kissed Me*; *Da Doo Ron Ron* and other singles that sold more than 20 million records.

NUMBER ONE SONGS:

1961
Runaround Sue by Dion (2)
1976
If You Leave Me Now by Chicago (2)

24

1936
Bill Wyman is born in London. Bass player for The Rolling Stones (Keith Richards, Charlie Watts, Mick Jagger, Brian Jones). Inducted into the Rock and Roll Hall of Fame in 1989. (See Charlie Watts, June 2.)

1962
James Brown's *Live at the Apollo* album is recorded at the Apollo Theater in New York City. It will become one of R&B's landmark albums.

NUMBER ONE SONGS:

1960
I Want to Be Wanted by Brenda Lee (1)
1987
Bad by Michael Jackson (2)

25

1944
Jon Anderson is born in Lancashire, England. Vocalist, percussionist and founding member of Yes (Chris Squire, Peter Banks, Tony Kaye, Bill Bruford, later Rick Wakeman, Steve Howe), one of the most important progressive-rock bands of the 1970s, which combined vocal harmonies with superb musicianship. Yes had more than 10 Top 40 albums but is best known for its early works, *Fragile* and *Close to the Edge*. In 1983 the band had its only No. 1 hit, *Owner of a Lonely Heart*.

1959
A charity rock 'n' roll dance takes place at the New York Coliseum hosted by WMCA disc jockey Scott Muni. Among the performers is Clyde McPhatter.

1964
The Rolling Stones perform for the first time on *The Ed Sullivan Show*. After the performance, Sullivan says he will never invite them back.

1991
Bill Graham, pioneering rock promoter who established the premiere concert venues Winterland and Fillmore West in San Francisco and Fillmore East in New York City, dies at age 60 in a helicopter crash near San Francisco.

NUMBER ONE SONGS:

1980
Woman in Love by Barbra Streisand (3)
1986
True Colors by Cyndi Lauper (2)

26

1911
Mahalia Jackson is born in New Orleans. One of gospel's greatest singers, she is the link between blues innovators Ma Rainey and Bessie Smith and the undisputed Queen of Soul, Aretha Franklin. She died January 27, 1972, in Chicago.

NUMBER ONE SONGS:

1974
Then Came You by Dionne Warwick & The Spinners (1)

27

1985
Saving All My Love for You by Whitney Houston (1)

1960
Ben E. King records his first solo material since leaving The Drifters, including *Spanish Harlem* and *Stand by Me*, produced by Jerry Leiber and Mike Stoller.

1977
Bruce Springsteen appears on the covers of both *Time* and *Newsweek*.

NUMBER ONE SONGS:

1973
Midnight Train to Georgia by Gladys Knight & The Pips (2)

28

1945
Wayne Fontana is born Glyn Geoffrey Ellis in Manchester, England. Lead singer for The Mindbenders (Bob Lang, Eric Stewart, Ric Rothwell, Graham Gouldman), the British Invasion group that had two top singles, the No. 1 *Game of Love* and No. 2 *A Groovy Kind of Love*.

1961
Brian Epstein first hears about The Beatles when Raymond Jones asks for a copy of *My Bonnie* by The Beatles in Epstein's record store in Whitechapel, Liverpool.

1964
The *TAMI* show on U.S. television in Los Angeles features performances by The Rolling Stones, James Brown, Marvin Gaye, Chuck Berry, The Beach Boys and others.

NUMBER ONE SONGS:

1978
Hot Child in the City by Nick Gilder (1)

LESLIE WEST, 1969

AN ILLUSTRATED RECORD OF ROCK 'N' ROLL

29

1944
Denny Laine is born Brian Hines in England. Guitarist, keyboardist and vocalist who began his career with The Moody Blues and left to join Paul McCartney's post-Beatles band Wings (Linda McCartney, Denny Seiwell). (See Linda McCartney, September 24.)

1946
Peter Green is born in London. Guitarist, vocalist and founder of Fleetwood Mac (Mick Fleetwood, John McVie, Jeremy Spencer, later Christine Perfect McVie, Bob Welch, Stevie Nicks, Lindsey Buckingham). Green left the group in 1970.

1971
Duane Allman dies in a motorcycle accident in Macon, Georgia, at age 25.

NUMBER ONE SONGS:

1966
96 Tears by ? & The Mysterians (1)
1983
Islands in the Stream by Kenny Rogers and Dolly Parton (2)

30

1939
Eddie Holland is born in Detroit. One third of the team of Holland-(Lamont) Dozier-(brother Brian) Holland, which wrote and produced most of Motown's biggest hits in the 1960s. Inducted into the Rock and Roll Hall of Fame in 1990. (See Brian Holland, February 15.)

1939
Grace Slick is born Grace Wing in Chicago. Vocalist for Jefferson Airplane (Paul Kantner, Marty Balin, Jorma Kaukonen, Signe Anderson, Bob Harvey, Skip Spence, later Jack Casady, Spencer Dryden, Papa John Creach, John Barbata, Aynsley Dunbar, among others) when the group had its first success with the Top 10 singles Somebody to Love

and White Rabbit. After the group became Jefferson Starship, it had hits with the Top 10 singles Miracles and Count on Me; as Starship, it had No. 1 hits with We Built This City and Sara. The various incarnations of the band have had 19 Top 35 LPs, including the No. 1 Red Octopus.

1947
Timothy B. Schmidt is born in Sacramento, California. Bass player and vocalist who replaced Randy Meisner first in the country-rock band Poco (Richie Furay, Jim Messina, Rusty Young, George Grantham) and later in The Eagles (Don Henley, Glenn Frey, Bernie Leadon, Don Felder).

1972
Elton John performs before Queen Elizabeth at a Royal Command Performance.

1975
Bob Dylan begins The Rolling Thunder Revue tour in Plymouth, Massachusetts. Among the touring musicians are Roger McGuinn, Joan Baez and Joni Mitchell.

NUMBER ONE SONGS:

1982
Who Can It Be Now by Men At Work (1)

31

NUMBER ONE SONGS:

1964
Baby Love by The Supremes (4)

1

1946
Rick Grech is born in Bordeaux, France. Bassist for Blind Faith, which made only one album and did only one tour but was the band that brought together Steve Winwood, Eric Clapton and Ginger Baker. Blind Faith's album reached No. 1 on the LP charts.

NUMBER ONE SONGS:

1969
Suspicious Minds by Elvis Presley (1)
1975
Island Girl by Elton John (3)

2

1937
Earl Carroll is born in New York City. Lead vocalist for the 1950s vocal group The Cadillacs (Robert Carroll, Robert Phillips, Laverne Drake, Gus Willingham). The group had two Top 30 hits, Speedo and Peek-A-Boo, which pioneered choreographed stage shows and flashy costumes. Carroll later became a member of The Coasters.

1941
Jay Black is born David Black in Brooklyn, New York. Lead vocalist for the vocal quintet Jay and the Americans (Kenny Vance, Sandy Deane, Marty Sanders, Howie Kane), which had 10 Top 25 singles hits in the 1960s, including She Cried, Come a Little Bit Closer, Cara Mia and This Magic Moment.

1944
Keith Emerson is born in Todmorden, England. Keyboard player who, with guitarist Greg Lake and percussionist Carl Palmer, formed the 1970s classically influenced progressive band Emerson, Lake & Palmer. ELP produced eight Top 40 albums, including Pictures at an Exhibition, based on Mussorgsky's classical work, and a Top 40 single, From the Beginning.

1947
Dave Pegg is born in London. Guitarist, vocalist and violist for Fairport Convention (Judy Dyble, Simon Nichol, Ashley Hutchings, Sandy Denny, Martin Lamble, Ian Matthews, Richard Thompson), the eclectic British folk-rock band that influenced British and American bands through the guitar work of Richard Thompson and the vocals of Sandy Denny.

NUMBER ONE SONGS:

1974
You Haven't Done Nothin' by Stevie Wonder (1)
1985
Part-Time Lover by Stevie Wonder (1)

3

1948
Lulu is born Marie McDonald McLaughlin Lawrie in Lennox Castle, Scotland. Vocalist who had a No. 1 hit with the title theme from the movie To Sir with Love, in which she costarred with Sidney Poitier. She later had four other Top 40 singles, including Best of Both Worlds, Oh Me Oh My, and I Could Never Miss You (More Than I Do).

1972
James Taylor and Carly Simon are married in New York City just prior to Taylor's performance at Carnegie Hall.

NUMBER ONE SONGS:

1956
Love Me Tender by Elvis Presley (5)
1962
He's a Rebel by The Crystals (2)
1979
Pop Muzik by M (1)
1984
Caribbean Queen (No More Love on the Run) by Billy Ocean (2)

4

1963
The Beatles perform on the U.K. television show Royal Variety Show, which reportedly is seen by the Queen Mother.

NUMBER ONE SONGS:

1972
I Can See Clearly Now by Johnny Nash (4)
1978
You Needed Me by Anne Murray (1)
1989
Listen to Your Heart by Roxette (1)

GRACE SLICK, 1969

November

AN ILLUSTRATED RECORD OF ROCK 'N' ROLL

5

1931
Ike Turner is born in Clarksdale, Mississippi. Early R&B guitarist who recorded with Howlin' Wolf, B. B. King, Johnny Ace and Junior Parker but gained fame with his soul revue, fronted by his wife, Tina. Ike & Tina Turner had six Top 40 singles, including the No. 4 *Proud Mary.*

1942
Art Garfunkel is born in New York City. Vocalist who, with singer-songwriter Paul Simon, formed the popular 1960s folk-rock duo Simon & Garfunkel, which had 15 top 30 singles, including Three No. 1 hits—*The Sounds of Silence, Mrs. Robinson* and *Bridge Over Troubled Water*—and eight Top 30 LPs, including three consecutive No. 1 albums: *The Graduate, Bookends* and *Bridge Over Troubled Water.* His solo career has included eight Top 40 singles and three Top 20 albums, including *Angel Clare.* Inducted into the Rock and Roll Hall of Fame in 1990.

1946
Gram Parsons is born Cecil Connor in Winterhaven, Florida. Influential singer-songwriter whose work with The Byrds and as a member of The Flying Burrito Brothers pioneered country-rock and influenced Emmy Lou Harris, Poco and The Eagles. He died September 19, 1973, in Joshua Tree National Monument, California, at age 26.

1947
Peter Noone is born in Manchester, England. Lead singer who took on the name Herman for the 1960s pop group Herman's Hermits (Karl Greene, Keith Hopwood, Derek Leckenby, Barry Whitham), which had 18 Top 40 hits, including the No. 1 songs *Mrs. Brown You've Got a Lovely Daughter* and *I'm Henry VIII, I Am.* He later pursued an acting career and became host of the VH-1 music video program *My Generation.*

1960
Johnny Horton, a pioneer in crossing over from country to the pop charts with *The Battle of New Orleans,* dies at age 33 in Milano, Texas, after an automobile accident.

NUMBER ONE SONGS:

1966
Last Train to Clarksville by The Monkees (1)
1988
Kokomo by The Beach Boys (1)

6

1945
George Young is born in England. Producer and guitarist for the Australian group The Easybeats (Dick Diamonde, Gordon Fleet, Harry Vanda, Stevie Wright), which had a No. 16 chart hit with *Friday on My Mind* in 1967.

1948
Glenn Frey is born in Detroit. Guitarist, vocalist and founding member of The Eagles (Don Henley, Bernie Leadon, Randy Meisner, later Don Felder). His solo career includes the No. 1 single *You Belong to the City.* (See Randy Meisner, March 8.)

1965
Bill Graham promotes his first concert, at the Fillmore Auditorium in San Francisco, with The Grateful Dead, The Charlatans and Jefferson Airplane.

1973
The Sex Pistols play their first concert, at St. Martins College of Art in London.

NUMBER ONE SONGS:

1961
Big Bad John by Jimmy Dean (5)
1965
Get off of My Cloud by The Rolling Stones (2)
1971
Gypsys, Tramps & Thieves by Cher (2)
1976
Rock'n Me by Steve Miller (1)
1981
Up Where We Belong by Joe Cocker & Jennifer Warnes (3)

7

1937
Mary Travers is born in Louisville, Kentucky. Vocalist who, with Peter Yarrow and Noel Paul Stookey, formed the influential folk group Peter, Paul and Mary. The group helped popularize Bob Dylan's songs and had 11 Top 25 albums, including the No. 1 LPs *Peter, Paul &* *Mary* and *In the Wind,* along with 12 Top 40 singles, including *If I Had a Hammer, Puff the Magic Dragon, Blowin' in the Wind* and the No. 1 *Leaving on a Jet Plane.*

1938
Dee Clark is born Delectus Clark in Blythsville, Arkansas. Early R&B vocalist who had six Top 35 hits, including the No. 2 single *Raindrops* in 1961.

1942
Johnny Rivers is born John Ramistella in New York City. Producer, talent scout and singer-songwriter who had 17 Top 40 singles hits, including the No. 1 *Poor Side of Town,* and eight Top 40 LPs between 1964 and 1977. Also known for discovering The 5th Dimension (LaMonte McLemore, Marilyn McCoo, Ron Townson, Florence LaRue Gordon, Billy Davis, Jr.).

1943
Joni Mitchell is born Roberta Joan Anderson in Alberta, Canada. Singer-songwriter whose early folk-pop work was recorded by other performers, including Tom Rush (*Circle Game*), Judy Collins (*Both Sides Now*) and Crosby, Stills & Nash (*Woodstock*). Her greatest success came from her 12 Top 30 albums, including *Court and Spark* and *Miles of Aisles.* Her four Top 25 singles hits included *Big Yellow Taxi* and *Help Me.*

NUMBER ONE SONGS:

1981
Private Eyes by Hall & Oates (2)
1987
I Think We're Alone Now by Tiffany (2)

8

1887
Emile Berliner obtains U.S. patent No. 372,786 for the gramophone.

1944
Bonnie Bramlett is born Bonnie Lynn in Acton, Illinois. Soul-voiced singer who with her husband, Delaney Bramlett, performed as Delaney and Bonnie, attracting sidemen such as Eric Clapton, Leon Russell, Dave Mason and George Harrison. The duo's best-selling album was *Delaney & Bonnie & Friends on Tour with Eric* Clapton in 1970. Bramlett began her career as a backup singer with Ike and Tina Turner. Her rough vocal style influenced many of today's female rock and blues singers.

1946
Roy Wood is born in Birmingham, England. Guitarist and songwriter who formed the British pop band The Move (Bev Bevan, Carl Wayne, Trevor Burton, Chris Kefford, later Rick Price, Jeff Lynne), which had success primarily in England. Later, with Jeff Lynne, Wood founded The Electric Light Orchestra, with which he stayed for only a year.

1947
Minnie Riperton is born in Chicago. Lead singer for The Rotary Connection, she had a No. 1 hit as a solo in 1975 with *Lovin' You.* She died at age 32 on July 12, 1979, from cancer.

1949
Bonnie Raitt is born in Los Angeles. Singer-songwriter best known for her reputation as a blues guitarist, she performed as a journeyman musician until her Grammy-winning LP of 1989, *Nick of Time,* rejuvenated her career.

NUMBER ONE SONGS:

1969
Wedding Bell Blues by The 5th Dimension (3)

9

1941
Tom Fogerty is born in Berkeley, California. Guitarist and founder, with his brother John, of the R&B-based rock group Creedence Clearwater Revival (Stu Cook, Doug Clifford), which had seven Top 15 albums, including the No. 1 hits *Green River* and *Cosmo's Factory,* and 14 Top 30 singles, including *Proud Mary, Bad Moon Rising* and *Travelin' Band/ Who'll Stop the Rain.* He died September 6, 1990, at age 48.

1961
Brian Epstein visits The Cavern, a club in Liverpool, to hear The Beatles for the first time. He later became the manager who pushed them to international fame.

1966
John Lennon meets Yoko Ono at the Indica Gallery in London, where she

will participate in an avant-garde art show.

1967
Jann Wenner publishes the first issue of *Rolling Stone* magazine.

1974
You Ain't Seen Nothing Yet by Bachman-Turner Overdrive (1)
1985
Miami Vice Theme by Jan Hammer (1)

10

1948
Greg Lake is born in Bournemouth, England. Vocalist, guitarist and bass player who with keyboard player Keith Emerson and percussionist Carl Palmer formed Emerson, Lake & Palmer. (See Keith Emerson, November 2.)

1958
It's Only Make Believe by Conway Twitty (2)
1973
Keep on Truckin' by Eddie Kendricks (2)
1979
Heartache Tonight by The Eagles (1)

11

1927
Mose Allison is born in Tippo, Mississippi. Influential jazz singer and pianist whose understated, cynical songs have been covered by a variety of rock performers, including Bonnie Raitt (*Everybody's Cryin' Mercy*), John Mayall (*Parchman Farm*) and The Who (*A Young Man Blues*).

1929
LaVern Baker is born in Chicago. Pioneering R&B singer during the early days of rock 'n' roll, when she toured the country with Alan Freed's showcases. She had seven Top 40 hits between 1955 and 1963, including *See See Rider, Tweedlee Dee, I Can't Love You Enough* and the No. 6 *I Cried a Tear*. Inducted into the Rock and Roll Hall of Fame in 1991.

1943
Chris Dreja is born in Surbiton, England. Original guitarist for The

IKE & TINA TURNER, 1969

Yardbirds (Keith Relf, Paul Samwell-Smith, Jim McCarty, Anthony Topham, later Eric Clapton, Jeff Beck, Jimmy Page), the pioneering band that set the style for blues-based guitar rock and was the link between the British R&B and Psychedelic eras that led to heavy metal when Page formed the New Yardbirds, which later became Led Zeppelin. The Yardbirds had limited chart success, with six Top 30 singles, including *For Your Love* and *I'm a Man*. Inducted into the Rock and Roll Hall of Fame in 1992.

1944
Jesse Colin Young is born Perry Miller in New York City. Singer-songwriter,

guitarist and founder of the folk-rock group The Youngbloods (Jerry Corbitt, Joe Bauer, Lowell "Banana" Levinger), which had a No. 5 hit with *Get Together*. His solo career included three Top 40 albums.

1945
Vince Martell is born in New York City. Guitarist and vocalist for Vanilla Fudge (Mark Stein, Tim Bogert, Carmine Appice), pioneering heavy-rock band that popularized recording the long version of songs on albums. The band's best-known song is *You Keep Me Hangin' On*, a No. 6 single from its debut album, *Vanilla Fudge*.

1965
The Velvet Underground plays its first concert, at a high school dance in Summit, New Jersey.

1972
Berry Oakley, original bass player for The Allman Brothers Band, dies in Macon, Georgia, at age 24 following a motorcycle accident.

1978
MacArthur Park by Donna Summer (3)
1989
When I See You Smile by Bad English (2)

NEIL YOUNG, 1970

November

12

1943
Jimmy Hayes is born in Hopewell, Virginia. Vocalist for The Persuasions (Jerry Lawson, Jayotis Washington, Joseph Jesse Russell, Herbert Rhoad, Willie Daniels). (See Joseph Jesse Russell, September 25.)

1943
Brian Hyland is born in Woodhaven, New York. Vocalist who launched his career with the quirky No. 1 hit *Itsy Bitsy Teenie Weenie Yellow Polkadot Bikini* and had seven other Top 25 singles, including *Sealed with a Kiss* and *Gypsy Woman.*

1944
Booker T. Jones is born in Memphis, Tennessee. Organist who, with his band the MGs (Lewis Steinberg, Al Jackson, Steve Cropper and Donald "Duck" Dunn) at Stax Records, pioneered the signature "Stax Sound" behind acts such as Wilson Pickett, Eddie Floyd, Sam & Dave and Otis Redding. He had seven Top 40 singles in the 1960s, including *Green Onions, Hang 'Em High* and *Time Is Tight.*

1945
Neil Young is born in Toronto, Ontario. Influential singer-songwriter who, through his association with Buffalo Springfield; Crosby, Stills, Nash & Young and Crazy Horse, as well as his eclectic solo work, has gained increasing respect through the years. His 15 Top 35 LPs include the No. 1 *Harvest,* which produced his only top single, *Heart of Gold.*

1957
The rock 'n' roll movie *Jamboree,* with a variety of rock artists, including Fats Domino and Carl Perkins, premieres in Hollywood.

NUMBER ONE SONGS:

1966
Poor Side of Town by Johnny Rivers (1)
1983
All Night Long (All Night) by Lionel Richie (4)
1988
Wild, Wild West by The Escape Club (1)

13

1966
The Four Tops perform in London in a concert produced by Brian Epstein.

NUMBER ONE SONGS:

1976
Tonight's the Night (Gonna Be Alright) by Rod Stewart (7)

14

1940
Freddie Garrity is born in Manchester, England. Vocalist, guitarist and namesake of Freddie and the Dreamers (Derek Quinn, Roy Crewsdon, Peter Birrell, Bennie Dwyer), which had a No. 1 hit in 1965 with *I'm Telling You Now* and a Top 20 success with a novelty dance song, *Do the Freddie.*

NUMBER ONE SONGS:

1960
Georgia on My Mind by Ray Charles (1)

15

1933
Petula Clark is born in Epsom, England. Pop vocalist who had 15 Top 40 singles between 1965 and 1968, including the No. 1 hits *Downtown* and *My Love.* Other Top 10 hits included *I Know a Place, This Is My Song* and *Don't Sleep in the Subway.*

1933
Clyde McPhatter is born in Durham, North Carolina. Founder and lead singer from 1953 to 1954 of The Drifters (Billy Pinkney, Andrew Thrasher, Gerhart Thrasher), a group whose blend of gospel-styled vocals with secular material helped create soul music. McPhatter had eight Top 40 hits as a solo, including the Top 10 hits *A Lover's Question* and *Lover Please.* He died June 13, 1972, in New York City. Inducted into the Rock and Roll Hall of Fame January 21, 1987.

1980
Double Fantasy, John Lennon's last LP, is released.

NUMBER ONE SONGS:

1980
Lady by Kenny Rogers (6)

16

1938
Toni Brown is born in Madison, Wisconsin. Vocalist, pianist and cofounder of Joy of Cooking (Terry Garthwaite, Ron Wilson, Fritz Kasten, David Garthwaite), one of the early rock groups led by women.

1949
Patti Santos is born in San Francisco. Vocalist and percussionist for the jazz-influenced It's a Beautiful Day (David LaFlamme, Linda LaFlamme, Val Fuentes, Bill Gregory, Tom Fowler, later Hal Wagenet, Michael Holman, Fred Webb), which pioneered the use of the violin in rock bands and became best known for the FM hit *White Bird.*

1956
Love Me Tender, Elvis Presley's first film, premieres at the Paramount Theater in New York City.

NUMBER ONE SONGS:

1959
Mr. Blue by The Fleetwoods (1)
1963
Deep Purple by Dale & Grace (1)
1974
Whatever Gets You Thru the Night by John Lennon with the Plastic Ono Nuclear Band (1)
1985
We Built This City by Starship (2)

17

1938
Gordon Lightfoot is born in Ortilia, Ontario. Singer-songwriter whose folk-rock style in the 1970s produced seven Top 40 LPs, including the No. 1 *Sundown,* which yielded a No. 1 single of the same name, and six Top 40 singles, including *The Wreck of the Edmund Fitzgerald* and *If You Could Read My Mind.*

1941
Gene Clark is born in Tipton, Missouri. Vocalist and guitarist with the pioneering folk-rock band The Byrds (Roger McGuinn, Chris Hillman, Michael Clarke, David Crosby). The group's early use of harmonies influenced many later bands. The Byrds had seven Top 40 singles, including two No. 1 hits, *Mr. Tambourine Man* and *Turn! Turn! Turn!* Clark left the group in 1966.

1942
Bob Gaudio is born in New York City. Vocalist and keyboard player for the white doo-wop group The Four Seasons (Frankie Valli, Tommy DeVito, Nick Massi), which had 30 Top 40 hits, including four No. 1 songs (*Sherry, Big Girls Don't Cry, Rag Doll* and *Walk Like a Man*) between 1962 and 1976. Inducted into the Rock and Roll Hall of Fame in 1990 with The Four Seasons.

1979
John Glasock, bass player for Jethro Tull, dies of a heart ailment in London at age 26.

NUMBER ONE SONGS:

1958
Tom Dooley by The Kingston Trio (1)
1962
Big Girls Don't Cry by The Four Seasons (5)
1979
Still by The Commodores (1)
1984
Wake Me Up Before You Go-Go by Wham! (3)

18

1936
Hank Ballard is born in Detroit. Vocalist and composer who led the R&B vocal group The Midnighters (Lawson Smith, Norman Thrasher, Billy Davis, Henry Booth, later Charles Sutton, Sonny Woods), which had seven Top 40 chart hits, including *Finger Poppin' Time* and *Let's Go, Let's Go, Let's Go.* He also wrote the 1960s dance hit *The Twist.* Inducted into the Rock and Roll Hall of Fame in 1990.

1956
Fats Domino sings *Blueberry Hill* on *The Ed Sullivan Show.*

1972
Danny Whitten of Crazy Horse dies of a drug overdose.

NUMBER ONE SONGS:

1986
Amanda by Boston (2)

DUANE ALLMAN, 1971
The Allman Brothers Band

19

1943
Fred Lipsius is born in New York City. Original alto saxophonist and pianist for Blood, Sweat & Tears (Al Kooper, Steve Katz, Jim Fielder, Bobby Colomby, Dick Halligan, Randy Brecker, Jerry Weiss), the pioneering jazz-rock group that had three consecutive No. 2 single hits with *You've Made Me So Very Happy*, *And When I Die* and *Spinning Wheel*, along with two No. 1 LPs, *Blood Sweat & Tears* and *Blood, Sweat & Tears 3*.

1971
B. B. King celebrates 25 years in the music business by beginning a tour of Europe in London.

1990
The National Academy of Recording Arts & Sciences takes back the Grammy awarded to Milli Vanilli (Rob Pilatus, Fabrice Moran) for *Girl You Know It's True* after the duo admit that they did not sing on the album.

NUMBER ONE SONGS:

1966
You Keep Me Hangin' On by the Supremes (2)
1988
Bad Medicine by Bon Jovi (2)

20

1942
Norman Greenbaum is born in Malden, Massachusetts. Singer-songwriter who had a No. 3 hit in 1970 with the electric jug band tune *Spirit in the Sky*. Earlier, he had formed Dr. West's Medicine Show and Junk Band, which had a song on the charts in 1966, *The Eggplant That Ate Chicago*.

1946
Duane Allman is born in Nashville, Tennessee. Guitarist and cofounder, with his brother Greg, of The Allman Brothers Band (Dickey Betts, Butch Trucks, Berry Oakley, Jai Johanny Johanson). His session work included the Derek and the Dominoes' session for *Layla* with Eric Clapton. His best work appears on the landmark Allman

Brothers album *At Fillmore East*. He died at age 24 on October 29, 1971, in a motorcycle accident in Macon, Georgia, before the band's period of greatest success. (See Jai Johanny Johanson, July 8.)

1947
George Grantham is born in Cordell, Oklahoma. Drummer for Poco (Richie Furay, Jim Messina, Rusty Young, Randy Meisner), the country-rock band formed out of the breakup of Buffalo Springfield. The band had two Top 20 singles, *Crazy Love* and *Heart of the Night*.

1955
Bo Diddley performs *Bo Diddley* on *The Ed Sullivan Show* as part of a 15-minute R&B segment hosted by Dr. Jive (Tommy Smalls), which also includes LaVern Baker and The Five Keys.

1965
I Hear a Symphony by The Supremes (2)
1971
Theme from Shaft by Isaac Hayes (2)

21 1941
Dr. John is born Malcolm Rebennack in New Orleans. Highly respected pianist and vocalist who has performed with Professor Longhair, Joe Tex, Frankie Ford, Eric Clapton, John Hammond, Jr. and Mike Bloomfield. He had a Top 10 single hit with *Right Place Wrong Time* in 1973.

1948
Lonnie Jordan is born in San Diego, California. Vocalist and keyboardist for the Latin-jazz-funk band War (Harold Brown, Papa Dee Allen, B. B. Dickerson, Charles Miller, Lee Oskar, Howard Scott). The group's nine Top 25 albums in the 1970s included the No. 1 *The World Is a Ghetto,* which produced two of the group's 11 singles, *The World Is a Ghetto* and *The Cisco Kid.*

1950
Livingston Taylor is born in Boston. Singer-songwriter who had two Top 40 singles, *I Will Be in Love with You* and *First Time Love,* and a minor hit with *Carolina Day.* Younger brother of '70s folk-rocker James Taylor.

1964
B. B. King's performance at The Regal Theater in Chicago is recorded and later released as *Live at The Regal.* The LP is considered one of the definitive blues albums.

1960
Stay by Maurice Williams & The Zodiacs (1)
1970
I Think I Love You by The Partridge Family (3)
1981
Physical by Olivia Newton-John (10)
1987
Mony Mony Live by Billy Idol (1)

22 1946
Aston "Family Man" Barrett is born in Kingston, Jamaica. Bass player for Bob Marley's reggae group The Wailers (Peter Tosh, Bunny Livingston, Carlton Barrett), the pioneering and influential Jamaican pop group that had two Top 20 albums in the 1970s, *Rastaman Vibration* and *Exodus.*

1955
Elvis Presley begins his record contract with RCA Records, following the expiration of his Sun Records deal.

1975
That's the Way (I Like It) by KC & The Sunshine Band (2)
1986
Human by Human League (1)

23 1940
Freddie Marsden is born in Liverpool, England. Drummer for Gerry and the Pacemakers (Les Maguire, John Chadwick,), led by his brother Gerry. (See Gerry Marsden, September 24.)

1974
I Can Help by Billy Swan (2)

24 1941
Donald "Duck" Dunn is born in Memphis, Tennessee. Bassist for Booker T. & The MGs, which pioneered the signature "Stax Sound" behind acts such as Wilson Pickett, Eddie Floyd, Sam & Dave and Otis Redding. Later the group had seven Top 40 singles in the 1960s, including *Green Onions, Hang 'Em High* and *Time Is Tight.* Dunn continued his career as a session player and resurfaced with MG guitarist Steve Cropper as sidemen for The Blues Brothers in 1979 to 1980, fronted by comedians John Belushi and Dan Aykroyd.

1945
Lee Michaels is born in Los Angeles. Organist who developed a unique hard-rock style through his keyboards and his drummer, Frosty. He had a No. 16 album, *5th,* which yielded a Top 10 hit, *Do You Know What I Mean.*

1954
Judge Carrol G. Walter bars Alan Freed from using the name Moondog as his radio name, after a brief trial brought on by Thomas Louis Harden, who claimed the name was his own invention. Freed later decided to rename his program on WINS *The Rock 'n' Roll Party.*

1972
In Concert premieres on ABC television, featuring performances by Blood, Sweat & Tears; Chuck Berry; Poco; Alice Cooper and The Allman Brothers Band.

1991
Freddie Mercury, lead singer for Queen, dies in Kensington, England, at age 45 of AIDS.

1973
Photograph by Ringo Starr (1)

1979
No More Tears (Enough Is Enough) by Barbra Streisand and Donna Summer (2)

25 1961
Phil and Don Everly are inducted into the U.S. Marine Corps Reserves at Camp Pendleton, California.

1976
The Last Waltz concert by The Band, billed as the group's final performance, takes place at the Winterland auditorium in San Francisco. Guests include Bob Dylan, Neil Young, Van Morrison, Joni Mitchell, Eric Clapton, Muddy Waters, Ringo Starr and others.

1982
The Jamaican World Music Fair is held at the Bob Marley Performing Center in Montego Bay before an audience of 45,000. Performers include Aretha Franklin, The Grateful Dead, Gladys Knight, The Clash and others.

1984
Do They Know It's Christmas is recorded by Band Aid at SARM Studios in London to benefit famine victims in Ethiopia. Musicians, led by Bob Geldof of the Boomtown Rats, include Phil Collins, Sting, Jody Watley, George Michael, Paul Young and Nick Rhodes.

1967
Incense and Peppermints by Strawberry Alarm Clock (1)
1989
Blame It on the Rain by Milli Vanilli (2)

26

1939
Tina Turner is born Anna Mae Bullock near Memphis, Tennessee. Influential vocal stylist who first gained fame with her husband, Ike Turner, in their soul revue, Ike & Tina Turner. The duo had six Top 40 singles, including the No. 4 *Proud Mary*, in the early 1970s. She gained success as a solo performer in the 1980s, with Top 5 albums including *Private Dancer* and *Break Every Rule*, which included the No. 1 hit *What's Love Got to Do with It* and the No. 2 *Typical Male*.

1949
John McVie is born in London. Bassist with Fleetwood Mac (Peter Green, Mick Fleetwood, Jeremy Spencer, later Christine Perfect McVie, Bob Welch, Stevie Nicks, Lindsey Buckingham), one of the longest-running British bands, whose only remaining original members are McVie and drummer Fleetwood. The group began its greatest success in the mid 1970s, when it launched six Top 40 LPs, including three No. 1 albums—*Rumours, Fleetwood Mac* and *Mirage*—and had 13 Top 25 singles, including the No. 1 *Dreams*.

1962
The Beatles record their second record, *Please Please Me*. The album was not released in England until January 1963 because the band returned to Germany to play club dates in Hamburg. It peaked on the Billboard charts at No. 3 in 1964 after its U.S. release.

1968
Cream's last concert is performed at The Royal Albert Hall in London.

NUMBER ONE SONGS:

1955
Sixteen Tons by Tennessee Ernie Ford (8)

27

1942
Jimi Hendrix is born in Seattle. Innovative singer and guitarist who influenced electric guitar styles for rock performers by using the instrument as a source of sound. He did session work with B. B. King, Little Richard, Jackie Wilson, Ike & Tina Turner, Sam Cooke, Wilson Pickett, The Isley Brothers and King Curtis. He died at age 28 of a drug overdose on September 18, 1970, in London. Before he died, he had five Top 19 albums, including the No. 1 *Electric Ladyland*. After his death, he had five more Top 20 LPs. Inducted into the Rock and Roll Hall of Fame with the Jimi Hendrix Experience in 1992.

1969
The Rolling Stones perform at Madison Square Garden in New York City in the first of two concerts that will later become part of the album *Get Yer Ya-Yas Out!*

NUMBER ONE SONGS:

1982
Truly by Lionel Richie (2)

28

1929
Berry Gordy, Jr. is born in Detroit. Pioneering record company executive who built Motown Records into a classic record factory. He made it possible for black artists to record and perform throughout the world. His discoveries include Smokey Robinson and the Miracles, The Supremes, Ashford & Simpson, Stevie Wonder, Mary Wells and the songwriting team of Holland-Dozier-Holland. Inducted into the Rock and Roll Hall of Fame January 20, 1988.

1944
Randy Newman is born in New Orleans. Singer-songwriter known for his biting lyrics, who gained a reputation after his songs were covered by other performers, including Three Dog Night (*Mama Told Me Not to Come*), Judy Collins (*I Think It's Going to Rain Today*) and Peggy Lee (*Love Story*). He had his greatest pop success with his No. 2 single *Short People* from his No. 9 LP *Little Criminals*. He also wrote the musical scores for the films *The Natural* and *Ragtime*.

1974
What will be John Lennon's last stage performance takes place at Madison Square Garden in New York City when he joins Elton John during a concert.

NUMBER ONE SONGS:

1960
Are You Lonesome To-Night by Elvis Presley (6)
1964
Leader of the Pack by the Shangri-Las (1)
1987
(I've Had) The Time of My Life by Bill Medley & Jennifer Warnes (1)

29

1941
Dennis Doherty is born in Halifax, Nova Scotia. Began his career as a member of The Mugwumps (John Sebastian, Cass Elliot) and became a vocalist with The Mamas & The Papas (John Phillips, Michelle Phillips, Cass Elliot). (See John Phillips, August 30.)

1943
John Mayall is born in Manchester, England. Innovative blues master who influenced British rock musicians through membership in his band, John Mayall's Bluesbreakers. Among the musicians he discovered were Jack Bruce, Eric Clapton, Mick Taylor, Mick Fleetwood, Peter Green, Aynsley Dunbar and John McVie. He had limited chart success, with three Top 35 LPs, *The Turning Point, Empty Rooms* and *USA Union*.

1944
Felix Cavaliere is born in Pelham, New York. Vocalist, keyboardist and cofounder, with Eddie Brigati, Dino Dinelli and Gene Cornish, of The Young Rascals (later The Rascals), which had 13 Top 40 singles between 1966 and 1969, including three No. 1 hits, *Good Lovin', Groovin'* and *People Got to Be Free*. The group's greatest hits LP, *Time Peace*, reached No. 1.

1963
I Want to Hold Your Hand by The Beatles is released as a single in England.

1968
John Lennon and Yoko Ono release *Two Virgins*, which becomes controversial because of the cover, which shows both of them naked.

1991
The American Museum of the Moving Image in New York City opens a six-week film series, *Play This Movie Loud: A History of Rock on Film*, which traces the 35-year history of rock music on film.

NUMBER ONE SONGS:

1969
Come Together/Something by The Beatles (1)
1986
You Give Love a Bad Name by Bon Jovi (1)

30

1929
Dick Clark is born in Mount Vernon, New York. Philadelphia disc jockey who succeeded Alan Freed as the most important proponent of rock 'n' roll as the host of *American Bandstand*, the television dance show that gave national exposure to bands, fads and the Rate-a-Record feature.

1937
Noel Paul Stookey is born in Baltimore, Maryland. Singer-songwriter and guitarist who, with Peter Yarrow and Mary Travers, formed the influential folk group Peter, Paul and Mary. (See Mary Travers, November 7.)

1944
Leo Lyons is born in Bedfordshire, England. Bassist for the rock-blues band Ten Years After (Chick Churchill, Ric Lee, Alvin Lee). (See Chick Churchill, January 20.)

1973
Kiss performs its first concert, at the Coventry Club in Queens, New York City.

1991
Billboard magazine changes the way it tracks the Hot 100, from rankings based on information obtained from radio stations and retailers to information based on sales compiled by computer data and monitored airplay.

NUMBER ONE SONGS:

1968
Love Child by Diana Ross & The Supremes (2)
1985
Separate Lives by Phil Collins and Marilyn Martin (1)

1

1934
Billy Paul is born in Philadelphia. R&B singer who had a No. 1 hit with *Me and Mrs. Jones* in 1972. He also had a Top 40 hit with *Thanks for Saving My Life* in 1974.

1935
Lou Rawls is born in Chicago. Popular R&B singer who has had chart success for more than 30 years, including six Top 30 singles and six Top 30 albums. His biggest hit was the No. 2 *You'll Never Find Another Love Like Mine.*

1945
Bette Midler is born in Paterson, New Jersey. Campy singer-songwriter who had eight Top 40 hits between 1973 and 1989, including the No. 1 *Wind Beneath My Wings.* She also has had a successful film career, including The Rose, in which she played a character based on Janis Joplin.

1946
Gilbert O'Sullivan is born Raymond O'Sullivan in Waterford, Ireland. Pop singer who had five Top 15 hits during 1972 to 1973, including the No. 1 *Alone Again (Naturally)* and the No. 2 *Clair.*

1957
The Crickets perform *That'll Be the Day* and *Peggy Sue* on *The Ed Sullivan Show.* Sam Cooke sings *You Send Me* on the same show.

1982
Thriller by Michael Jackson, the best-selling album of the rock era (more than 40 million), is released.

NUMBER ONE SONGS:

1958
To Know Him Is to Love Him by the Teddy Bears (1)
1973
Top of the World by The Carpenters (2)
1974
Cat's in the Cradle by Harry Chapin (1)

2

1941
Tom McGuiness is born in London. Bass player for Manfred Mann (Manfred Mann, Paul Jones, Mike Hugg, Michael Vickers), the English pop band that had 16 singles hits on the British charts in the 1960s and U.S. success with *Mighty Quinn (Quinn the Eskimo)* and the No. 1 *Do Wah Diddy Diddy.*

NUMBER ONE SONGS:

1957
You Send Me by Sam Cooke (3)
1967
Daydream Believer by The Monkees (4)

1972
Papa Was a Rolling Stone by The Temptations (1)
1978
You Don't Bring Me Flowers by Barbra Streisand and Neil Diamond (2)

AN ILLUSTRATED RECORD OF ROCK 'N' ROLL

LITTLE RICHARD, 1969

3

1940
John Cale is born in Wales. Bass player, keyboardist and violist for the 1960s avant-garde group The Velvet Underground (Lou Reed, Nico, Sterling Morrison, Maureen Tucker), which influenced the punk-rock movement in the 1970s. He established his own solo career and also performed with Brian Eno and the McGarrigle sisters, Kate and Anna.

1948
Ozzy Osbourne is born John Osbourne in Birmingham, England. Heavy metal singer who began his career with Black Sabbath (Geezer Butler, Tony Iommi, Bill Ward) and had five Top 25 LPs in the 1980s.

1957
Great Balls of Fire by Jerry Lee Lewis enters the charts. It will go to No. 2 and remain on the charts for 13 weeks.

1960
The Federal Trade Commission charges RCA with payola, beginning the payola hearings and trials.

1961
Brian Epstein invites The Beatles to his record store to discuss the future of the band.

1968
Elvis Presley returns to his roots of rock 'n' roll performing on the NBC television special *Elvis*. The highlight of the show is a jam session with Alan Fortas, Charlie Hodge, Scotty Moore and D. J. Fontana.

NUMBER ONE SONGS:

1966
Winchester Cathedral by The New Vaudeville Band (3)

1988
Baby, I Love Your Way/Freebird Medley (Free Baby) by Will To Power (1)

4

1940
Freddy Cannon is born Frederick Anthony Picariello in Lynn, Massachusetts. Singer-songwriter and guitarist who had eight Top 35 singles, including *Tallahassee Lassie*, *Way Down Yonder in New Orleans* and *Palisades Park*.

1942
Chris Hillman is born in Los Angeles.

Bass player and vocalist for the pioneering folk-rock band The Byrds (Roger McGuinn, Michael Clarke, Gene Clark, David Crosby). The group's early use of harmonies influenced many later bands. The Byrds had seven Top 40 singles, including two No. 1 hits, *Mr. Tambourine Man* and *Turn! Turn! Turn!* Hillman had a solo career after The Byrds and later formed the country group The Desert Rose Band. Inducted into the Rock and Roll Hall of Fame with The Byrds in 1991.

1944
Dennis Wilson is born in Hawthorne, California. Drummer and vocalist for The Beach Boys (Brian Wilson, Carl Wilson, Mike Love, Alan Jardine), the group that established California rock and expanded Jan & Dean's "Surfing Sound" in the 1960s. The Beach Boys had 34 Top 15 singles and 20 Top 35 LPs. Their No. 1 hits include *I Get Around; Help Me, Rhonda; Good Vibrations* and *Kokomo.* He died December 28, 1983, when he drowned near Marina Del Ray, California. Inducted into the Rock and Roll Hall of Fame with The Beach Boys January 20, 1988.

1956
An impromptu recording session takes place at Sun Records in Memphis when Jerry Lee Lewis, Elvis Presley and Carl Perkins play together.

1976
Tommy Bolan, guitarist for Deep Purple, dies at age 25 of a drug overdose in Miami.

1988
Roy Orbison gives what will be his last performance, in Cleveland, Ohio.

NUMBER ONE SONGS:

1963
Dominique by The Singing Nun (Sister Luc-Gabrielle) (4)
1965
Turn! Turn! Turn! by The Byrds (3)
1971
Family Affair by Sly & The Family Stone (3)

5

1935
Little Richard is born Richard Wayne Penniman in Macon, Georgia. One of rock 'n' roll's pioneering free spirits, he was the personification of rock's sexuality and rebellious nature. He has influenced generations of rock singers and piano players with his style. Little Richard had Top 10 hits with *Long Tall Sally; Jenny, Jenny; Keep A Knockin'* and *Good Golly Miss Molly.*

1947
Jim Messina is born in Maywood, California. Singer-songwriter-guitarist who was a member of Buffalo Springfield and Poco before becoming a producer. His early production with Kenny Loggins resulted in a return to performing. Loggins & Messina produced six Top 25 LPs and had a Top 5 singles hit with *Your Mama Don't Dance.*

1956
The Alan Freed movie *Rock Rock Rock* premieres in New York City, featuring Chuck Berry, LaVern Baker, Frankie Lyman & The Teenagers and The Moonglows.

NUMBER ONE SONGS:

1964
Ringo by Lorne Greene (1)
1987
Heaven Is a Place on Earth by Belinda Carlisle (1)

6

1943
Mike Smith is born in London. Lead vocalist and songwriter for the Dave Clark Five (Dave Clark, Rick Huxley, Lenny Davidson, Denis Payton), which had 17 Top 35 singles between 1964 and 1967, including *Glad All Over, Bits and Pieces, I Like It Like That, Catch Us If You Can* and the No. 1 *Over and Over.*

1949
Leadbelly, pioneering folk-blues singer-songwriter and member of the Rock and Roll Hall of Fame who influenced folk singers and folk-rock performers, dies at age 60 in New York City.

1961
The Beatles agree to have Brian Epstein become their manager.

1969
The Rolling Stones hold a free concert at Altamont Speedway in Livermore, California, to close their U.S. tour. During the concert, Meredith Hunter is stabbed to death by Hells Angels, who had been hired as security.

1970
The film of The Rolling Stones in concert, *Gimme Shelter,* opens in New York City.

NUMBER ONE SONGS:

1969
Na Na Hey Hey Kiss Him Goodbye by Steam (2)
1986
The Next Time I Fall by Peter Cetera with Amy Grant (1)

7

1942
Harry Chapin is born in New York City. Singer-songwriter who established his career as a musician and then devoted most of his performances to raising money for charitable causes. He had four Top 40 singles hits, including the No. 1 *Cat's in the Cradle* and No. 2 *W-O-L-D.* He died July 16, 1981, in an automobile accident in Jericho, New York.

1949
Tom Waits is born in Pomona, California. Singer-songwriter whose songs have been recorded by a variety of artists, including Crystal Gayle, The Eagles, Rikki Lee Jones and Bette Midler. He also established a career scoring music for films.

1967
The Beatles open the Apple Shop boutique at 94 Baker Street in London.

1988
Roy Orbison dies of a heart attack at age 52 in Nashville, Tennessee, during a visit with his mother.

NUMBER ONE SONGS:

1985
Broken Wings by Mr. Mister (2)

8

1939
Jerry Butler is born in Sunflower County, Mississippi. Soul singer who formed The Impressions (Arthur Brooks, Richard Brooks, Sam Gooden) with Curtis Mayfield. He had a Top 15 hit with *For Your Precious Love* with the group and found chart success as a solo with 13 Top 40 singles, including the Top 10 hits *He Will Break Your Heart* and *Only the Strong Survive.* The Impressions were inducted into the Rock and Roll Hall of Fame in 1991.

1943
Jim Morrison is born in Melbourne, Florida. Lead singer and spiritual leader of The Doors (Ray Manzarek, Robby Krieger, John Densmore), which had 11 Top 40 albums and eight Top 40 singles, including the Top 10 records *Hello, I Love You* and *Touch Me* and the No. 1 *Light My Fire.* The band disbanded soon after Morrison's death on July 3, 1971.

1947
Greg Allman is born in Nashville, Tennessee. Vocalist, keyboardist and cofounder, with his brother Duane, of The Allman Brothers Band (Berry Oakley, Dickey Betts, Jai Johanny Johanson, Butch Trucks). He had solo success with a Top 20 single, *Midnight Rider,* while continuing to perform with the group. (See Jai Johanny Johanson, July 8.)

1958
Lonely Teardrops by Jackie Wilson enters the Billboard charts, where it will stay for 16 weeks, reaching No. 7. The song was also the first hit for its composer, Berry Gordy, Jr., who later founded Motown Records.

1980
John Lennon, founding member of The Beatles and a member of the Rock and Roll Hall of Fame, is shot and killed by Mark Chapman in front of The Dakota building in New York City.

NUMBER ONE SONGS:

1956
Singing the Blues by Guy Mitchell (10)
1979
Babe by Styx (2)
1984
Out of Touch by Hall & Oates (2)

9

1943
Rick Danko is born in Simcoe, Canada. Vocalist and bass player for The Band (Levon Helm, Richard Manuel, Garth Hudson, Robbie Robertson). (See Garth Hudson, August 2.)

NUMBER ONE SONGS:

1972
I Am Woman by Helen Reddy (1)
1978
Le Freak by Chic (5)
1989
We Didn't Start the Fire by Billy Joel (2)

AN ILLUSTRATED RECORD OF ROCK 'N' ROLL

10

1910
John Hammond, Sr. is born in New York City. Record company executive long associated with Columbia Records, he discovered many of the best-known jazz and rock stars, including Billie Holiday, Count Basie, Charlie Christian, Pete Seeger, Aretha Franklin, The Four Tops, Bob Dylan and Bruce Springsteen. Inducted into the Rock and Roll Hall of Fame January 20, 1986.

1945
Chad Stuart is born in England. With Jeremy Clyde formed the vocal duo Chad and Jeremy, which had seven Top 35 singles between 1964 and 1966, including *Yesterday's Gone* and *A Summer Song*.

1967
Otis Redding, influential soul singer and a member of the Rock and Roll Hall of Fame, dies in an airplane crash near Madison, Wisconsin, at age 26.

1973
The rock club CBGB opens in New York City, providing a stage for new musicians, including Talking Heads, Blondie, the Ramones and Patti Smith.

NUMBER ONE SONGS:

1966
Good Vibrations by The Beach Boys (1)
1983
Say Say Say by Paul McCartney & Michael Jackson (6)
1988
Look Away by Chicago (2)

11

1940
David Gates is born in Tulsa, Oklahoma. Vocalist and guitarist for Bread (James Griffin, Larry Knetchel , Mike Botts), the 1970s pop group that had 12 Top 40 singles, including *It Don't Matter to Me, Baby I'm-A Want You, Lost Without Your Love* and the No. 1 *Make It with You*.

1944
Brenda Lee is born Brenda Mae Tarpley in Atlanta, Georgia. Vocalist who began in pop music and crossed over to country after having 29 Top 40 singles between 1960 and 1967, including *I'm Sorry, Sweet Nothings, All Alone Am I, Losing You* and the No. 1 *I Want to Be Wanted*.

1957
Jerry Lee Lewis marries his 13-year-old cousin, Myra Brown, in Hernando, Tennessee, while he is still married to Jane Mitcham. When this later becomes public, his career is in ruins.

1960
Aretha Franklin sings a program of standards in her New York City stage debut at the Village Vanguard.

1964
Sam Cooke, a member of the Rock and Roll Hall of Fame, is killed at age 29 by a gunshot fired by Bertha Franklin, the manager of the Hacienda Motel in Los Angeles, who claimed that he attacked her.

NUMBER ONE SONGS:

1961
Please Mr. Postman by the Marvelettes (1)
1982
Mickey by Toni Basil (1)

12

1941
Dionne Warwick is born in East Orange, New Jersey. Pop vocalist who became synonymous with performing songs written by Burt Bacharach and Hal David. She has had almost 30 Top 40 singles over a 20-year period, including *Walk on By, Message to Michael, I Say a Little Prayer, I'll Never Fall in Love Again* and the No. 1 *That's What Friends Are For*, a collaboration with Elton John, Gladys Knight and Stevie Wonder.

1942
Mike Pinder is born in Birmingham, England. Keyboardist and vocalist for The Moody Blues (Denny Laine, Ray Thomas, Clint Warwick, Graeme Edge, later Justin Hayward, John Lodge). (See Justin Hayward, October 14.)

1943
Dickey Betts is born in West Palm Beach, Florida. Guitarist and vocalist for The Allman Brothers Band (Duane Allman, Greg Allman, Berry Oakley, Jai Johanny Johanson, Butch Trucks), which influenced southern rock bands throughout the 1970s and 1980s with its blend of blues, country, gospel and R&B, highlighted by lengthy jams. The group had eight Top 40 albums in the 1970s, including the No. 1 *Brothers and Sisters*, which produced a No. 2 single, *Ramblin' Man*, for which Betts performed lead vocals.

1946
Clive Bunker is born in Blackpool, England. Drummer for Jethro Tull (Ian Anderson, Mick Abrahams, Glenn Cornick, John Evan). (See Ian Anderson, August 10.)

1949
Paul Rodgers is born in Middlesborough, England. Vocalist for the hard-rock group Bad Company (Mick Ralphs, Simon Kirke, Boz Burrell), which had six Top 30 LPs, including the No. 1 *Bad Company*, and two Top 10 singles, *Can't Get Enough* and *Feel Like Makin' Love*, in the 1970s.

NUMBER ONE SONGS:

1964
Mr. Lonely by Bobby Vinton (1)
1970
The Tears of a Clown by Smokey Robinson & The Miracles (2)
1987
Faith by George Michael (4)

13

NUMBER ONE SONGS:

1986
The Way It Is by Bruce Hornsby & The Range (1)

14

1932
Charlie Rich is born in Colt, Arkansas. Singer-songwriter and pianist who first made his reputation as a rockabilly session man at Sun Records with such stars as Roy Orbison and Johnny Cash. He found success as a country performer in the 1970s with the Top 10 LP *Behind Closed Doors*, which included the No. 1 single *The Most Beautiful Girl*.

NUMBER ONE SONGS:

1959
Heartaches by the Number by Guy Mitchell (2)

15

1968
I Heard It Through the Grapevine by Marvin Gaye (7)

1939
Cindy Birdsong is born in Camden, New Jersey. Vocalist with Patti LaBelle and the Blue Belles who replaced Florence Ballard in The Supremes (Diana Ross, Mary Wilson), the most successful female group of the 1960s, which helped establish the Motown Sound. The Supremes had 30 Top 40 hits between 1963 and 1976, including the No. 1 hits *Where Did Our Love Go, Baby Love, Come See About Me, Stop! In the Name of Love, I Hear a Symphony* and *You Can't Hurry Love*.

1942
Dave Clark is born in London. Drummer, songwriter and founder of the Dave Clark Five (Mike Smith, Rick Huxley, Lenny Davidson, Denis Payton), which had 17 Top 35 singles between 1964 and 1967, including *Glad All Over, Bits and Pieces, I Like It Like That, Catch Us If You Can* and the No. 1 *Over and Over*.

1946
Carmine Appice is born in Staten Island, New York. Drummer for Vanilla Fudge (Mark Stein, Tim Bogert, Vince Martell), the pioneering heavy-rock band that popularized recording extended versions of songs on albums. The band's best-known song is *You Keep Me Hangin' On*, a No. 6 single from its debut album, *Vanilla Fudge*. Appice later formed a power trio with Jeff Beck and Tim Bogert before establishing himself as a session man.

1959
The Everly Brothers record *Let It Be Me* at Bell Studios in New York City. It is the first time they record with an orchestra. The song reaches No. 7.

NUMBER ONE SONGS:

1973
The Most Beautiful Girl by Charlie Rich (2)

16

1943
Anthony Hicks is born in Nelson, England. Guitarist for The Hollies (Graham Nash, Allan Clarke, Donald Rathbone, Eric Haydock), second only to The Beatles as singles hitmakers in Britain. The group had 12 Top 40 singles between 1966 and 1983, including *Bus Stop; Carrie-Anne; Stop Stop Stop; On a Carousel; He Ain't Heavy, He's My Brother; Long Cool Woman (in a Black Dress)* and *The Air That I Breathe.*

NUMBER ONE SONGS:

1957
April Love by Pat Boone (6)
1972
Me and Mrs. Jones by Billy Paul (6)

AN ILLUSTRATED RECORD OF ROCK 'N' ROLL

17

1939
Eddie Kendricks is born in Union Springs, Alabama. Vocalist who for 11 years was the lead tenor for The Temptations (Otis Williams, Paul Williams, Melvin Franklin, Eldridge Bryant, later David Ruffin, Dennis Edwards), the most popular male vocal group of the 1960s and early 1970s. The Temptations had 35 Top 40 songs, including *I Wish It Would Rain, Cloud Nine, Psychedelic Shack, Ball of Confusion (That's What the World Is Today)* and four No. 1 hits: *My Girl, I Can't Get Next to You, Just My Imagination (Running Away with Me)* and *Papa Was a Rollin' Stone.* Kendricks's solo career included five Top 40 singles, including the No. 1 *Keep On Truckin' (Part 1).* Inducted into the Rock and Roll Hall of Fame as a member of The Temptations January 18, 1989.

1942
Paul Butterfield is born in Chicago. Blues guitarist who was influential in reviving the blues for American musicians in the 1960s. He performed with blues masters Howlin' Wolf, Otis Rush, Buddy Guy and others. His Paul Butterfield Blues Band included Mike Bloomfield and Elvin Bishop. He died May 4, 1987, in North Hollywood, California, at age 44.

1948
Jim Bonfanti is born in Windber, Pennsylvania. Drummer for The Raspberries (Eric Carmen, Wally Bryson, Dave Smalley), the 1970s pop group that had four top 35 singles, including the No. 5 hit *Go All the Way* and the top 20 songs *I Wanna Be with You* and *Overnight Sensation (Hit Record).*

1950
Carlton Barrett is born in Kingston, Jamaica. Percussionist for Bob Marley's reggae group The Wailers (Peter Tosh, Bunny Livingston, Aston Barrett), the pioneering and influential Jamaican pop group that had two Top 20 albums in the 1970s, *Rastaman Vibration* and *Exodus.*

18

1918
Professor Longhair is born Henry Roeland Byrd in Bogalusa, Louisiana. Innovative piano stylist who pioneered early rock 'n' roll piano techniques and influenced Fats Domino, Dr. John and Allen Toussaint. He died January 30, 1980, in New Orleans. Inducted into the Rock and Roll Hall of Fame in 1992.

1943
Keith Richards is born in Dartford, England. Guitarist, songwriter and founding member of The Rolling Stones (Mick Jagger, Charlie Watts, Bill Wyman, Brian Jones). Inducted into the Rock and Roll Hall of Fame in 1989. (See Charlie Watts, June 2.)

1948
Chas Chandler is born Bryan Chandler in Newcastle-upon-Tyne, England. Bass player for The Animals (Alan Price, Eric Burdon, John Steel, Hilton Valentine), the British Invasion group based in R&B. The group had 14 Top 40 singles and is best known for the No. 1 hit *The House of the Rising Sun.*

NUMBER ONE SONGS:

1961
The Lion Sleeps Tonight by the Tokens (3)
1982
Maneater by Hall & Oates (4)

19

1944
Alvin Lee is born in Nottingham, England. Singer and guitarist for the blues band Ten Years After (Chick Churchill, Leon Lyons, Ric Lee), which had five Top 40 albums and one Top 40 single, *I'd Love to Change the World,* but is remembered for its performance at the Woodstock Music and Art Festival in 1969, particularly *Goin' Home,* which featured Alvin Lee's nimble guitar and vocals.

1945
John McEuen is born in Long Beach, California. Guitarist and vocalist for the country-rock group The Dirt Band, originally the Nitty Gritty Dirt Band (Jeff Hanna, Jimmie Fadden, Jackson Browne, Jimmy Ibbotson, Ralph Barr, Les Thompson, Bruce Kunkel), which had a Top 10 single hit with *Mr. Bojangles* but is known for its landmark album *Will the Circle Be Unbroken,* which brought together many of country music's biggest names.

1955
Carl Perkins records *Blue Suede Shoes* at Sun Records.

1956
Elvis Presley has nine records on the Billboard Hot 100 at the same time, a record broken only by The Beatles on April 4, 1964. Presley's chart hits include *Love Me, When My Blue Moon Turns to Gold Again, Paralyzed, Old Shop, Don't Be Cruel/ Hound Dog, Blue Moon, I Don't Care If the Sun Don't Shine, Anyway You Want Me* and *Love Me Tender.*

1962
The Motown Revue begins a 10-day series of performances at the Apollo Theater in Harlem. Performers include Marvin Gaye and The Supremes.

NUMBER ONE SONGS:

1964
Come See About Me by the Supremes (2)

20

1944
Bobby Colomby is born in New York City. Drummer for Blood, Sweat & Tears (Al Kooper, Steve Katz, Jim Fielder, Fred Lipsius, Dick Halligan, Randy Brecker, Jerry Weiss), the pioneering jazz-rock group that had three consecutive No. 2 single hits with *You've Made Me So Very Happy, And When I Die* and *Spinning Wheel,* along with two No. 1 LPs, *Blood Sweat & Tears* and *Blood, Sweat & Tears 3.*

1957
Elvis Presley receives his draft notice from the U.S. Army, inspiring the Broadway musical *Bye, Bye Birdie.*

1973
Bobby Darin dies during heart surgery in Los Angeles at age 37.

NUMBER ONE SONGS:

1969
Leaving on a Jet Plane by Peter, Paul and Mary (1)

1986
Walk Like an Egyptian by The Bangles (4)

21

1921
Alan Freed is born in Johnstown, Pennsylvania. Disc jockey who is credited with coining the phrase *rock 'n' roll* to describe the music he played on Cleveland radio station WJW, where his show was originally called *Moondog Rock 'n' Roll Party.* He became the country's top disc jockey when he moved to WINS and WABC in New York City. Always a controversial figure, he promoted rock 'n' roll shows, received writing credits on records and was accused of accepting money for playing records. The film *American Hot Wax* was based on his life. He died January 20, 1965, in Palm Springs, California, at age 43. Inducted into the Rock and Roll Hall of Fame January 20, 1986.

1940
Frank Zappa is born in Baltimore, Maryland. Versatile musician, songwriter and arranger who developed a cult following for his unique fusion of jazz and classical forms with rock. He has had nine Top 40 LPs and a Top 35 single, *Valley Girl.*

1944
Carl Wilson is born in Hawthorne, California. Guitarist and vocalist for The Beach Boys (Brian Wilson, Dennis Wilson, Mike Love, Alan Jardine). Inducted into the Rock and Roll Hall of Fame with The Beach Boys January 20, 1988. (See Mike Love, March 15.)

NUMBER ONE SONGS:

1985
Say You, Say Me by Lionel Richie (4)

22

1939
Ma Rainey, influential blues singer and member of the Rock and Roll Hall of Fame, dies in Rome, Georgia, at age 53.

1949
Robin and Maurice Gibb are born in Isle of Man, Australia. Twins who with younger brother Barry formed The Bee Gees, one of the most

successful pop groups of the 1970s. (See Barry Gibb, September 1.)

1962
Telstar by The Tornadoes (George Bellamy, Heinz Burt, Alan Caddy, Clem Cattini, Roger Laverne Jackson) becomes the first single by an English group to become No. 1 in the U.S., where it remains for three weeks.

1979
The first of four concerts to raise money for the boat people of Kampuchea takes place at Hammersmith Odeon in London. Performers include Elvis Costello, The Who, Paul McCartney &

Wings, Robert Plant, The Pretenders and Rockpile.

NUMBER ONE SONGS:

1979
Escape (The Piña Colada Song) by Rupert Holmes (2)

1984
Like a Virgin by Madonna (6)

1940
Jorma Kaukonen is born in Washington, D.C. Guitarist and vocalist who was an original

member of Jefferson Airplane (Marty Balin, Paul Kantner, Signe Anderson, Bob Harvey, Skip Spence, later Jack Casady, Grace Slick, Spencer Dryden, Papa John Creach, John Barbata, Aynsley Dunbar, among others) when the group had its first success with the Top 10 singles *Somebody to Love* and *White Rabbit*. Formed the blues-based Hot Tuna with Casady as an acoustic band and later went electric. Known for his intricate guitar work, based in the Mississippi Delta blues style of the Rev. Gary Davis.

1941
Tim Hardin is born in Eugene, Oregon. Singer-songwriter best known for his

work performed by others, including *If I Were a Carpenter*, *Misty Roses* and *Reason to Believe*. He died December 29, 1980, of a heroin overdose in Los Angeles.

NUMBER ONE SONGS:

1989
Another Day in Paradise by Phil Collins (4)

AN ILLUSTRATED RECORD OF ROCK 'N' ROLL

24

1920
Dave Bartholomew is born in Edgard, Louisiana. Trumpeter, arranger and producer who established the 1950s New Orleans sound personified in Fats Domino's hits *I'm Walkin'* and *Blueberry Hill*. Also worked with Bobby Mitchell and Lloyd Price, among others. Inducted into the Rock and Roll Hall of Fame in 1991.

1924
Lee Dorsey is born in New Orleans. Vocalist who performed Allen Toussaint's songs and had four Top 30 singles, including two Top 10 hits, *Ya Ya* and *Working in the Coal Mine*.

1954
Fifties balladeer Johnny Ace dies at age 25 while playing Russian roulette in Houston.

NUMBER ONE SONGS:

1977
How Deep Is Your Love by The Bee Gees (3)

1988
Every Rose Has Its Thorn by Poison (3)

25

1937
O'Kelly Isley is born in Cincinnati, Ohio. Founding member, with brothers Ronald and Rudolph, of the R&B-soul group The Isley Brothers, which had 11 Top 40 singles between 1962 and 1980, including the Top 10 hits *It's Your Thing*, *That Lady (Part 1)* and *Fight the Power—Part 1*, and a dozen LPs, including the No. 1 *The Heat Is On*. Inducted into the Rock and Roll Hall of Fame in 1992.

1958
Alan Freed's Rock 'n' Roll Spectacular, a 10-day event, begins at Loew's State Theater in New York City. Performers include Chuck Berry, Jackie Wilson, Eddie Cochran, Bo Diddley and The Everly Brothers.

NUMBER ONE SONGS:

1965
Over and Over by The Dave Clark Five (1)

1971
Brand New Key by Melanie (3)

26

1935
Abdul Fakir is born in Detroit. Vocalist with The Four Tops (Levi Stubbs, Renaldo Benson, Lawrence Payton), one of Motown Records' most successful groups, producing 22 Top 40 singles hits over almost two decades, including *Bernadette*, *Standing in the Shadows of Love*, *It's the Same Old Song*, *Ain't No Woman (Like the One I've Got)* and the No. 1 hits *I Can't Help Myself* and *Reach Out I'll Be There*. The Four Tops were inducted into the Rock and Roll Hall of Fame in 1990.

1940
Phil Spector is born in New York City. Innovative record producer who created the overdubbing technique known as the "Wall of Sound," typified by The Righteous Brothers' No. 1 single *You've Lost That Lovin' Feelin'* and *River Deep, Mountain High* by Ike & Tina Turner. Also was writer and/or producer of hit singles by The Crystals, The Ronettes, Darlene Love, Bob B. Soxx and The Blue Jeans and The Righteous Brothers in the 1960s. Inducted into the Rock and Roll Hall of Fame January 18, 1989.

1967
The Beatles' *Magical Mystery Tour* film premieres on BBC-1 television in England.

NUMBER ONE SONGS:

1964
I Feel Fine by The Beatles (3)

1970
My Sweet Lord by George Harrison (4)

27

1941
Les Maguire is born in Wallasey, England. Pianist for Gerry and the Pacemakers (Gerry Marsden, John Chadwick, Freddie Marsden). (See Gerry Marsden, September 24.)

1960
The Beatles' performance at Litherland Town Hall in Liverpool is billed as *The Beatles, Direct from Hamburg* and is a watershed that unleashes the group's new style of rock 'n' roll. The audience responds with a near riot.

NUMBER ONE SONGS:

1969
Someday We'll Be Together by Diana Ross & The Supremes (1)

1975
Let's Do It Again by The Staple Singers (1)

1980
(Just Like) Starting Over by John Lennon (5)

28

1915
Roebuck "Pops" Staples is born in Drew, Mississippi. Patriarch and guitarist for the gospel-R&B-rock group The Staple Singers (Mavis, Pervis, Cleo, Yvonne Staples), which had eight Top 40 singles in the 1970s, including two No. 1 hits: *I'll Take You There* and *Let's Do It Again*.

1924
Johnny Otis is born. Bandleader and songwriter who helped promote R&B artists in the 1950s and who had a Top 10 single, *Willie and the Hand Jive*.

1946
Edgar Winter is born in Beaumont, Texas. Vocalist and keyboardist who is best known for his No. 1 hit *Frankenstein*, which was from the No. 3 LP *They Only Come Out at Night*, one of his three Top 25 LPs in the mid 1970s.

NUMBER ONE SONGS:

1959
Why by Frankie Avalon (1)

1974
Angie Baby by Helen Reddy (1)

29

1942
Ray Thomas is born in Stourport-on-Severn, England. Flute player and vocalist for The Moody Blues (Denny Laine, Mike Pinder, Clint Warwick, Graeme Edge, later Justin Hayward, John Lodge). (See Justin Hayward, October 14.)

1963
Sunday Times of London critic Richard Buckle calls John Lennon and Paul McCartney "the greatest composers since Beethoven."

NUMBER ONE SONGS:

1973
Time in a Bottle by Jim Croce (2)

30

1928
Bo Diddley is born Ellas Bates in McComb, Mississippi. Pioneer of the syncopated "hambone" rhythm guitar technique that is a foundation in rock 'n' roll, the "chink-a-chink, a-chink-chink" that is heard in his own *Who Do You Love*. His only Top 40 hit was *Say Man* in 1959, but his style influenced many rock guitarists. Inducted into the Rock and Roll Hall of Fame January 21, 1987.

1931
Skeeter Davis is born Mary Frances Penick in Dry Ridge, Kentucky. Vocalist who had four Top 40 hits in the early 1960s, including the Top 10 songs *The End of the World* and *I Can't Stay Mad at You*.

1939
Del Shannon is born Charles Westover in Coopersville, Michigan. Pioneering singer-songwriter who was one of the earliest rock performers to write his own songs. He had nine Top 40 singles, including *Hats Off to Larry*, *Keep Searchin' (We'll Follow the Sun)* and the No. 1 *Runaway*.

1943
Mike Nesmith is born in Houston, Texas. Singer, songwriter and guitarist for The Monkees (Mickey Dolenz, Davy Jones, Peter Tork), the made-for-TV pop group styled after The Beatles. The group had 12 Top 40 singles, including three No. 1 hits—*Last Train to Clarksville*, *I'm a Believer* and *Daydream Believer*—and seven Top 35 LPs, including four consecutive No. 1 albums—*The Monkees*, *More of the Monkees*, *Headquarters* and *Pisces, Aquarius, Capricorn & Jones, Ltd.* Nesmith went on to have a successful career as a record producer and country performer.

1945
Davy Jones is born in Manchester, England. Singer for The Monkees. (See above entry for Mike Nesmith.)

1947
Jeff Lynne is born in Birmingham, England. Guitarist, vocalist, keyboardist

and arranger for The Electric Light Orchestra (Roy Wood, Bev Bevan, Rick Price), which had 19 Top 40 singles and 10 Top 40 LPs between 1974 and 1986. ELO's best-known singles are *Telephone Line, Hold On Tight, Don't Bring Me Down* and *Evil Woman*. Lynne later became a member of The Traveling Wilburys (George Harrison, Roy Orbison, Tom Petty, Bob Dylan).

NUMBER ONE SONGS:

1967
Hello Goodbye by The Beatles (3)

31

1930
Odetta is born Odetta Holmes in Birmingham, Alabama. Influential blues singer whose style in the folk-blues tradition was important in influencing Janis Joplin, Joan Armatrading and others.

1943
John Denver is born John Henry Deutschendorf in Roswell, New Mexico. Pop-country singer-songwriter who had 12 Top 30 albums and 15 Top 40 singles in the 1970s and early 1980s, including the No. 1 singles *Sunshine on My Shoulders, Annie's Song, Thank God I'm a Country Boy* and *I'm Sorry*.

1946
Patti Smith is born in Chicago. Poet turned punk-rock singer who had a Top 15 single, *Because the Night*, and two Top 20 LPs, *Easter* and *Wave*.

1947
Burton Cummings is born in Winnipeg, Manitoba. Vocalist and keyboardist for The Guess Who (Chad Allan, Bob Ashley, Randy Bachman, Garry Peterson), which had 14 Top 40 singles between 1965 and 1974, including *These Eyes, Laughing, No Time, Share the Land* and the No. 1 *American Woman*. Cummings had a Top 10 single after the group broke up with *Stand Tall*.

1951
Tom Hamilton is born in Colorado Springs, Colorado. Bass player for Aerosmith (Joe Perry, Brad Whitford, Steven Tyler, Joey Kramer), the heavy metal band based in the blues that has had seven Top 40 singles and nine Top 40 LPs. The band's top

RAY THOMAS, 1978
The Moody Blues

singles include *Dream On, Walk This Way* and *Janie's Got a Gun.*

1961
The Beach Boys perform for the first time, at the Ritchie Valens Memorial Dance in the Municipal Auditorium in Long Beach, California.

1970
The Beatles begin a legal separation

when Paul McCartney files suit in London to dissolve their partnership.

1978
Bill Graham closes the Winterland Theater in San Francisco with performances by The Blues Brothers and The Grateful Dead.

1985
Rick Nelson, a member of the Rock

and Roll Hall of Fame, dies at age 45 with several members of his band when their chartered plane crashes near DeKalb, Texas.

NUMBER ONE SONGS:

1966
I'm a Believer by The Monkees (7)

Bibliography

Amburn, E. *Dark Star: The Roy Orbison Story*. New York: Carol, 1990.

Ayres, B., Fornatale, P., and Macken, B. *The Rock Music Source Book*. Garden City, N.Y.: Anchor Books, 1980.

Bacon, T. *Rock Hardware*. New York: Harmony Books, 1981.

Bego, M. *TV Rock*. New York: Paperjacks, 1988.

Berry, C. *Chuck Berry: The Autobiography*. New York: Harmony Books, 1987.

Bronson, F. *The Billboard Book of Number One Hits*. New York: Billboard Publications, 1988.

Bronson, F. *Billboard's Hottest Hot 100 Hits*. New York: Billboard Books, 1991.

Brooks, T., and Marsh, E. *The Complete Directory to Prime Time Network TV Shows 1946–Present*. New York: Ballantine Books, 1988.

Carr, I., Fairweather, D., and Priestley, B. *Jazz: The Essential Companion*. New York: Prentice-Hall, 1987.

Carr, R., and Tyler, T. *The Beatles: An Illustrated Record*. New York: Harmony Books, 1975.

Clifford, M. (consultant). *The Harmony Illustrated Encyclopedia of Rock*. (6th ed.) New York: Harmony Books, 1988.

Davies, H. *The Beatles: The Authorized Biography*. New York: Dell Books, 1969.

Dearling, R., and Dearling, C., with Rust, B. *The Guinness Book of Music Facts & Feats*. (2nd ed.) Enfield, Middlesex, England: Guinness Superlatives, 1981.

Dellar, F., Green, D. B., and Thompson, R. *The Illustrated*

Encyclopedia of Country Music. New York: Harmony Books, 1977.

Elliott, M. *The Rolling Stones Complete Recording Sessions 1963–1989*. London: Blanford, 1990.

Facts On File. New York: Facts on File, 1973, 1982, 1987, 1990.

Flip Magazine Editors. *Flip's Groovy Guide to the Groups*. New York: Signet, 1968.

Fornatale, P. *The Story of Rock 'n' Roll*. New York: William Morrow, 1987.

Jackson, J. A. *Big Beat Heat: Alan Freed and the Early Years of Rock & Roll*. New York: Schirmer Books, 1991.

Jancik, W. *The Billboard Book of One-Hit Wonders*. New York: Billboard Books, 1990.

Lazell, B., with Rees, D., and Crampton, L. *Rock Movers & Shakers*. New York: Billboard Books, 1989.

Lewisohn, M. *The Beatles Recording Sessions: The Official Abbey Road Studio Session Notes 1962–1970*. New York: Harmony Books, 1988.

Lewisohn, M. *The Beatles Day By Day*. (2nd ed.) New York: Harmony Books, 1990.

Logan, N., and Woffinden, B. *The Illustrated Encyclopedia of Rock*. New York: Harmony Books, 1977.

Marsh, D. *Born to Run: The Bruce Springsteen Story*. Garden City, N.Y.: Doubleday, 1979.

Miller, J. (ed.). *The Rolling Stone Illustrated History of Rock & Roll*. New York: Rolling Stone Press, 1976.

Nite, N. N. *Rock On: The Illustrated Encyclopedia of Rock 'n' Roll*. New York: Thomas Crowell, 1974.

Pareles, J., and Romanowski, P. (eds.). *The Rolling Stone*

Encyclopedia of Rock & Roll. New York: Rolling Stone Press, 1983.

Planet Magazine. *A Tribute to The Fillmore*. New York: N.P.P. Music, 1971.

Rees, D., and Crampton, L. *Rock Movers & Shakers*. (2nd ed.) New York: Billboard Books, 1991.

Ribowsky, M. *He's a Rebel: The Truth About Phil Spector—Rock and Roll's Legendary Madman*. New York: E. P. Dutton, 1989.

Roxon, L. *Rock Encyclopedia*. New York: Grosset & Dunlap, 1969.

Sia, J. *Woodstock '69: Summer Pop Festivals*. New York: Scholastic Book Services, 1970.

Smith, S., and The Diagram Group. *Rock Day By Day*. Enfield, Middlesex, England: Guinness Books, 1987.

Stambler, I. *The Encyclopedia of Pop, Rock and Soul*. New York: St. Martin's Press, 1974, 1989.

Television Critics Association National Cable Forum Directory. Washington, D.C.: Television Critics Association, 1990.

Tosches, N. *Unsung Heroes of Rock 'n' Roll*. New York: Harmony Books, 1984.

Wheeler, T. *American Guitars: An Illustrated History*. New York: HarperCollins, 1982.

Whitburn, J. *The Billboard Book of Top 40 Albums*. New York: Billboard Publications, 1987.

Whitburn, J. *The Billboard Book of Top 40 Hits*. (3rd ed.) New York: Billboard Publications, 1987.

Whitburn, J. *Top 1000 Singles 1955–1990*. Milwaukee, Wis.: Hal Leonard, 1991.